"I can't think of a better book than *Remarkable Leadership* to put into the hands of aspiring leaders—or people who want to become more effective leaders. It's well-written, filled with practical suggestions, and, for my money, hits the truly important aspects of leading inside an organization."

—Rick Maurer, author of *Beyond the Wall of Resistance* and "Change Management News" blog

"What is so remarkable about *Remarkable Leadership* is that Kevin has found that the key to being a great leader doesn't have to come with being a remarkable person. His book can take the ordinary and human in all of us and help us meld ourselves into remarkable leaders. His book invites all of us to find what kind of leader we can truly be."

—Rusty Rueff, CEO, SNOCAP, Inc.

"One of the most thought-provoking and creative activities I invest in as a leader is to have breakfast with Kevin Eikenberry. Innovative, cost-effective, and practical ideas jump out of his head. Now, he has graciously written an entire book of these ideas around leadership, creating a practical asset for all leaders. Kevin does a great job balancing a leader's need for a checklist with the need for practical tips and tools. He combines ideas from many leaders, melding them into cohesive lessons. For example, he helps you learn the difference between being a good leader who delegates and a great leader who empowers. This is a book that will help you get from where you currently are as a leader to where you strive to be."

—Lou Russell, bestselling author and president of Russell Martin & Associates

"Kevin's ability to focus, empower, and push leaders to a higher standard is what makes his insights illuminating. He has proven to be one of our association's greatest friends and trusted advisors. I wouldn't just recommend his book. I recommend you dog-ear it, highlight it, scratch random thoughts in it, and then buy a copy for your second-in-command as required reading."

—Tony Scelzo, founder of Rainmakers

"When you're ready to unleash the remarkable leader within you, you must read this book and apply its simple yet profound principles. Kevin Eikenberry has broken down leadership in a bottom-line, user-friendly way. By the time you are done with this book, you will realize that personal leadership is both your birthright and natural legacy."

—Tami Walsh, president of TeenWisdom.com

"Reading this book inspires you to want to be a better leader in all aspects of your life. What's great about the book is that it gives you a hands-on, practical approach that you can use right from Chapter 1 to jump-start your journey to becoming a truly remarkable leader. Learning is a choice and if you make the choice to read this book, you are investing in yourself, in making yourself a better leader, learner, and active participant in the world around you. *Remarkable Leadership* is like your own leadership playbook for the twenty-first century. This book is a must-have for all managers and leaders!"

—Michelle Zant, Ph.D., education marketing manager, Arrow Enterprise Computing Solutions

More Praise for Remarkable Leadership

"Buy this book if you want to read about leadership. *Use* this book if you want to be challenged to move out of your leadership comfort zone and develop skills that will release your untapped potential. Kevin has included every competency it takes to be a remarkable leader. He not only identifies and explains them, but goes on to challenge you to assess and further develop each competency in your life. From a human developmental standpoint, this book should be required reading, and learning, for anyone assigned the responsibility of being in leadership."

—Greg Shaffer, training supervisor, Chevron Phillips Chemical Company

"An important book that combines profound simplicity with practical instructions for leadership greatness. Buy two copies—one for your desk and one for your bedside. Its poignant lessons will bear fruit at work and at home."

—Chip R. Bell, author of *Customer Loyalty Guaranteed*

"The best measurement of success is the number of choices available to you. In this book, Kevin Eikenberry infinitely increases those choices for you. Choose to devour this book. It's brilliant!"

—Jim Canterucci, author of *Personal Brilliance*

"In my assessment, Kevin Eikenberry is leading one of the most powerful and inspiring conversations about leadership now occurring on our planet. *Remarkable Leadership* brings the reader a concise distillation of all the most useful insights and actions regarding *what actually works* in leadership into one enjoyable volume. If you ever thought to yourself, 'I could never be a great leader,' reading this book will not only change your mind, it will launch you on a journey of fulfillment you hadn't thought possible. At a time when many are cynical and resigned, Kevin's book injects fresh new DNA into the intellectual gene pool of possibility. I urge you to read this book. Then go out and make a difference."

—David Chard, regional director, Edelman Asia Pacific Academy

"This book will equip you with all the skills you need to become a remarkable leader. Remarkable leaders can be made, if we choose to live and improve in our strength zones. Regardless of title, position, or station in life, each of us can become a remarkable leader. This book gives you all the tools you'll need; the only question is, will you choose to use them or will you settle for being mediocre?"

—Phil Gerbyshak, author of *10 Ways to Make It Great!*

"Kevin Eikenberry knows what it takes to be a remarkable leader and shares his secrets, tips, and examples in this compelling and enjoyable book. *Remarkable Leadership* is elegant, powerful, and actionable. The book is full of excellent self-assessments and stories that illustrate what you can do to improve your impact as a leader. I love that Kevin zooms in on the leadership practices that can supercharge any company environment. Anyone can be a great leader by reading and following his guidance."

—Lisa Haneberg, author of *Two Weeks to a Breakthrough* and *Focus Like a Laser Beam*

REMARKABLE LEADERSHIP

REMARKABLE LEADERSHIP

Unleashing Your Leadership Potential
One Skill at a Time

Kevin Eikenberry

John Wiley & Sons, Inc.

Published by Jossey-Bass
A Wiley Imprint
989 Market Street, San Francisco, CA 94103-1741—www.josseybass.com

Wiley Bicentennial logo: Richard J. Pacifico

Jossey-Bass books and products are available through most bookstores. To contact Jossey-Bass directly call our Customer Care Department within the U.S. at 800-956-7739, outside the U.S. at 317-572-3986, or fax 317-572-4002.

Jossey-Bass also publishes its books in a variety of electronic formats. Some content that appears in print may not be available in electronic books.

Library of Congress Cataloging-in-Publication Data

Eikenberry, Kevin, 1962–
     Remarkable leadership : unleashing your leadership potential
     one skill at a time / Kevin Eikenberry.
     p. cm.
     ISBN 978-0-7879-9619-2 (cloth)
     1. Leadership.   I. Title.
     BF637.L4E37 2007
     158′.4—dc22

                            2007008061

Printed in the United States of America
FIRST EDITION
HB Printing   10 9 8 7 6 5 4 3 2 1

CONTENTS

*For Lori, who shows me a picture of remarkable every day,
and for my Dad, the first leader I observed and followed*

FOREWORD

WHEN YOU THINK of the greatest leaders you've ever experienced, either firsthand or from a distance, I'm guessing you don't think of their technical prowess. To be effective in an organizational context, leaders must know their business and the unique aspects of that organization. They must be able to think strategically, budget, implement, and do a variety of these sorts of things well.

But when you think of the greatest, most remarkable leaders, you most likely don't think of these skills—or at least these aren't the things you think of first. If you are like me, what you think of first are leaders who are remarkable people: leaders who engender trust, create great teams, are innovative, have a vision, and are great communicators. You think about the skills that are explored in the following pages of this book.

I congratulate you for choosing this book. The fact that you are reading it says that you have a picture in your mind of becoming a more successful, confident, and valuable leader. This picture of your own potential is an important first step in your ultimate success.

Kevin Eikenberry accurately reminds us that whatever our job title or position, we are all leaders, and we all have the potential to become truly remarkable. His belief in us and our ultimate success is real and stands out on every page. This belief is inspiring and empowering. As you read these pages, his belief in you will build your own belief in yourself, an important ingredient in any successful learning journey.

In my book *The Success Principles*, I outline a series of principles that lead to greater success in any aspect of your life. Similarly in this book, Kevin Eikenberry identifies and illustrates principles that will help you become a remarkable leader. Through these principles, you will find a map that can lead you to great success, satisfaction, and fulfillment as a truly remarkable leader.

In my talks, I often quote my friend Tony Robbins, who says that "success leaves clues." In this book, Kevin has provided the clues, and he has provided something even more important: he has given you specific action steps to apply those clues to your own great benefit and those you lead. Although you can't do everything at once, with this book you have a clear set of actions that, when applied, will lead consistently and predictably to your success.

Santa Barbara, California   JACK CANFIELD
March 2007

REMARKABLE LEADERSHIP

THE LEADER IN YOU

ARE LEADERS MADE OR BORN? The question seems to be eternal, yet the answer seems clear. I've never received a birth announcement in the mail, or read one in the newspaper, that announced the birth of a leader. Yet on any given day, we can read the obituaries in any newspaper and see that leaders have died. This simple analysis shows that leaders *must be made*. People can do and learn the skills of leadership. People can become leaders.

In fact, I know that at some level, you already believe this or you wouldn't be holding this book. After all, if you didn't think it was possible to develop your leadership skills—if you thought they were skills people were born with—what would be the point of spending time reading this or any other book on leadership?

We all are born with a unique set of skills and innate abilities. Some of us are born with talents that make us more easily successful as musicians, mathematicians, or mechanics. Others are blessed with talents that make empathy, persuasion, vision, or communication come more easily. We all are given a unique bundle of talents at birth, and it is our job/opportunity to use that personal set of skills and abilities to maximize our potential throughout our life. Some of our unique talents will help us in our journey to becoming a remarkable leader, and other skills may not come as naturally to us, and so we may need to be more diligent or conscious in developing them.

So while leaders are most definitely made, I hope you will agree that within our personal package of potential, we each are given tools that will aid us in our leadership development. There *is* a leader in you. Part of that leader you may already see; other parts may not yet be revealed.

My Goal

This book is designed to help you identify the parts of your personal leadership package working in your favor and help you develop those parts, and any others you wish to work on, to become the leader you are capable of becoming. In other words, my goal is to help you become a remarkable leader by unleashing the leadership potential that is already within you.

A secondary goal of this book, which may not be quite as obvious, is to help you develop leaders around you. Remarkable leaders are those who lead *and* develop others, and this book will help you do that as well.

My Philosophy

When I read a book, I always appreciate knowing the author's perspective and philosophy. Once I learn an author's underlying beliefs, I am in a better position to learn from him or her. I've actually already shared part of that philosophy, but here is some more context.

Our Potential Is Vast

Think about the last time you were in a room of people where a baby was present. Where was most of the focus in the room? On the baby, of course! We all are drawn to babies, like metal to a magnet. We all sense that there is something magical about their presence. However, on a purely logical level, this doesn't make much sense.

Babies cry. Babies smell (really bad) sometimes. Babies are high maintenance. And they aren't attractive by the standards we use to determine physical attractiveness in adults. Yet we are still drawn to them. We want to look at them (or their pictures in their absence). We want to hold them, smile at them, and talk to them in strange voices. Why is this true? Because deep down we know that every baby we hold, every baby we look at, every baby we hear has the chance to be anyone and anything. That baby could be a president of the United States, a Nobel Prize–winning scientist, a best-selling author, a preacher, a teacher, a star athlete—anyone. We know that a baby's potential is limitless.

Because you were once a baby too, that same limitless potential that we know resides in babies still resides in us. Our potential is vast: we are capable of far more than we can ever imagine. This potential exists in all parts of our life, including our potential to be a truly remarkable leader.

We Can Choose

One of the most valuable abilities we all have—something that distinguishes humans from other animals—is the ability to choose. We make choices all day, every day. Many are subconscious and taken for granted, but we can choose how to respond to a situation, what to say, and how to view something. We also have the power to make a choice to learn and grow, or to stay and stagnate.

This book is about helping you use your power of choice wisely to help you become a remarkable leader.

Opportunities Abound

Chances are you are reading this book because you want to become a more effective leader in one part of your life: at work, in your church, in a volunteer organization, or in some other role. Having a focus is a perfect way to approach this book, but you shouldn't limit your view.

The skills of a leader are transferable across all the roles you play in all parts of your life. So while you may read this book through the lenses of your leadership role at work, recognize that you can practice and use those skills in your community, in your church, with your neighbors, and even at home.

We Shouldn't Settle

If you believe, even if only intellectually at this point, that your potential is huge, then it should be easy to see why you shouldn't settle for less than your best. You didn't decide to read this book because you thought you could be a slightly-better-than-mediocre leader. You didn't decide to learn more about leadership skills so you could get by. Deep down you know you can be remarkable. You shouldn't settle for anything less than your best self, reaching ever closer to your potential—whether as a leader or in any other part of your life.

This isn't the time or the place for compromise. Now is the time to take action to become what you are capable of being. This book is about helping you move up your ladder of success, increasing your confidence and competence as a leader—to become remarkable.

What Are the Skills?

Before you read any further, get a mental picture of a person you consider a remarkable leader: a person who personifies leadership to you. This person can be living or dead, someone you know well or have worked with or someone you have only read about or observed from afar. Once you have that person in your mind, write his or her name below.

My remarkable role model leader:

_____

Now write down five skills, attributes, behaviors, or habits that make this person a model of leadership for you:

1. _____

2. _____

3. _____

4. _____

5. _____

We all have a picture in our mind's eye of what a great leader looks like or of how a great leader behaves. You've just now identified part of your personal picture.

Organizations build these pictures too. They are reinforced through culture and often codified by a list of leadership competencies or leadership behaviors used to describe the traits they value and use to evaluate potential leaders within the organization. Each organization has a different list of competencies. The lists I've seen range from five to twenty-three competencies. In the end, although those skills may be stated somewhat differently, there are some core skills or competencies that usually are included. This book focuses on thirteen of those core competencies:

○ Remarkable leaders learn continually.

○ Remarkable leaders champion change.

○ Remarkable leaders communicate powerfully.

○ Remarkable leaders build relationships.

○ Remarkable leaders develop others.

○ Remarkable leaders focus on customers.

○ Remarkable leaders influence with impact.

○ Remarkable leaders think and act innovatively.

○ Remarkable leaders value collaboration and teamwork.

○ Remarkable leaders solve problems and make decisions.

○ Remarkable leaders take responsibility and have accountability.

○ Remarkable leaders manage projects and processes successfully.

○ Remarkable leaders set goals and support goal achievement.

These are the competencies I have identified through experience, consultation, observation, and study as those broad, core competencies that lead to remarkable leaders.

What Makes a Leader Remarkable?

I recently spent time with a Canadian client group that included many hockey fans. I asked them who the greatest hockey player of all time was. After some good-natured teasing and verbal jousting, they agreed that if it wasn't Wayne Gretzky, he was clearly one of the greatest.

I then asked them if he was the greatest skater, the fastest skater, the best defenseman, the best goal tender, or the most physical player ever. On each of these questions, the whole group answered no: they agreed that he was none of these things.

Then I asked if he was the best passer, the best scorer, the best at anticipating where play was going, and the most competitive ever to play the game. These answers were much different from the ones to my first set of questions. Although there wasn't complete consensus on each of these, there was general agreement that Gretzky was the best, or among the very best, in hockey history at these skills.

This led to an interesting discussion about strengths, weaknesses, and greatness. The group determined that it wasn't necessary that the greatest player be the greatest at every individual skill. In fact they generally agreed that there were some skills where Gretzky was far from the best.

If I had asked people to write down what they thought of when asked to think about Gretzky, they would have written down all of his great strengths and not mentioned any of his weaknesses at all.

Think about the outstanding leader you identified a minute ago. When you thought of your role model leader, did you focus on what he isn't good at, or did you remember and marvel at all that she is best at?

I'll bet your results aren't very different from my hockey loving participants.

What makes us remarkable are those skills at which we truly excel. What makes *you* remarkable are those things at which *you* truly excel.

If you have two or more skills at which you truly excel, you will likely be seen by others as highly effective. This is true for a sport, a hobby, or any other endeavor, including leadership.

Of course, if Wayne Gretzky couldn't skate, his other great skills would be all for naught *as a hockey player*. The same is true for us. There are some underlying skills for any pursuit that are absolutely critical: we must have some skill in these competencies even to be in the game.

If you took a person unwilling or unable to learn, with extremely low interpersonal or communication skills, it would be hard to see a remarkable leader because such a flaw (like Gretzky not being able to skate) would overshadow or negate other great skills they possess.

It is a freeing thought to consider, especially after looking at a list of thirteen competencies such as those explored in this book, that anyone can become remarkable by becoming truly outstanding at a few of these rather than needing to become very good or excellent at all thirteen of them.

 Remember that what makes you remarkable are those skills at which you truly excel.

Strengthening Strengths Versus Working on Weaknesses

Does all of this excuse us from improving our skills even in areas that aren't already strengths? Of course not! Remember that people at the top of their professions, whether in hockey, horseshoes, or leadership, continue to work on all of their skills, but recognize the importance of their natural gifts.

Before we go any further, get a piece of paper and a pen. Once you have that in front of you, draw a tree. (If you don't have a pen and paper handy, stop and draw the tree in your mind.) Once you have drawn your tree, continue reading.

I don't know whether you drew a palm tree, a tree with leaves, an evergreen tree, or something else, but I do know that about 90 percent of people following that direction will draw only half of a tree: they don't draw any roots (or draw only some just below ground level). In fact, about half of the total plant mass of trees is below the ground's surface. That is, the mass of the root system is as large as the mass of the tree's branches and leaves.

What does this have to do with our strengths and weaknesses? Everything. Just like a tree, most people who want to improve at something focus on only what they can see. And what they can see are their weaknesses. If you want to excel at something, including leadership, you typically are looking for areas where you can improve—that is, the things you see as weaknesses. You may want to be as good at a particular skill as someone you admire. In this analysis, you forget about the root half of your skills tree—the part that nurtures you and gives you strength and balance and stability.

Have you ever had someone compliment you for something that you thought was easy or that you otherwise took for granted? Did you ever stop to think that the compliment was valid and heartfelt, and that the reason you didn't give that behavior much thought was that it was something that came extremely easy to you?

Those things that we are best at are often the things we take for granted. Just like the roots of a tree, your strongest skills are what allow your tree to grow. The stronger and deeper the roots are, the taller the tree can and will grow.

When given feedback on your performance from a reliable (a person we trust), powerful (our boss), or diverse (through a 360-degree assessment perhaps) source, you will have a list of strengths and weaknesses to consider.

Most people look immediately to the weaknesses to determine what to work on and improve. If you consider our analysis of stars in any field, you quickly realize that it is precisely the strengths that made them stars that make people effective. If this is equally true for all of us (and not just the easily recognizable stars), and I believe that it is, then it makes sense for you to spend at least as much time strengthening your strengths as working on your weaknesses.

There is a growing number of books that explore this concept in far greater detail—*Now, Discover Your Strengths* (2001) by Marcus Buckingham and Donald Clifton is one I recommend—but the concept is important for you to consider as you read this book.

You will read chapters or portions of chapters that you consider or know to be your strengths. It will be to your greatest advantage to consider these chapters at least as strongly as those areas where you know you need to improve.

Before You Go

I close this chapter the way I started it.

You were born with a unique set of skills and innate gifts. In many ways, you have been a leader throughout your life. Regardless of your past experience or success, you have the capacity and the potential to be a remarkable leader.

You are already a leader. Read and use this book, and you can become remarkable.

LEADERSHIP DEVELOPMENT IN THE REAL WORLD

TARA AND JILL MET IN COLLEGE and became close friends and sorority sisters. Active in most of the same activities on campus, they often thought they would take jobs in the same organization after graduation. But when their offer letters arrived, the women chose different companies, though within the same industry. Not surprisingly, both had success in the first few years of their careers. As it turned out, they both were promoted to their first leadership roles within a few weeks of each other, just before homecoming at their alma mater.

During a gathering that weekend, Tara and Jill caught up and compared career experiences. Once they realized they recently received similar promotions, they resolved to stay in closer touch. In fact, they decided to get back together for a weekend in about six months to compare experiences and see what they could learn from each other.

True to their word, in the early spring, they met for a weekend. They quickly found their challenges had been quite similar, but their experiences had been somewhat different.

Tara's Experience

Soon after the homecoming weekend and less than a month after being named a supervisor, Tara was sent to a four-day company-sponsored leadership training workshop. Attended by people from across the organization, it was clearly a company priority. It was well planned and executed, in depth, and relevant to Tara's needs as a new supervisor. In fact, Tara learned that everyone in the session had been named a supervisor within the past few weeks.

Tara found the training to be interesting, and she returned to work eager to apply what she learned. Unfortunately, on her return she found herself busier than ever before. Not only had she been gone for four days, leaving some of her work undone, but she found herself staring at 142 e-mails that had arrived during her short absence that all needed to be answered.

She quickly moved into overdrive, putting out fires, answering e-mails, and generally trying to catch up with her backlog. After several days of playing catch-up, she found a small bit of time to reflect on the workshop and decided to try a couple of the techniques she had learned.

About a month after her return to the office, she had a brief conversation with her boss to review her progress and see how he could help her be more comfortable and successful in her new role. She appreciated this opportunity and tried to use the advice and counsel he offered, but generally she was too busy to apply that advice (or most of the ideas she had learned in the workshop for that matter).

In preparation for her weekend with Jill, Tara reviewed her action plan from the workshop. Although she didn't think she had the opportunity to apply much of what she learned or even take many of the action steps she had committed to, she realized that there had been a couple of things that she had successfully applied from that workshop session several months before.

Jill's Experience

Jill returned after the homecoming weekend to a large stack of work too. She suddenly found her department one person short, and she was busier than ever before. Some days it seemed okay, because as a top performer, she always had been able to get a lot of work done. But now things were different: she was expected to get the work done *and* lead others. However, this expectation was mostly hers, because no real expectations had ever been shared with her. She was given a new job title, some new business cards, a bigger office, and lots of congratulations—but not much else.

Each week seemed like more of the same. She never seemed to catch up enough to have time to read the book she bought that would help her with her supervisory and leadership skills. She hadn't had much of a conversation with her boss either. He occasionally stopped by to talk, but about the time she was going to ask a question about her new role, he'd be out the door, telling her to keep up the good work.

One day she learned the company offered a leadership class for new supervisors. Ecstatic, she e-mailed her boss about the course. He replied that he had put her name on the list and proudly replied that he had fought to get her in the next available course—three months away. Although she was pleased with that news, she was dismayed that she would have to wait more than ten months from the time she started her job until she would finally get some training.

She arrived at her weekend with Tara confused, frustrated, and tired. She had started with high hopes of being the kind of supervisor she had always wanted to be—knowledgeable, supportive, and inspiring—but instead she found herself harried and far too often at a loss for what to do in situations she'd never experienced before.

Their Weekend

After Tara and Jill discussed their six-month experiences, they realized that while Tara had initially been given a better chance to succeed, neither had been provided with the experiences, skills, counsel, and support needed to become the kind of leaders they both wanted to be.

Unfortunately, if they expanded their viewpoint to two years, the women likely would find their experiences to be quite similar: not enough skill development or support, or what they were given often being too late to make a difference. They both knew there had to be a better way to learn the skills both really needed and were eager to learn.

The Traditional Leadership Development Process

The experiences of Tara and Jill are not uncommon. Your own experience may be similar to theirs. Although some organizations have a leadership development process that goes beyond the first-line supervisor development described in this story, for the most part, the process in many organizations looks much like what Tara and Jill experienced:

1. Be identified as a leader.
2. Get to work on your new job.
3. Attend the prescribed workshop (when it is scheduled and you can attend).
4. Go back to work (to a very busy job).
5. Apply what you learned (presumably in your "spare" time).

I call this the spray-and-pray approach to leadership development. Even with the best intentions, high-quality training designs and experiences, and willing learners (like Tara and Jill), the chances for a significant impact with this traditional approach are slim. When any one of these three assumptions (good intentions, good training, and willing learners) is not present, the chances for success are slimmer yet. And it can be much worse: some organizations have no leadership development process at all.

Although the traditional approach is certainly better than having no program or process at all, it is far from desirable. It is flawed due to its underlying philosophy that a training event alone will create new performance.

Developing a New Model

You must recognize that training alone won't solve performance gaps (whether in leadership development or any other sort of development). Only then can you begin to create a process that will create real, lasting performance improvement. This recognition is built from the following principles:

○ *Training is an event, but learning is a process.* Training can be an important part of the learning process, but new skills require practice, and even the best training workshops provide only limited opportunities for practice. For real performance improvement to occur, people must use the skills they learned in real-life settings. Your leadership development model must be viewed as a process.

○ *People must want to learn.* Tara and Jill were willing learners and eager to be successful, both for themselves and those they were supervising. Unfortunately not everyone shares this mind-set. Your leadership development model must engage participants in a way that creates their desire to learn the new skills.

○ *People will succeed faster with help.* You can't learn in a vacuum. Organizations are groups of people with varying experience and knowledge, and much of this experience and knowledge can help leaders develop their skills faster—if it is offered to them. Your leadership development model must engage more than just the participant; it must engage others in the organization as well.

○ *People, and especially leaders, are busy.* Leaders often have a hard time applying what they have learned because they are so busy. Whether that busyness is real or perceived, it is a significant obstacle to leadership development. Your leadership development model must account for the huge quantity of work expected from your leaders and help them manage both their work and their development.

○ *Leadership success comes from a wide variety of skills used in complex human systems.* Because there are so many skills, behaviors, techniques, and approaches to learn, leaders often become discouraged by the size of the task and the amount of material available to them. There is a lot to learn to be a remarkable leader. Your leadership development model must help your leaders focus and succeed in a complex system.

These beliefs can become the foundation of a leadership development model for you as well as your department or organization. Now let's look more at what that model might look like.

A New Leadership Development Model

Although the specifics of your model may vary, it must be based on the principles described to ultimately be successful. An effective leadership development program consists of more than a workshop or series of workshops, even if the workshop is stellar. To develop remarkable leaders, you must build an integrated approach to leadership development. Here are some of the steps you'll want to consider in this integrated approach.

1. *Create discovery and desire.* People must want to learn new skills (that is, they must have a felt need for change). When was the last time you were a successful learner of anything when you weren't interested in learning the material? A common complaint of high school and college students is, "I'm never going to use that information." I'm sure your experience matches mine, in school or out. When we become truly interested in the topic and see relevance, we become more willing to learn.

2. *Set a goal and make a plan.* In the story, Tara left her training workshop with an action plan to help her implement the ideas and techniques she learned. This is a great approach, but it can take you only so far. It is far better to build a process that sets goals (see Chapter Sixteen) and makes a plan to reach those goals before attending any formal training. This step will focus you on what you most want to learn during any workshops and put your overall leadership development into a clearer context. Most important, doing this at the beginning will help create the desire necessary for significant improvement.

3. *Focus on strengths.* This point was discussed at some length in Chapter One, so you already recognize that any development plan should focus on more than just those things identified as weaknesses. Rather, it should recognize and provide an opportunity to continue to reinforce and strengthen your greatest strengths.

4. *Find ways to learn.* Recognize that there are many ways to learn, including training. Look for books (it looks like you've already done that), magazines, and blogs to read. Seek out role models to observe and emulate. Find a mentor to help you regularly with your development plan. Gather with like-minded colleagues to talk through some of your successes and challenges. Use a journal to reflect on and learn from your own experiences. Learning can happen anywhere you let it.

5. *Find ways to practice.* Leadership development is skill development. As with any other skill, your learning process must include opportunities to practice. However, one of the keys for success is to be clear on what you are practicing. The skills of remarkable leaders are many, and you will become overwhelmed if you try to work on all of them at once. Identify and practice one skill at a time. Internalize that skill, and lock in the improvement gained from those new habits before practicing another.

6. *Build systems organizationally to support the model.* To be successful, leadership development requires more than an aspiring leader and some training. Organizations can create repeatable processes to make any individual's leadership development more successful. In short, an organization must consider leadership development more holistically.

AN EXAMPLE OF PRACTICE

When you learned to drive a car, you didn't start out knowing all of the details and complexities that would be required for you to be a successful driver. You were taught where to place your hands on the wheel, how to engage the transmission, and how to begin using the accelerator. Once these skills began to come automatically, additional skills (using the mirrors, scanning the gauges and the road, driving defensively, and others) were added to your training. Whether learning to drive, playing a board game, or developing leadership skills, once a skill becomes part of your subconscious repertoire, you are consciously ready to practice another one.

KEY ROLES IN EFFECTIVE ORGANIZATIONAL
LEADERSHIP DEVELOPMENT

Many people can contribute to an organization's leadership development process:

- *The direct supervisor.* Assists in goal setting and action planning, provides context and support for any training the leader attends, and serves as a consistently available coach.

- *Senior-level management.* Recognizes the strategic importance of developing leaders internally. Supports and funds resources and tools for successful leadership development.

- *Human resources and training.* Create or manage the tools, systems, and training. When given the opportunity to operate within a broader vision, exciting tools and processes can emerge. Remember that the best leadership development models leverage the skills and knowledge of these professionals but do not rely completely on them.

- *Peers.* Support each other in their mutual leadership development. Peer support, feedback, and coaching are critical components for developing remarkable leaders.

- *Those led by the leader.* Use the team. In many ways, these people are in the best position to help: they likely interact with the leader and see the results of their skill development more than anyone else. Make them part of the development team by having the leader share his or her goals with them. When leaders do this and are open to feedback, they will benefit from a perspective no one else can provide. Involving the team not only aids the leader but jump-starts the leadership development of other team members too.

This discussion may seem to be organizationally focused: how organizations can build a leadership development process (especially point 6). All of the components certainly apply to organizations. But as an individual reader of this book, I encourage you to think about how you can craft your own leadership development process using these components as your guide. This work is far too important to delegate to your organization. Ultimately you are responsible for becoming the remarkable leader you are meant to be.

The Bottom Line

Results come down to time and focus. Every well-meaning leader I've ever met, regardless of job title, maturity, or skills as a leader, has told me in one way or another that the biggest barriers to developing and using their leadership skills are time and focus. Beyond all of the great concepts and philosophies, any leadership development process must take these two factors into account. The first two components described earlier in this chapter, desire and a goal, are the linchpins to unraveling the challenges presented by time and focus.

Desire

Think of a time in your life when you desperately wanted something: a new skill, a new habit, or something material, for example. Whatever it was, when you reflect on it carefully, you will recognize the power of desire. Desire propels us toward our goals. In fact, there's nothing else that can propel us as quickly.

This leads to part of the problem with most leadership development programs: they impose the program on people when it's convenient for the program (or schedule), even if the leaders are not ready or do not see the relevance at that time. For the program or training to be most successful, the decision to learn must come first. As leaders wanting to develop others, we must remember this key concept: make sure people have developed the desire to learn first. As learners ourselves, we must leverage this idea. When we have the internal motivation to learn something, we will do what it takes, investing the time and asking the questions to create the learning. I assume you are reading this book because you have the desire to become a more effective leader. Couple this book with your desire, and you are on your way to becoming a remarkable leader.

Focus

Most leaders have too much to do. People often tell me they'd love to work on their leadership skills, but they don't have time: they are too busy fighting fires or getting the work out the door. When people are this busy, they often compare themselves to a drowning person. As much as a drowning person might want to be doing something else, his or her only thought at the moment is getting air. Too many leaders find themselves constantly focused only on "getting air."

The appropriate answer is that leadership is the leader's main job. Once leaders realize this and have a way to work on developing leadership skills, the number of fires they will have to contend with will drop. Their leadership skills will be helping them develop the confidence and competence of their team to manage or eliminate the fires themselves.

This problem of focus is exacerbated by the workshop process where we come back from training with several great ideas we want to apply all at once. Your development program will be much more successful when you focus on one skill, behavior, or habit at a time. Your mind was not designed to consciously work on four or five things at once. Rather, we function most effectively when we work on or think about one thing at a time. Once you have completed and successfully mastered that one skill, you can then move on to another. Choosing to focus is an investment in yourself. Remember that you don't have to do everything different all at once to become a remarkable leader. You must instead become remarkable one new skill at a time.

Final Thoughts

The real world poses challenges for leaders at all levels, yet it is in this real world that we must operate. The real world also is the best place for you to practice and hone your skills. Rather than curse the challenges in the real world, leverage reality to your benefit. As a leader, consider using the suggestions and ideas in this chapter to create your own leadership development model or process.

Beyond that, your challenge (no matter your role or title) is to find ways to support the development of other leaders using these same principles and ideas. Translating these principles, one at a time, into relevant practices for yourself and others helps you become a truly remarkable leader.

3

HOW TO GET THE MOST OUT OF THIS BOOK

THIS BOOK CAN HAVE A SIGNIFICANT IMPACT on your life and your success as a leader if you apply what you read and learn. Consider this book a significant part of your own personal leadership development process.

If you have gotten this far or reviewed the Contents page, you will recognize that this book covers a broad range of topics. You might even consider it a survey of leadership skills. This is somewhat true but actually misses the point. This book has been written and designed to help you accelerate your journey toward remarkable leadership. It provides a framework, mentions many topics and ideas, and gives specific actions to help you apply each of these skills.

As you read some sections of this book, you may think, "I already know that" or "That's not new to me." If you do already know the material, that's wonderful—though somewhat irrelevant. What's relevant is whether you are *applying* what you know. As you read, ask yourself this important question: "How well am I applying this?" Answering that question honestly and then applying those things that you don't consistently do will take you far down the road to becoming a remarkable leader. Once you have mastered not only the knowledge but the use of the ideas and tools, then you can delve into a specific area in greater depth, and I strongly encourage you to do so.

The Book Structure

A quick scan of the Contents shows that each chapter focuses on one leadership competency. Within each chapter (starting with Chapter Four), you will find several common components:

o *Self-assessment.* Each chapter begins with a brief self-assessment based on that chapter's competency. These reflective questions will help you think about your current skill level and help you determine your strengths and weaknesses. This is designed to help you prioritize and focus your reading for that chapter. To get the most out of this book, take the time to answer and reflect on the self-assessment questions before reading each chapter.

o *Skill areas.* Each competency is divided into skill areas designed to help you dissect the larger competency to find specific skills inside that may be especially relevant to you now. The purpose of this book is to give you the relevant information, tools, and techniques that will make a real difference in your leadership results. The material selected for inclusion in each of these areas will, when applied, help you become a remarkable leader.

o *Your Now Steps.* At the end of each section are action items called "Your Now Steps," designed to help you take immediate action on what you've just learned. These ideas are quick to apply and relevant to your growth as a leader. Yes, I know you are busy, but if you want to become remarkable (or even just better), these are the first steps. Even so, you may not be able to do all of the Now Steps. Don't let your inability to do all of them prevent you from doing some of them. Apply something, and get started.

o *Bonus Bytes.* There was no way to get everything I wanted into each chapter. The Bonus Byte icon shown here is your alert to additional materials to support the content of the chapter. You have access to all of the Bonus Bytes on their own Web site: RLBonus.com. Each can be obtained with the use of a keyword or phrase so that you can quickly and easily find the additional resources you need.

o *Your Remarkable Principles.* Each skill area was included because of the importance of an underlying principle. By identifying these principles, I hope to help you solidify your understanding and knowledge of the ideas you read.

○ *Remarkable Resources.* At the end of each chapter is a link to other writing related to each skill. Whereas Bonus Bytes typically are tools to help you apply specific concepts of the chapter, Remarkable Resources are extensions of the content. They explore additional thoughts, skills, and ideas within the overall chapter competency.

This book is designed this way because it is meant to be a development resource, not just a book to read. I love to read books, but reading alone won't change anything. Only action creates change.

How to Read This Book

According to Jerrold Jenkins of the Jenkins Group (1999), 57 percent of new books aren't read to their conclusion. If you are reading this sentence I'm betting you've decided to read it all. Congratulations and thanks!

Most people were taught in school to read a book from front to back, one chapter at a time. That is one way to read this book, but it's not the only way, and it may not be the most effective way for you.

I suggest that you next read Chapter Four. Then you have at least three options and can decide which will work best for you:

Option 1: Start with a quick full read, and then decide where to focus.

Option 2: Browse quickly, and then decide where to start.

Option 3: Start with the skill you are most interested in.

If you create option 4, send me an e-mail. I would love to hear about it!

How to Apply This Book

Any of the reading approaches will get you started. Ultimately it doesn't matter how you start; what matters is that you get into a chapter and put it to use. Start with the self-assessment; then read the chapter thoroughly with a highlighter handy to mark the concepts that speak to you.

After you've read the chapter, decide which skill area you want to focus on first. Remember that your best success will come by focusing on one skill at a time. Use Your Now Steps as a guide, and get to work.

If you don't currently keep a journal, I encourage you to use one as an aid for your learning process (for this book and beyond).

WHAT TO WRITE IN YOUR LEARNING JOURNAL

- *Ideas.* Use your journal to write down ideas that come to you as you read or while you work on your skills.

- *Action items.* You may choose to rewrite Your Now Steps so that you can work without the book in front of you. You may also identify other action steps you want to take.

- *Questions.* As you study, you likely will have questions. Write those questions in your journal, whether you have the answers or not. The process of capturing the question is an important part of the learning process. When you review your journal at some future date, you'll be surprised how many of your questions you have now answered.

- *Reflections and results.* After you've applied something, tried something, or experienced something, take the time to reflect. Your journal is the perfect place to write reflections and your results. Perhaps you've applied a Now Step and had limited results. Remember that practice is a precursor to perfection, and that without reflecting on the practice, you'll never achieve all that is possible.

- *Quotations.* When you read something in this book that you like, agree with, or want to remember, capture it. Perhaps you will think of other quotations that you have read or heard people say that apply to your study and application of the skill; if so, capture those as well. These quotations will become a valuable part of your journal over time and something you will treasure for many years.

- *Anything else.* Maybe you don't like the title "Learning Journal." If not, call it a leadership log, a notebook, a diary, or something else. It truly doesn't matter what you call it or exactly how you use it. Your journal will be highly personal, and you should feel free to adapt this tool to fit your own personal needs and style. Whatever you include is exactly the right stuff for you.

This book can be extremely valuable, but you must do more than read it. *Use* the book, and you will become a remarkable leader.

I wish you great success, and appreciate being invited along for your journey.

4

REMARKABLE LEADERS LEARN CONTINUALLY

OFTEN WHEN I AM WITH A GROUP helping them think about or work on their leadership skills, I do the following exercise (feel free to play along):

1. Close your eyes, think of the most effective leader you know, and get a mental picture of him or her. This person can be alive or dead, someone you know personally or have only read about or observed from afar. Whoever it is, see the person in your mind's eye.
2. Make a list of the behaviors or skills that this person exhibits—the things that make him or her so successful as a leader.

After people complete this simple exercise, I ask them to share the skills and behaviors they have identified. The lists I hear are long and cover many of the competencies explored in this book—except one. The skill that is almost always is missing from these lists is being a lifelong learner.

There is absolutely no question in my mind that being a continual learner is a key skill for leaders. In fact, I believe that it is the most important skill of all for leaders, yet it usually doesn't make people's lists. (Did it make yours?)

Why don't people consider learning and add it to the list of traits of great leaders? Because it is the underlying skill—the skill without which improvement in any other area is nearly impossible. If leaders aren't learners, they can't be remarkable. Perhaps learning is a skill that we don't think about because it is assumed, considered a given, or deemed obvious. Whatever the reason, it doesn't change the fact that we must start with learning. And while we all know how to learn, remarkable leaders know that because it is the underlying foundational skill, as they get better at it, it will help them in all of their other leadership development efforts.

Why Learning Is So Important to Us as Leaders

There are several specific reasons that we must focus on continual lifelong learning as the cornerstone skill on the path to remarkable leadership.

Leadership Is a Complex Endeavor

Humans are complex, and a leader is dealing with more than just his or her own complexities. Leaders are tasked with understanding the complexity of human behavior and coordinating interactions across many people. (When we put it this way, the role can seem daunting.) Something this complex won't be mastered quickly. Remarkable leaders know that the mastery of these complexities is a lifelong journey with no defined end point. The result? The need and desire to have a learning mind-set continually.

Status Quo Requires No Leadership

If everything in the current situation was great, that is, if there was no need for change, how much leadership would be needed? Leadership is required because we want to move somewhere. The need for leadership is predicated on change, and so leaders must be prepared to work under changing conditions. If conditions change, then learning is required to continually adapt to and work within the changing conditions.

How static is your situation? Unless you are unlike anyone in any organization in which I've worked, change is everywhere. Remarkable leaders know their job is to help move people through the status quo. Therefore, they know that they must continue to grow themselves to meet the needs of the situations and the people they are leading.

It Will Make Us Better and Our Job Easier

Let's get to the bottom line: you want to be more effective in your work and accomplish things more easily. Because of the two reasons I've already shared, it is clear that when you have a learning mind-set, you will be able to handle complexities more successfully, and that will make your job easier and you more successful.

We Must Model It for Others

When you are a leader, whether by position or reputation, people are looking to you. You are a role model, which means there's even more incentive to learn, since you are learning for more than just yourself. Of course, we need to be learning for our own competency and confidence, but we also need to be learning to better serve those we are leading. It is our role to set a tone and model for those following us.

Do you want those you lead to be consistently learning and improving? If the answer is yes, how can you honestly expect them to do that if you aren't consistently modeling those behaviors? You cannot expect your teams to continue to grow and develop if you aren't growing yourself.

Better Leader = Better Human

Warren Bennis, the renowned leadership thinker, wrote, "Effective leaders understand that there is no difference between becoming an effective leader and becoming a fully integrated human being" (quoted in Baker, 2003). The best leaders are learners for all of the reasons above (and for many other reasons), but they also know something else: In the end, the skills that make them better leaders also make them more highly functioning, successful, confident, and satisfied human beings. Remarkable leaders are learners because they want to be better leaders and better people. For example, learning how to communicate more effectively makes you more effective in more than just your role as a leader. That skill development, that growth, spills out into every other part of your life. If none of the other reasons listed are compelling enough for you to focus on learning, this one should be.

Learning is a skill, and this chapter will help you hone and develop that skill. But as the points suggest, learning also is a choice. You can choose to have a learning mind-set and be open to new ideas and techniques. It is from these choices that you can develop your proficiency as a learner and the habit of learning continually.

Remarkable Principle ▷ **Leaders become remarkable through learning.**

Self-Assessment

Here is a quick assessment to help you think about your skills as a relationship builder. Use the following scale of 1 to 7 on each question:

1. Almost never
2. Rarely or seldom
3. Occasionally
4. Sometimes
5. Usually
6. Frequently
7. Almost always

I consciously think about learning.   _____

I consider myself a learner.   _____

I am open to new ideas and approaches.   _____

I am observant.   _____

I am curious.   _____

I reflect and/or keep a journal.   _____

I find learning fun.   _____

The Cycle of Learning

The challenge posed by this chapter (and in fact this entire book) is to be more intentional about what, when, and how we learn. We have all invested lots of time in school, and so we think we ought to be expert learners because we've spent all this time "learning." Unfortunately, time in school doesn't ensure that we become proficient learners. After all, how many classes have you taken on learning? But if we are going to be intentional, we need to look at the underlying learning process rather than just move forward assuming our learning competence.

As you can see from Figure 4.1, there are four elements in the human learning cycle. Let's examine each one.

Step One: Have an Experience

At the top, to start the cycle, there must be an input—some event or experience.

I'm guessing that you have learned how to ride a bicycle. You went through a learning process to master that skill. I'm also guessing that you can remember the first time you got on a bicycle. What happened during that first experience? There may have been some initial success, but pretty quickly there was a fall. That fall was clearly an experience,

Figure 4.1. The Cycle of Learning

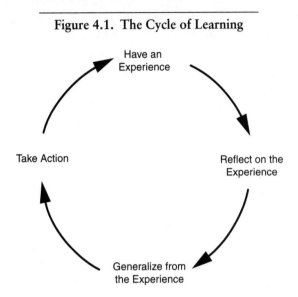

but not necessarily a learning experience yet. At the fall stage, it's just an experience. I put myself on the seat of the bicycle, I put my feet on the pedals, I start to do something, I wobble around, and then I fall down, and so I've had an experience: the first step in the learning cycle.

You learn to ride a bicycle, learn a new procedure at work, read about a new technique, listen to a lecture, or do any of a thousand other things to create an experience (either directly or in the third person) to help you start the learning process. Some impetus is required, and that's the experience. To initiate learning, there must be the input of an experience.

Step Two: Reflect on the Experience

The second step begins as you think about the experience, but even as you move into that second step, you will aid your learning by observing.

We'll look more at observing later in this chapter, but for now, observing means *becoming aware of your actions and results*. You'll be a more effective learner in any situation when you are observing during the experience and thinking about what's going on around you. The more aware you are and the more you keep your attention focused in the present and on that situation (say, of getting on the bicycle), the more you'll gain from the experience.

In this step, you begin thinking about the facts: what actually happened. For example, as you analyze your fateful bike ride, you realize that you started to fall when you leaned this way, or that you started to fall when you stopped pedaling, or you started to fall when you did something else.

Beyond the facts, completing this step fully includes thinking about what was going on around you and how you felt during the experience. Consider questions like: "Beyond the facts, what was going on from an emotional perspective?" And "How do those feelings relate to what happened?"

You may stay in this second step for a long time, or you may complete it almost instantaneously. You fall off the bike, notice that your knee is scraped, and make a couple of quick decisions before moving on. You may already be thinking about what happened, analyzing it, and deciding what you did wrong or want to change almost immediately, and that's great. But in many work and life situations, people do not intentionally spend enough time in this step.

Step Three: Generalize from the Experience

You've had an experience and have some new insights. Now the questions are, How do you apply what you are thinking to your situation? How do you relate it to what you already know? How do you translate it? How do you generalize it?

When you are learning to ride the bicycle, there will be some very specific things you can gain from the experience of falling, but you also may be able to generalize the experience for greater learning. Perhaps that experience reminds you of something else, and that connection will help you to be more successful in the future. Generalizing is asking this trilogy of questions: How does this relate? What did I learn? What do I do next?

Step Four: Take Action

This all leads directly to the fourth step: taking action on what we have learned. It doesn't matter what action we decide we should take. All that really matters is that we actually take an action. Until we do something, nothing is going to happen. You undoubtedly know some people who are highly experienced on their jobs in terms of years of service, but they still tend to make rookie mistakes. (They say they have ten years of experience, but really, they have one year of experience ten times.) Those people probably are stopping after the third step in the learning cycle because they are not applying what they learned. (They might even be stopping after the second step.)

The linchpin of this cycle of learning—of making your learning intentional—is applying what you have learned. You must take steps Two and Three to understand what you learned: ask the questions and reflect on both the experience and the questions. And then you must then translate all of that into what to do now. It is these next steps that will lead to your continuous growth and success.

Reinforcing the Learning Cycle

Looking at the cycle of learning here, flat on the page, can be a bit deceiving. Actually this series of steps is not two-dimensional. Instead, look at this cycle as an upward spiral (Figure 4.2).

When we apply the experience after going through this cycle, our skill level is higher than it was when we had the experience the first time. And as we go through the cycle the next time, we are continuing on an upward spiral for that experience. We are truly learning not only from the mistakes we made but also by continuing to reinforce, reactivate, and repeat the things that were successful.

Figure 4.2. The Upward Spiral of Learning

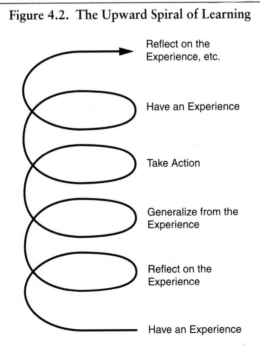

Reflect on the Experience, etc.

Have an Experience

Take Action

Generalize from the Experience

Reflect on the Experience

Have an Experience

We have already agreed that we learn from our mistakes and from strengthening our strengths. While you certainly want to think about the things that did not go as planned, you also want to think about what did go well so you can replicate those. This reinforces the concept of the learning cycle as an upward spiral of growth, improvement, and greater success.

Your Now Step

1. Before you read any further, think about a situation that you've been in recently where you have applied this cycle or wish you had applied it. As you reflect, make some notes. Think about how the cycle applied—whether you recognized it—and what you can do differently next time.

 Intentionally completing the cycle of learning helps you learn more from every experience.

The Learning Mind-Set

Once we have a clear motive to improve or learn, there are two other major components to having a learning mind-set: having a beginner's mind and self-awareness.

The Beginner's Mind

Shunryu Suzuki wrote in his book *Zen Mind, Beginner's Mind* (2006), "If your mind is empty, it is always ready for anything; it is open to everything. In the beginner's mind there are many possibilities; in the expert's mind there are few" (p. 1).

How likely are you to learn something new if you already consider yourself an expert? You've probably been to a training workshop where people have walked in with arms folded and thinking (or even saying), "I already know this. This is a waste of my time." How much do those people learn in that situation?

We all want to be experts, and as leaders, there are particular pressures—whether cultural expectations, the expectations of our boss, or our own beliefs—that we need to know for what we are doing. But there is a difference between being proficient or "knowing what we are doing" and assuming we have (or need to have) all of the answers.

Remarkable leaders know they don't have all the answers and want to be on a path of learning some of the answers, as well as the new questions, every day.

We have common phrases to describe this phenomenon: "We are writing the book as we go." "This is new for all of us." "It's a whole new ballgame." Each of these statements is an indication of operating with a beginner's mind: people know they have a lot to learn. In these cases, you may allow yourself to be a beginner, but in many other cases, people don't, especially when they are talking or thinking about themselves as opposed to a group or team. Somehow it is okay for the group to have a beginner's mind-set, but *I* better know what *I'm* doing! You must get past this mental obstacle if you want to have a learning mind-set: you must know and behave as if there is always more to be learned on any subject.

So what does a beginner's mind look like?

o Beginners are secure enough in themselves that they can say, "I don't know," to themselves and to others. Interestingly, I have heard many people say they admire others who can admit when they don't know something, but it's much more infrequent that people are comfortable saying it themselves.

o Beginners don't connect their self-worth to their expertise. They are more likely to tie their internal worth to their ability to get the answer, to be adaptable, and to be resourceful in learning what is needed.

o Beginners are willing to ask for help, and they actively seek out experts as resources to help with the quest for continual learning.

o Beginners recognize other beginners and support them however they can.

o Beginners recognize there is always more to learn about learning. As such, they learn not only about things they want to know or be able to do, but they learn about learning and spend time and effort on improving as a learner.

o Beginners realize that all learning is a journey or a process without a final destination. They recognize the value of learning something new every day and aren't discouraged by the fact that there is no real end. They recognize learning as valuable in and of itself.

Interestingly when we truly are starting to do something for the first time—a new job, a new procedure, a new hobby, a new sport—and are a beginner by the classical definition of the word, we naturally do the first four items above. Our challenge, and opportunity, is to continue to do those four when things aren't new and to add the last two to our regular habit patterns.

Self-Awareness

Along with motivation and a beginner's mind, a learning mind-set also requires us to be self-aware. You must be aware of the learning process and your proficiency at it. Beyond that, you must also consider your biases, prejudices, and beliefs about the topic you are learning about. Each of these can have a massive impact on what you observe and learn, and with self-awareness, you can monitor that learning much more effectively. You also must notice your reactions to situations and understand why you respond in the ways you do. This self-awareness and understanding provide necessary preparation for your success as a continual learner.

Your Now Steps

Here are some things you can do right now to develop your learning mind-set. These are actions you can take at any time to instantly change your approach and increase your success:

1. Think of something you need to get better at now. Write down two or three reasons that learning more about this will benefit you.
2. Say, "I don't know," out loud. Say it loud; say it proud. Now say it adding some important words: "I don't know, *but I can find out*!" Adding these five words will change your attitude and approach. Saying it now is practice for the next time you have the opportunity to say it. (I'm guessing that chance will come before the end of the day.)
3. Read the rest of this chapter. (It is going to help you develop your learning mind-set.)

 Remarkable leaders consciously cultivate a learner's mind-set.

Curiosity

I'm sure you would agree that kids are the most prolific learners, and I'm guessing you also would agree that kids are the most curious people you know.

That is no coincidence: curiosity and learning go hand-in-hand. Our minds want to know the answer to questions we care about, and so our minds search for that answer. Curiosity combines the concepts of motivation (eagerness) and being a beginner (looking for an answer).

Our curiosity is expressed through the questions we ask. And the number one question that kids—our masters of curiosity—ask is, "Why?"

Why? When you ask, "Why?" you are open and eager to learn or know, you are searching, and you are on the path to understanding.

Many problem-solving techniques include a step of getting to the root cause of a problem. One component of root cause analysis is asking, "Why?" Specifically, the method is known as the "Five Whys." In this approach, you start with a problem and continue to ask (and answer) the why question until you can no longer ask, and answer, a why question. At this point, you have found the root cause of the problem. You can usually get to the root cause in "five whys" or fewer—hence the name of the method. You will learn more about problem solving in Chapter Thirteen.

 To learn more about the Five Whys technique and how to use it, download this Bonus Byte at www.RLBonus.com using the keywords "five whys".

When is the last time you used the Five Whys (or something similar) to analyze something other than a work-related issue? Remember the "why" question is the key to our curiosity and so asking, "Why?" helps us to understand and helps us to stay on a learning path.

OTHER WAYS TO ASK WHY

The "why?" question is powerful, so be careful when asking it of others unless they know your purpose. Posing "why" questions can lead people to be defensive. Let people know why you are asking them "Why?" or use some of these alternative questions:

- How do you mean?
- Then what happened?
- Tell me more...
- What do you think?
- What do you think was the cause?

Beyond "Why?" there are many other questions to ask. And remember that questions in general are the stuff of our curiosity.

Curiosity is not something we outgrow. Research shows that our capacity to learn doesn't fall off as we grow older. Although kids seem to be faster, more agile learners, age alone doesn't determine our ability to learn. But declining amounts of curiosity do play a part in our declining learning prowess. The good news is that we can choose to be curious; we can make curiosity and questioning a habit.

Your Now Steps

Here's what you can do right now to develop and invigorate your curiosity:

1. Think about something you have wondered about within the past hour and ask "Why?" Ask it again if you wish to use the answer as a platform for your learning.

2. When you encounter something new or something you are curious about, act like an investigative reporter or journalist. This is your chance to be Anderson Cooper or Barbara Walters.

 Remarkable leaders are curious leaders.

Observation

I have had many opportunities to help people learn to be better trainers and presenters. In all these cases, the most valuable tool I can bring to those learning experiences is a video camera. Few people like to see themselves exposed on a television screen, but once they get past how they look and sound, they realize how valuable it is to watch themselves perform. This third-person observation triggers deeper insights and understanding of both their strengths and the things they want to improve. Nevertheless, you don't need a video camera to benefit from observing.

Observation is a skill to employ in the learning cycle during Step One (the experience itself) and Step Two (thinking about the experience). It is a powerful and drastically overlooked skill.

The fact that you can observe during the experience in Steps One and Two is an important point. People often don't recognize that they can observe things while they are experiencing something (admittedly it takes willingness and practice) and delay observation for afterward. As you become more skilled, you can actually observe in the moment. That will become easier when you understand the two major keys to observing: attention and filters.

Attention

Attention is what you choose to notice among the thousands of stimuli your brain receives each moment. Those things you notice are the things you think about, analyze, and process in a more meaningful way.

Your attention is naturally drawn to one of two types of things: things you recognize and things that are significant because they are surprising. When we see someone we know in a room crowded with strangers, our attention is on that acquaintance. Alternatively if there is one person wearing a clown suit at a black tie dinner, it would be hard to not keep looking at the clown. These are the types of things—the very familiar and the very unusual—that we naturally notice, but as a continual learner we are more intentional about the things we notice and observe.

In their book *The Prepared Mind of a Leader*, Bill Welter and Jean Egmon wrote, "Attention is a requirement for the skill of observing. It is the filter through which we choose what to sense and what to make sense of" (2005, p. 50).

Observing requires us to bring things into our consciousness, and the things we pay attention to are those that we have made conscious. You will become a more effective observer when you are clear on what you choose to pay attention to because it is only those things that you can consider and analyze further.

Filters

Have you ever watched a movie with someone and when you discuss it later, you're pretty sure you weren't watching the same screen? Two people can easily watch the same movie or read the same book and have very different perspectives on the most powerful parts, the most important roles, and the most crucial scenes. One person feels the power was in the relationship in the story; the other is touched by the cinematography. Each person sees the movie through different eyes, clouded by his or her current thoughts and preoccupations, as well as past experiences, ideas, beliefs, and values. All of these form the filters through which we see.

The importance of our filters is described well by this quotation, attributed to many sources: "We do not see things as they are, but as we are." Your filters are a powerful magnet for your observations. As with your attention, you need to be self-aware enough to understand that these natural tendencies exist. With this awareness, you can choose a different set of filters (see a situation from another perspective) or drop your filters altogether to observe without judgment—to observe as the video camera does, simply recording the images and facts.

The Reticular Activating System

A few years ago we bought a new black Ford Expedition that we loved. Right after we bought it, I began to see Expeditions everywhere: on ads, in parking lots, on the streets. It was as if everyone had decided to buy an Expedition at the same time we did.

Of course, that's not true. There were Expeditions on the road, in commercials, and on billboards long before we bought ours, but I hadn't noticed them. The number of vehicles or commercials didn't change; what changed was my new combination of attention and filters. I noticed Expeditions now because I was paying attention to them. Because of the experience of shopping for and buying an Expedition, my filters were letting this information through. I've shared this story with many others who have a similar story.

The technical reason for this filter is the reticular activating system, which is the brain's filtering system. This system helps us sort what we see, and it brings to our consciousness those things that we deem important. The reticular activating system helps us explain assumptions, prejudices, and lots more in our lives. Beyond that, it keeps us from being in constant sensory overload.

What to Observe

Now let's look at what to observe in any situation in which you want to learn.

CONTENT. Whatever experience you are having, whether sitting through a lecture, doing a task, or having a conversation, the content of the situation is important. You need to be observant of what is being said—the facts of the situation. This may seem obvious: the content of a situation is what we typically think about as the source of learning.

PROCESS. Highly effective observers are noting more than the words that are being said; they also are paying attention to what is happening while the words are being said. For example, if you are leading or facilitating a meeting, you might be observing the process of what is going on, in addition to the outcomes (the content).

Observing process in this example means to pay attention to the group dynamics: what is being said, the body language in the room, how people react to the behaviors of others, what is working or not working from these perspectives. As mentioned earlier, you can observe later by replaying an experience in your mind, but you also can become skilled at observing during the actual experience, giving you better insights for the later sections of the cycle of learning. This approach also allows modifications to be made while you are experiencing something, not just reflecting after the fact.

MORE THAN WHAT WE SEE. Most people consider *observing* as a synonym for *seeing*. We certainly can observe with our eyes, but we also can observe with all of our other senses, as well as with our intuition. Your observations will become more useful to you as fodder for learning when you adopt a multisensory approach to observation.

BEING IN THE MOMENT. You likely will be thinking about all of these ideas the next time you are in a situation you consider to be a learning opportunity. Remember that although you want to build your observation skills, you don't want them to be such a conscious part of your thinking that you aren't present in the experience. In other words, you still need to listen to the team member who needs your help rather than becoming completely preoccupied with your own observations on how you are doing. Observing during an experience is valuable, but remaining present with the situation and the others in it should be your first priority.

 To learn seven ways to help you stay in the moment, download this Bonus Byte at www.RLBonus.com using the keyword "moment."

Your Now Steps

Here's what you can do right now to develop your observation skills and habits:

1. Determine one thing you'd like to improve on today. Think about the last time this situation occurred, and notice what you observed.

2. Think about the last movie you watched or the last fiction book you read. Think of the three things that most struck you about the story,

and determine how your filters might have played a role in your experience of the story.

3. In your next interaction with another person, be aware of both the content and process of that situation as a way to practice observing both things.

 Your ability to observe is your most underused and underappreciated learning skill.

Reflection

When people first think of the word *reflection,* they typically think of a mirror. After all, most of us use the reflection from a mirror as part of our normal morning routine. We do that, out of habit, to see how we look and to help us improve our appearance for the day ahead.

Mirrors are useful tools: in an instant, we get information about ourselves that helps us have a more successful and enjoyable day. Most of us would miss them if we didn't have them around, and some people think they couldn't live without one.

It puzzles me that most of us use the power of reflection with a mirror as a tool, but too few of us, and far too infrequently, use the greater power of reflective thinking to bring much greater things to our lives. We use a mirror to improve our outward appearance but do not always use reflection tools to help us improve from the inside, in our minds and behaviors.

Experience can be our greatest teacher. And we become our best teacher when we step back and reflect.

What Keeps Us from Reflecting

Most of our deep beliefs and ideas about learning come from our school experiences. In school, reflection typically didn't play much of a role in the learning process. We were always learning the next thing, solving the next kind of problem. Rarely were we asked to look back and review our experiences to help us improve or learn more in the future. We were tested on what we learned, the grade being the outcome, and then moved on to the next subject.

Because of this training and experience, many people walk through their lives without reflecting. They do some work, get a result, and move

on to the next task or event, without ever (or only rarely) looking back
to reflect and learn.

How to Do It

In its simplest form, reflecting is thinking about what happened. Reflection doesn't mean looking for blame or looking for regrets. Your reflection will be most valuable when it considers events and their results (whether desirable or not). In general, your reflection will be most valuable to you when you think about and answer these types of questions:

o What happened (both the process and the end results)?

o How did I feel about it?

o Why did it happen that way (what contributed to the results)?

o How does this remind me of other situations?

o What will I do differently in the future based on these answers?

These questions form the backbone of effective, reflective learning. They help us look at the events and results from a variety of angles and lead us to the all-important Step Three generalizing question: "Knowing what I now know, what will I do differently next time?"

When to Do It

Reflecting can be part of your everyday routine. You might reflect on the previous day and see how you can apply any lessons in the coming day. You might take time during the day to reflect on a project or specific event. In general, once you have the basic pattern of questions in your mind, you can reflect before going to bed, in your car on the way to work, while you exercise, or at any other time when you are doing routine things that don't require your full mental attention.

St. Ignatius Loyola, founder of the Jesuits, developed a form of prayer called Examen of Consciousness. The major component was called "reviewing your day" (originally done two to three times per day). In this activity, you review the portion of your day since your last reflection, watching it like a movie in your mind. While you replay your experiences, you notice the details of the experience, the context of what happened, and how you acted. You reflect too on your motives and feelings. This is not psychoanalysis; rather, it is a time for you to discern your daily motives, actions, and reactions.

This is a great example of consciously and consistently applying reflection to your life. You can choose this more rigorous approach, or you can choose to reflect on any particular situation or experience that you want to examine.

Your reflection can take the form of thinking only, or it can be expanded to writing in a journal of some sort, or in talking about your reflections with a friend, colleague, or peer.

To learn more about using a journal for learning reflection, download this Bonus Byte at www.RLBonus.com using the keywords "learning journal."

Just like looking in the mirror, reflective thinking can become a habit. It will help you see yourself better, and after taking action on what you see (just as you presumably improve your appearance after acting on what you see in the mirror), you will improve accordingly.

Your Now Steps

Here's what you can do right now to develop your reflection skills:

1. Apply the reflective questions above to some event or experience in your day so far.
2. Write those insights in a notebook or journal, or type them into your computer.
3. Share those insights with someone who is supportive of your ongoing development.

Remarkable leaders reflect on their experiences to continue their improvement.

Fun

Think about some of the most emotional times in your life—the times when you were stressed or faced a major challenge. It is often in our darkest and most challenging times that we learn things that we will remember and use for a lifetime. We all have had these experiences and have had these sometimes hard lessons, but you may not have stopped to think about why those lessons are so engrained in your mind.

The reason is that learning is firmly anchored when it is connected to an emotional event, and it doesn't matter if the emotional event is negative or positive. That's good news because it means that connecting your learning to pleasure, joy, or fun is an effective way to deepen your lessons and remember those lessons longer.

In my organization, we always are looking for ways to make learning more relevant, focused, and valuable for our clients. Equally important, we intentionally design ways to make the learning experience more fun. Research tells us this is the right strategy, and our experiences confirm it. When learning is more fun, people are more receptive and remember the lessons much longer.

Why It Matters to You

I've just shared this concept from the perspective of someone who creates training and other learning experiences. If you are thinking that this doesn't matter to you because you aren't a trainer, you are wrong. As a member of a team, you want to help others learn. As a leader, you have skills and behaviors you want others to know and practice. If you are a parent or a community volunteer, for example, you have a teaching role. And of course, if none of the other things are true, you are still responsible for your own personal learning.

Here are five things you can do to incorporate more fun into the learning you lead and your personal learning:

○ *Learn with others*. Students know that studying together in a group can be a good strategy. This can be true for adults too. Read a book, and talk about it with others (this book perhaps). Get three or four people together to work on your next presentation. Do a project as a team. The results, enjoyment, and learning will all likely increase.

○ *Plan for fun*. If you are doing a presentation or training, use an exercise to lighten up the session. Don't do this just for fun; make sure you connect it to the lessons or message of the session. This works for you personally too: keep a playful and fun mind-set when you find yourself in any learning situation.

○ *Laugh and learn*. The next time you make a mistake, laugh about your foible. While you are reflecting on and laughing about your mistake, think about what you can learn from the experience. Use the learning and the laughter to ensure the mistake isn't repeated.

○ *Think about it.* When you've experienced something fun, take a few minutes to see what you can learn from the fun. What made it fun? How can you repeat those elements in another situation or with other people?

○ *Allow fun in.* The lesson you are trying to learn may be serious, but things can be both serious and enjoyable. When we allow fun in, we can help the learning process and cement the learning. The efforts you make to lighten the spirit during a serious and important situation can be richly rewarded.

This is just a start. Once you recognize the power of connecting learning and fun, you will find yourself enjoying yourself and learning more than ever before.

Your Now Steps

Here's what you can do right now to infuse more fun into your learning:

1. Think about the last mistake you made. Look for the humor or silliness in it. Take the lesson, but see the humor too.
2. Take five minutes right now to do something fun or enjoyable (even if you are reading this on the job). Then get on with an important task, and observe how much better the task goes.

 Remarkable leaders make learning last by making learning fun.

Some Final Thoughts

This chapter has been about learning both consciously and subconsciously. But don't let the fact that you have learned many things in your life cloud the most important concept raised by this chapter: learning is a choice.

Everything in this chapter becomes more powerful when you consider learning to be an intentional activity and choose to make it an underlying component of what you do every day. We all have the choice of what to do with any given situation or event. Remarkable leaders choose to learn from these situations.

The following chapters describe twelve competencies necessary to become a remarkable leader. All of them are important. Learning to do any one of them more effectively will require you to practice and use your skill of learning, which is one reason that this chapter came first. The other reason is that I want you to be thinking about not only learning the skills and techniques that can make you remarkable, but the meta skill of learning to learn. In that way, this chapter is meant as both preparation for the rest of the book and a challenge to you for the rest of your life.

 Go to remarkableleadershipbook.com/resources for more information, writing, tools, and other highly recommended resources to help you make learning a more intentional part of your daily life.

REMARKABLE LEADERS
CHAMPION CHANGE

IF EVERYTHING IS PERFECT, no change is needed. If an organization is achieving at the highest possible levels, all employees are thrilled, customers are flocking to buy products of perfect quality, and supply is always at the right place at the right time, so no change is needed. Oh—and no leaders would be required either.

Of course we know this isn't reality. There are problems, and there are opportunities. There are mergers, reorganizations, product launches, new software to be implemented, new facilities to build, quality problems to solve, customer service challenges, and a host of other things. These are the fabric of modern work, and all of them require change by someone (or, in many cases, everyone). When considered from this perspective, change is the currency of leaders.

Although understanding and championing change is important, organizations aren't very good at implementing it. According to Rick Maurer (1996), author of *Beyond the Wall of Resistance*, only 23 percent of mergers recoup their costs, 43 percent of quality improvement efforts are good investments, and 9 percent of major software applications are worth what you pay for them. This is not to say change can't be successful. Rather, it is a reminder that remarkable results require more successful approaches. This chapter gives you the approaches to help you beat those odds.

To be a remarkable leader, you must understand change from both an individual and organizational perspective, and you must be able to influence, manage, lead, and champion change within your organization and your teams. In this chapter, we explore four key change skills:

1. Using the levers of change
2. Planning and implementing successful change

3. Being a change champion

4. Moving past resistance to acceptance

Before we get to those important skills, let's discuss change itself a bit more. When you read or hear the word *change,* what do you think of? In your journal, on a piece of paper, or in the space below, write the first six words or phrases that come to mind:

1. _____

2. _____

3. _____

4. _____

5. _____

6. _____

We'll come back to your words shortly. A quick look in any thesaurus will give you a long list of synonyms for the word *change;* here are just fourteen:

Addition	Innovation
Adjustment	Refinement
Advance	Revolution
Break	Shift
Conversion	Transformation
Diversification	Transition
Excitement	Variation

Here is another list of words. I gathered these by asking other people their thoughts about change:

Dread	Too expensive
Fear	Too soon
Risk	Not necessary
Too fast	Uncertainty

Do you see the difference between the two lists? The words in the second list have a decidedly more negative tone. And yet all of the words, both positive and negative (and a bunch of other neutral ideas in between), are part of what comes to mind when people think about change.

Now go back to your own list. Place a plus sign beside your words and phrases that you think or feel positively about, a minus sign by those that you think or feel negatively about, and an N by those that are neutral to you. Chances are that not all of your words have a plus sign beside them (and I hope they don't all have a minus sign either). Almost everyone has mixed feelings and experiences about change, and these all play a part in how readily someone will accept or adopt any change.

Why Our Feelings Matter

Thoughts, feelings, and experiences relating to change are important to us as leaders in at least three ways:

1. *How we feel about change at any point in time will change based on our current or most recent experiences.* If an organization has just been through a tough or challenging change, even the most change-welcoming people might be a bit more reticent. Conversely if a team is on a roll of adopting new procedures, they are likely to be more open to the next suggested change.

2. *Most people tend to feel that they are more open to change than the general population is.* This leads to people expecting significant resistance to new change. Whether accurate or not, those expectations change people's approach to introducing change.

3. *Leaders are people too!* Your feelings and experiences regarding change, whether positive or negative, are important to your ability to lead a new change. Your awareness of how your thoughts are affecting your reaction to change will help you become a more effective leader of change.

Self-Assessment

Here is a quick assessment to help you think about your skills as a relationship builder. Use the following scale of 1 to 7 on each question:

1. Almost never
2. Rarely or seldom
3. Occasionally
4. Sometimes
5. Usually

6. Frequently

7. Almost always

I see the positive in changes I'm involved in. _____

I understand organizational change. _____

I recognize the forces that impact change. _____

I create and share a vision of the future after change is
implemented. _____

I adapt to change easily. _____

I support organizational changes. _____

I deal with resistance productively. _____

The Change Levers

Imagine that you are sitting in my living room on a cool fall Sunday after-
noon. I'm lounging on my couch, extremely comfortable, and watching
football on television. I comment to you that life is good: I have the couch,
the game, and my team is winning. In this situation, how likely am I to
get up off of the couch? Not very, because I am completely comfortable.

When you are in your comfort zone, how likely are you to want, let
alone look for, change? Not very likely.

As we continue to watch the game I notice a number of commercials
for a certain cold adult beverage. The more of these commercials I watch
(and in any professional football game, there are many), the more likely
I am to get thirsty for a cold adult beverage. As I notice and then develop
my thirst, my comfort level begins to drop—not because any of the other
factors of my comfort have changed, but because I have become aware
of something new that is desirable to me. Notice that my comfort level
dropped because my worldview changed. But I'm still on the couch. I am
still there not because I don't know how to get this beverage (there is
probably some in my refrigerator just a few steps away), but because of
the risks of getting up: I might miss a key play, I might lose my seat (or
the remote) to someone else in the house, or I might not be able to settle
back into a spot quite as comfortable as I am in now. Notice that none
of these risks is immense, but they still keep me in my comfort zone.

So when will I get that drink? I'll get up when I get thirsty enough
(when my dissatisfaction gets high enough) or when a commercial comes
(which might lower the risks of getting up), or I might get a drink when
someone walks through the room and I ask that person to please get the

beverage for me (which makes the change easier for me to implement and lowers my risk factors).

This simple story illustrates the four levers of change:

1. Dissatisfaction with the current situation
2. Vision of a desired future
3. A plan for achieving or implementing the goal
4. The costs or risks (both real and perceived) of the change

These four levers are the keys to understanding the current state of any change and how to advance it. They work for both personal or professional changes for individuals, teams, and full organizations.

Before I explore each of these levers more fully, let me introduce a case study.

A CEO client of mine had a vision of a workplace that people loved working in, where they felt supported, where they felt their work really mattered, where there were high levels of trust (across and up and down), and, because of all of these factors, a workplace where productivity and quality soared. This wasn't an organization that was failing, but it didn't meet his criteria to any widespread degree either. As he and I began working together, we started to identify a plan to create a new organizational culture using these four levers.

Dissatisfaction

If there is no dissatisfaction with the way things are now, no person or group will be interested in change. Another word for this situation is *complacency*. In order to raise the dissatisfaction level, there are two basic choices: help people see how bad something is now or help them see a picture that is even better than what they have now.

Taking the "life is awful" approach can create dissatisfaction and unrest; in organizations, this approach typically leads to long periods of complaining, cynicism, and arguing, which are not conducive to high productivity. As a leader trying to create change within a group or organization, taking this approach can be dangerous. First, you are stimulating negativity, which in many cases leads to hopelessness and a sense of futility. Beyond that, when you create dissatisfaction from the position of lack, you aren't providing people with the option of something better.

The other option for creating dissatisfaction is to acknowledge how things are now, and likely how good (or at least comfortable) people feel about the current state. As the leader, you may not be very happy with the way things are (your level of dissatisfaction is already raised), but it is best to start with an acknowledgment of how people feel about the situation and then help them see something better. As you raise the vision of a different future, people create their own dissatisfaction—exactly what the commercials did for me.

The first obstacle that Steve, the CEO in our case study, needed to overcome was the current comfort zone: in general, people were pretty happy with their work and their workplace environment. Overall satisfaction was pretty good, turnover was manageable, and financial results weren't too bad either. Steve needed to develop some level of dissatisfaction, and he chose to do it by helping people create a vision of something even better.

Vision of a Desired Future

Think about the most successful changes you have created in your own life. Chances are the vision lever played a powerful part in those situations. The stronger your vision is, the more compelling it is. The more desired the vision becomes, the more leverage it provides to catapult you through your change. There are four keys to creating a vision that will compel and drive individual and group change. The vision must be:

1. *Highly desirable.* Perhaps this goes without saying, but if a change is to be truly compelling, it must be something that people really want. Beyond the other three factors, the more desirable, the better.

2. *Real.* The more real the vision is, the better. As a leader you can help people see what it will look like, feel like, taste like, and sound like. When they immerse themselves and their senses into a picture of a desired future, the vision becomes more powerful.

3. *Believable.* People must believe that the goal—the future state—is possible. If you have never walked around the block, running a four-minute mile probably doesn't feel believable. The vision should be a stretch, which will make it more motivating, but it should still be within the realm of belief.

4. *Personal.* This factor is the most important of all. It doesn't matter to your organization or team how desirable, real, and believable the vision is to *you*. It matters only if those things are true for *them*. People can't argue with their own data, so you must help them personalize the vision. Help your team answer and understand what is in it for them to make or support the change.

To get some specific help on making the vision personal, download this Bonus Byte at www.RLBonus.com using the keywords "personal vision."

Look at any change you have attempted in the past or any change you are involved in currently (individually or as a leader), and you can diagnose how successful or how easy the change was or will be by looking at it in terms of these four factors. Objectively look at your change through this vision lens. This exercise will help you see which areas you can develop. As you strengthen each of these four factors, change will come more quickly and be more successfully maintained.

THE IMPORTANCE OF A CLEAR VISION

This concept of a clear vision is critical to many of the skills of remarkable leaders. The reason is that your mind cannot tell the difference between something real and something vividly imagined. When you help people create a three-dimensional vision of what they desire, their subconscious mind begins drawing them toward that picture. The concept is the same no matter the competency. The clearer, more believable, real, and personal we can make a vision, the more powerful it will become. (Chapters Fifteen and Sixteen provide more information about vision.)

Company vision statements litter conference room walls throughout the world, and they all serve as a reminder that these four very logical factors aren't well understood or implemented.

Rather than trying to force his vision on others, Steve created a cross-organizational culture team of volunteers to begin to describe, communicate, and personalize his initial vision. This process continues and is creating great success. People are beginning to own the change for themselves (and not just the team), and internally it is no longer "Steve's new culture" but "*our* new culture."

The Plan

The part of any change management plan that is most important is clear first steps.

Have you ever faced a major task or project and knew you needed to get started, but each day you procrastinated and did something else? Maybe you were overwhelmed by the size of the task. Often that is how people feel about change. You can be dissatisfied and even see a vision of a much better situation, but if you don't know how to proceed or what to do first, you are often immobilized by the change.

As the leader, you are often in the best place to give people a clear pathway. When people know what they need to do or what they can do to get started, they are more likely to get moving. When possible, involve others in creating these steps, but sometimes it is best to create these first steps for those you lead.

If the change is large, people don't need to see every step from the beginning to the end of the change, but they need enough steps to get started just like you needed on your big project. Trust plays a part in this lever as well. The greater the trust is between you and your team, the fewer initial steps people need to know. In organizations where trust is low, people may require or even demand a more complete plan from the start.

Steve, our CEO, had a series of high-level steps in mind to create the new culture he envisioned. Now he is creating the more detailed next steps with the help of his culture team. As their process moves forward, people are asking, "What's next?" "What can we do?" "How can we keep this moving forward?" These kinds of questions are proof that people are onboard mentally and emotionally and need some way to take action. As the leader, you must continue to provide these steps or help the group create those next steps themselves.

The Risks or Costs of Change

The first three factors of change (dissatisfaction, a vision, and a plan) must all be present. If just one of them is not, nothing will happen. But even when all of those are present, before making a change, people are going to compare the relative risk, or costs, of any change to the potential outcome. And these are the perceived risks to the person doing the changing, not the perceptions of the person (likely you) implementing the change.

Look back at the exercise for the word *change* at the start of this chapter. The more minus signs are associated with the list of words, the more likely it is that the person will be more cautious about change and therefore perceive greater risks or costs. Often leaders are confused as to why people are resisting a change, and this factor is important to remember. The leader is undoubtedly fired up for the change, and so the risks for them have already been reduced, or they see risks they are willing to live with. But each of us independently computes those costs and risks, and our perceptions of these costs are the reality for us. The higher the perceived risks, the less likely it is that an individual is going to welcome change, no matter how great the potential benefits seem.

In his conversations across the organization and with the help of his culture team, Steve has identified some of the risks and costs perceived by the larger organization. Once they are identified, leaders and members of the culture team can address them in conversation and begin to reduce those perceived risks in a variety of ways.

Your Now Steps

Understanding these change levers is the first and best step you can take to lead, manage, and champion change more successfully. These steps are designed to help you understand and begin to apply these levers:

1. Identify any change you've recently experienced. It can be individual or organizational in nature.

2. Determine how successful the change was.

3. Think about the change from the perspective of each of the levers. If it was a highly effective and successful change, consider how each of these levers played a part in that success. If it was (or is) a less successful change, use your knowledge of these levers to understand what was missing and what steps you could have taken to improve the success of the change.

4. Capture your insights and lessons learned in your journal.

5. Using these insights, make any adjustments to current changes you are involved in as a leader or a participant.

 Remarkable leaders create faster and more successful change by using the change levers.

Planning Change Efforts

Now that you understand the four powerful levers that can create or block change, you have a template for making change implementation work. Any successful change plan will include the development and implications of these four levers. The Now Steps you just worked through provide a clue to building your change plan, but the timing must be reversed. Ask yourself the questions about each lever *before* you implement the change to help create the information, communication, and insight required for your plan to be successful.

Figure 5.1. The Diffusion of Innovation

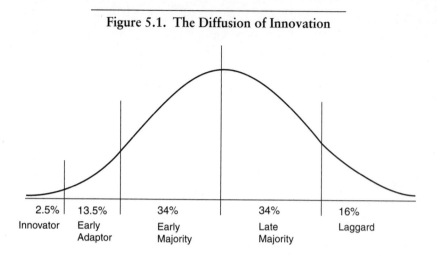

2.5%	13.5%	34%	34%	16%
Innovator	Early Adaptor	Early Majority	Late Majority	Laggard

The Diffusion of Innovation

In 1962, Everett Rogers wrote the first edition of *Diffusion of Innovations*, which formalized the diffusion of innovations theory and became a classic in sociological literature. It used statistics to look at populations of people and categorize their reactions to technological change. Through this work, Rogers stated that a population could be classified into one of five categories based on their adoption of an innovation or idea (Figure 5.1):

- *Innovators.* These are the people most willing to take risk. They are adventurous, eager, and well informed on the particular innovation. The research found innovators to be just 2.5 percent of the population.
- *Early adopters.* These are those on the leading edge of change. While the innovators come to the change first, the early adopters are watching them closely and come on board next. They represent 13.5 percent of the population.
- *Early majority.* Representing 34 percent of the population, the early majority is deliberate regarding a particular change.
- *Late majority.* Representing another 34 percent of the population, these people are even more deliberate, and perhaps even skeptical, regarding a change. They are more swayed by the experiences of people they know in regard to adopting the change.

o *Laggards.* The final 16 percent of a population to accept a change. These people are sometimes seen by others as hostile to change or unwilling to change. In reality, they are the most deliberate and typically rely on the direct experiences of those they trust.

While much can be learned about change implementation from this well-documented research, there are a couple of specifics to remember:

o Not everyone will see the risks and costs of a change in the same way. Even if two people both have high levels of dissatisfaction, have a clear vision, and know the early change steps required, they won't necessarily be ready to change at the same time because of the differences in their perceived risks (and perhaps their propensity to change in general).

o Although an individual might fall into a different category for different changes (for example, a typical early adopter might not like to be accessible 24/7 and chooses not to have a cell phone, making this person a laggard in that area), most people fall into one category most of the time, especially when you reduce the scope to work-related changes. Even if you can't categorize each individual, recognize that within your target population, you will have people across this full spectrum of innovation categories.

 To learn more about the diffusion of innovation and how it can affect your change plans, download this Bonus Byte at www.RLBonus.com using the keyword "diffusion."

Targets and Timing

The diffusion of innovation model is especially helpful when you add in a time component. Rogers' research took the bell-shaped curve and plotted it against the time line of adoption. The resulting S curve looks like Figure 5.2. This graphic illustrates a couple of points critical to your change planning and implementation process:

o If you can get your change to point A on the slope in Figure 5.2, you will gain the advantage of momentum as the early and late majority begin to adopt or accept the change. This is important because leaders often get discouraged as the change seems to be moving slowly. The S curve gives you hope that once you get to point A, the change will move much more quickly.

Figure 5.2. A Change Time Line

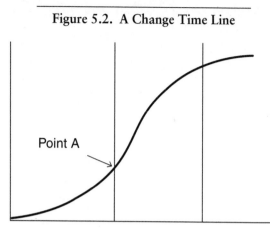

- ○ Your implementation and communication efforts should focus first on those who can become the first agents of change. Your focus as a leader should be to get to point A as quickly as possible.

- ○ Don't worry about your most cynical or critical people first (they may well sit on the far right of the S curve). Although you don't want to ignore them, focus positive energy on persuading the people who will help you get the change to point A.

If you can engender the support and adoption of your change by a person often seen as a cynic or a laggard early, often that can speed up overall adoption ("If Lisa in operations who *never* wants to change thinks this is a good idea, maybe I should take a closer look.")

A Planning Model

You can find fifty sources of change planning models, and you may already have one that you or your organization uses. What plan you follow matters much less than making sure it has all the right components. Make sure your plan includes pieces to address each of the four levers. Regardless of the size or complexity of your change, consider writing your plan at both the strategic and tactical levels.

Strategically your plan needs to outline how this change fits into organizational goals and objectives. People need to see how this change aligns with other efforts and organizational initiatives. The plan also should address the roles various people will play in the development of the tactical plans related to the change. Remember that people will be more committed and empowered by the plan when they have a hand in its creation. Stating this approach at the strategic level will help others understand your intentions and help remind you of this throughout your change implementation.

Tactically the plan needs to address the specific next steps required. Depending on the change, you may not need to identify every tactical step from the beginning all the way to the conclusion of the implementation. Build as much of the detail as your audience needs to feel good about the change.

Communicating the Plan

There are two keys to communicating a change plan: direction and frequency. If you review the levers again and reflect on them, you won't be surprised by my advice on either count.

When leading change, leaders typically focus on what they need to communicate. I hope that at this point, you recognize that the most effective change communication is dialogue. For people to have a personal vision of the results of the change, they must be *involved* in the conversation, not simply hear the message. For them to be more committed to the change, they need to feel part of the planning. The message here is clear: although there are things you must communicate as a leader, change communication cannot ultimately be successful if it is consistently delivered in just one direction.

Not everyone will be persuaded to support or adopt a change at the same time, and what you as the leader think is clear or obvious about a change won't be to others. This suggests the second important point about change communication: it must be frequent.

You want open dialogue about the change early and often. Talk about the purpose for and vision of the change. Provide people with an opportunity to discuss the change, the benefits, and the implications and to voice their concerns. Too often leaders don't want to talk about a change that everyone knows is coming until they believe they "are ready" and "have all of the answers." When you remember that people don't expect you to have all of the answers, you will be more open to starting the conversation sooner.

Your Now Steps

If you have an imminent change, you need to be building a change plan for it. However, that planning likely will take longer than typical Now Steps, so here are some ideas you can integrate into your existing work today:

1. Talk to someone you think is typically in a different category on the diffusion of innovation curve than you are.

2. Explore this person's feelings and experiences with change. Work to understand what motivates him or her to change and what information lowers the costs and risks to the individual.

3. Use these insights the next time you are planning a change.

 Change will be more successful with a plan for success.

Being a Change Champion

Although this chapter is titled "Remarkable Leaders *Champion* Change," I have somewhat interchangeably used the verbs *manage, lead,* and *champion.* Perhaps this has led you to think that I consider them to be synonyms. At one level they are synonyms, but let's take a closer look.

The Power of Language

The following list shows each of these three words with some synonyms. Look at this list and answer the questions that follow.

Manage	Lead	Champion
Administer	Steer	Support
Run	Shepherd	Advocate
Supervise	Move	Believe
Organize	Convey	Nurture

- Which of these columns best describes you?
- Which of these columns best defines who you aspire to be?
- Which of these columns is most needed in your organization?
- Which column will make you remarkable?

Organizations need all of these skills. Do you need change managers? Of course. In my experience, most organizations have the skills to manage change pretty well. These skills, though, are not enough. Peter Drucker wrote that "the most effective way to manage change successfully is to create it" (2004, p. 3). He succinctly stated the need for more than change supervisors and administrators. We need people to steer and shepherd and move people.

But organizations also need change champions: people (leaders by title or not) who actively support and advocate for change. They are most effective when they do this not because it is their job but because they believe in the change. Change leaders focus on the change; change champions focus on people. Change leaders focus on the change; change champions focus on the vision. Change leaders communicate about the change; change champions create a dialogue about the change.

All three skill sets are needed for change to succeed. You become remarkable when you can do all three.

How to Introduce Change

In reality, what matters to the organization doesn't matter; what matters to each individual matters.

Change champions recognize that organizational change is about the decision and the commitment of each individual. Here are the five high-level things a change champion does to introduce change:

1. Change champions build a reputation as a change champion in advance. They are known as long-time proponents of change.
2. Change champions help people see the current situation clearly and completely.
3. Change champions help people see a postchange vision.
4. Change champions provide or help develop clear first steps.
5. Change champions are optimistic about the change and its progress without being a Pollyanna.

These map directly back to the change levers because a change champion operates based on the principles of change.

The Nine Tactics

Those five steps provide an overview and a strategic road map; admittedly, they are not very tactical. Here are nine specific tactics you can use to champion change with any group, large or small:

1. *"Sell" individuals.* You might be championing a change affecting hundreds of people; even so, champion that change one on one. Find ways to create small group conversations, and speak individually with as many people as possible.
2. *Help people take ownership.* First, you must be willing to share ownership with them. Then build that ownership with small changes, gaining

their assistance in planning next steps. Once they feel empowered, you can help by removing obstacles in their path.

3. *Let people see your process.* Leaders often don't want to communicate about a change until they know everything. You will seldom know everything, and while you are waiting, the organization is wondering what is going on—and hypothesizing the worst-possible scenario. Let people know where you are as early as possible—and earlier than your instincts might suggest.

4. *Call the change a journey (because it is).* People will more easily accept things this way, and this positive view makes it easier for people to join in.

5. *Ask questions.* If you want to create a dialogue and engagement, talk less and ask questions more.

6. *Start small, and build a new status quo.* Perhaps your vision is a massive difference from where things are today. The best way to get there is in small chunks. Get people to see the value in small change, and get them there. Once they have successfully navigated a small change, you will have helped them build their willingness and confidence for the next step.

7. *Give it words.* Help people describe the change. Having common language across the group makes it easier for people to support and create the change.

8. *Ask questions.* This tactic is here twice on purpose. Remember to ask questions to create a useful change dialogue. (For more on this, see Chapter Thirteen.)

9. *Take responsibility.* You are the leader and the champion. While you are trying to do everything you can to get the group involved and committed to the change, take the responsibility to do everything you can to make it happen.

Your Now Steps

Spend a few minutes thinking about the differences among a change manager, leader, and champion:

1. Review the twelve verbs listed in this chapter.
2. Reflect on which of these actions you are most comfortable with and likely best at. Capture your thoughts in your journal.

3. Select another verb from the list you would like to do more effectively. Write that new target skill in your journal.

4. Think about your next change opportunity, and identify two things you will do to help you execute the new skill you have identified, putting your ideas and next steps in your journal.

 Remarkable leaders champion change.

Moving Past Change Resistance

You have read more than 75 percent of a chapter about change, and we haven't yet discussed resistance. It isn't that I was resisting talking about it; rather, I chose to wait until the end of the chapter because I wanted to give it more than a passing mention and explain how you can use resistance to your *advantage* as a remarkable leader.

Ask most people how they feel about resistance, and they likely will wrinkle their nose at least a little bit: they think that resistance to change is something that must be beaten down or overcome. However, rarely do we feel our own resistance, and if we do, we certainly don't see our own resistance as bad. Resistance is simply, as Peter Block said in Rick Maurer's *Beyond the Wall of Resistance*, "a reluctance to choose" (1996, p. 62).

The reality is that resistance is a wonderful thing. If everyone on your team thought exactly the same way, had exactly the same opinions, and lived in perfect harmony, would you have the most effective team? That description might sound blissful, but the reality is that without the dissonance that comes from different opinions and perspectives, you will never get new ideas, creative solutions, a competitive edge, or the synergy that creates greater results.

Remarkable leaders have a different attitude about resistance. They know it is natural and not by definition negative.

> Resistance = engagement

Typical Responses to Resistance

Because most people think of resistance as negative or bad, they typically want to overcome it as quickly as possible by breaking it down, discounting it, or avoiding it altogether. Unfortunately, these sometimes short-term processes typically lead to short-term results (at best) and add to the resistance later in the change journey.

People attempt to break down resistance by arguing, bullying, or using what they think of as logic to get past the resistance—in effect, to get others to acquiesce to the change. This approach assumes that the resistance isn't deeply felt and can be overcome by force, will, or logic. This approach may lead to acquiescence: people may be willing to move forward with a change, albeit reluctantly. But is acquiescence what you are looking for? Grudging acceptance clearly won't create the same results that willing participation will. Attempts to break down or wait out the resistance will seldom create willing participation; instead, it will bury the resistance for another day.

Rather than confronting resistance directly, some people prefer to discount it. They say their resistance is "no big deal," or if they just "go along," it will be okay. People with strong skills of persuasion often find good use for those skills in this situation.

Perhaps the most dangerous approach of all is to deny or avoid the resistance entirely. Have you ever been in a meeting where you could cut the tension with a knife? It was clear that there was unspoken resistance to an idea, approach, or next step. How many of these situations led to great outcomes? How many of these situations led to a team fully engaged in the next steps? How many of these situations led to poor results and further problems? In these cases, resistance has been stifled or ignored. Ignoring or avoiding it severely hampers the success of any change.

Instead, you should do the exact opposite of denying it: you must bring resistance to the surface and talk about it. In letting the resistance be heard, you will unleash people's emotions attached to the change, bring forward new ideas, and allow people to work through their concerns and better prepare themselves to commit to the change.

Five Better Steps

Once you are no longer daunted by resistance and believe that it can be your friend, there is a five-step process of actions you can take to get resistance on the table:

1. *Surface it.* This step is critical. People may not be used to being asked to identify their resistance, so you must be patient while they decide if you are serious. You will improve your chances of hearing the resistance when you make it safe to share it. You must ask for it, and then you must be quiet and listen. If the levels of trust among the team (or with

you) are low, it may take a long time for the real resistance to surface. It is worth making the time. Let the resistance flow, and make sure, through questioning, that you have surfaced all of it. (Now is not the time to justify, rationalize or further explain the situation; just listen.) In some cases, this process might be best led by a neutral facilitator.

2. *Honor it.* People need to know that you appreciate their concerns even if you don't agree with them. If you ask for the resistance and then immediately begin to justify or become defensive, you may well be worse off than if you never asked at all. Once you surface the resistance, you must honor it. Listen carefully, acknowledge it, and remind them that you appreciate their perspective and concerns. Remind them as well that the purpose of this exercise is to find the cracks or flaws in the change effort and create a plan for solving those issues.

3. *Explore it.* After all of the issues are on the table, it is time to sort them out, look for the real opportunities, and build a plan for overcoming that resistance. Remember that not everything identified is real. Now it is time to separate the real concerns from the babble and excuses. Usually the group quickly identifies the difference.

4. *Build a plan for overcoming it.* Once the issues have been surfaced and explored, you can create options for overcoming these challenges. Often important issues have been raised, and these may not have been considered by the implementation plan. This is why you wanted to surface the resistance in the first place: to create solutions that overcome all of the real issues.

5. *Map the solutions.* Once you have identified improvements to the change plan, check back to the initial resistance. Determine how much of the resistance will be eliminated or made manageable by the actions identified. If there is a pocket of resistance left, loop back and look for an action that might address that as well.

SURFACING RESISTANCE OR CREATING A BITCH SESSION?

If you think that surfacing resistance may create the never-popular bitch session, you are partly correct. Most people have lived through many organizational bitch sessions—those meetings where everyone complains about what is wrong. Typically these meetings make people feel good (except perhaps the leader) for a short time as they vent, but they usually leave these sessions feeling hollow because no action is taken.

> Remember that surfacing the resistance is only the first step in this process. When you complete all of the steps, you will get the positive benefits from the venting process, but make sure you close the loop and raise the resulting energy by completing the other four steps in this process.

Now that you have engaged the group in identifying these challenges and creating the solutions, this process takes the energy of resistance and uses it to further the change.

The Three Levels of Resistance

Rick Maurer, in his excellent book *Beyond the Wall of Resistance* (1996), identifies three levels of resistance. Consider how each of these levels can play into the process I've just outlined:

> *Level 1: "I don't get it."* Level 1 is the logical level of facts, presentations, and logical arguments. Resistance here comes from lack of information or a disagreement with the findings. According to Maurer, many make the mistake of treating all resistance as if it were level 1 resistance, so they schedule more meetings to tell people about the change and use their newest PowerPoint slides to try to overcome the resistance. More information will address level 1 resistance, but it won't do anything for the other two levels.
>
> *Level 2: "I don't like it."* This is the emotional reaction to change. When you use the five-step process to surface resistance, you will begin to explore and reduce level 2 resistance.
>
> *Level 3: "I don't like you."* Maybe the resistance is with you, or maybe it's with whom you represent (they trust you but don't trust the motives of the home office, senior management, or fill-in-the-blank). This third level of resistance can be surfaced with the five-step process, but only if you recognize that it might exist. If you believe this is a part of the resistance (or even if you think it might be), using a neutral facilitator may be the right answer to help surface these issues. Maurer puts it perfectly in a 2006 white paper update to his thoughts on these three levels of resistance: "So maybe they like you, but they don't trust you—or have

confidence in your leadership. That's a hard pill to swallow, I know" (2006, p. 3).

 If you are looking for ways to lessen this type of resistance in the future, download this Bonus Byte at www.RLBonus.com using the keyword "resistance."

Your Now Steps

Recognizing, surfacing, and valuing resistance is a huge key to successfully championing change. This outlines a process that will help, but it all starts with how you feel about resistance. Your Now Steps are designed to help you think about that. Capture your thoughts and reflections in your journal:

1. Think about the times you have faced resistance to changes you were proposing. What was your natural reaction? How did you respond?
2. Examine your beliefs about resistance itself. Do you believe there is good that can come from it?
3. Identify three times when resistance you have experienced (either as the leader, the resister, or as an observer) was acknowledged and had a positive impact on the overall change.

 Resistance is energy that can be used to move your change forward.

 Go to remarkableleadershipbook.com/resources for more information, writing, tools, and other highly recommended resources to help you lead change more successfully.

6

REMARKABLE LEADERS COMMUNICATE POWERFULLY

According to John Durham Peters in his book *Speaking into the Air: A History of the Idea of Communication* (2000), the word *communication* comes from the Latin *communicare,* meaning to impart, share, or make common. The key root is *mun-* (not *uni-*), related to such words as *munificent, community,* and *meaning.*

This etymology is instructive for leaders who want to be more powerful communicators. Communicating powerfully isn't about being glib or an exceptional conversationalist. It isn't about using the right words at the right time or having a great vocabulary. Communicating powerfully is about being able to "share or make common." As a leader, when you "make common," you are forming a connection between you and those with whom you are communicating and forming a community based on common meaning.

In this chapter, we examine three ways for creating common meaning and building connections with those you lead: the importance of communication style, the value of stories, and presenting to groups. To build those connections you must do more than talk; you must connect. The best way to do that is to think about the other person and how to best help that person receive your message. All three of these skills will help you do just that.

Effective communication is about connecting. It creates a community of understanding.

Self-Assessment

Here is a quick assessment to help you think about your skills as a relationship builder. Use the following scale of 1 to 7 on each question:

1. Almost never
2. Rarely or seldom
3. Occasionally
4. Sometimes
5. Usually
6. Frequently
7. Almost always

I understand the differences in communication styles. _____

I adjust my communication style to meet the needs
of the other person. _____

I communicate clearly and concisely. _____

I use stories as a way to communicate more effectively. _____

I am a confident presenter. _____

I present in groups effectively. _____

Communication Styles

The leadership team was gathering to discuss its plan for communicating the strategies for the new year. John, the CEO, brought together his four vice presidents for this discussion. John had a high level of faith in each member of his team: Frank, the head of human resources, and Danielle, the head of sales, were newer members and brought great previous experience to the team. Tom, who led operations, and Ingrid, who led finance, had been with the organization longer and knew it well.

John opened the meeting by setting the expectation that they leave with a complete communications plan. Danielle seemingly couldn't wait to begin the dialogue. "People here are pretty knowledgeable about our business and these strategies won't surprise them, so I think a quick meeting to communicate the high points will be all we need. We need to make the communication short and to the point," she stated with a bit of finality in his voice.

Frank spoke up next, excitedly: "I see Danielle's point, but I feel that we need to make sure people buy into the plan. Maybe the initial comments can be brief as Danielle said, but we have to include time, both in our meetings and more informally afterward, to get people's reactions to and feelings about the plan. This will encourage them and help them buy in to the work they'll be doing."

Danielle countered that "while getting input is fine, the goals are clear and ambitious, so they need to get to work on them as soon as possible."

After Danielle and Frank continued to explore their points for a couple of minutes, Tom chimed in: "I've been thinking about what you two have been saying, and I think you both make excellent points; however, I think we need to give people a bit more background on the strategies. They will need to know how we came up with these strategies and why they will be our focus for the year. In planning for this meeting, I've put together some draft PowerPoint slides that give the history and background of our planning process and share the details of the markets that led to these strategies. I think that is important to share as well."

Ingrid, energized by the discussion, added, "This is all great. There are clearly lots of great ideas about how to do this. And here's one more: I think we need to make sure that people see this year's goals in the context of our organizational vision. We can't talk about this year without talking about the next five years. We need to give people the vision for where we are headed in the longer term. One way I thought of is that we could do a skit as a team to show people what our success in reaching these goals would look like."

Although Danielle couldn't argue with the vision component, she still wanted to keep it short and was against anything involving a skit. Tom hated the skit idea too.

The conversation continued for some time, with John mostly staying out of it. When there seemed to be a longer lull, he spoke: "One of the reasons I love you all as my team is that you can have such different perspectives on a situation and talk about your opinions in a rational and respectful way. In that spirit of respect, here is what I am observing in this conversation. Each of you is coming at our communications challenge from one perspective: yours. Consciously or not, you are thinking back to times when you were in the shoes of our team and how you would have liked to receive this type of information. This is a good approach but somewhat limited. Since our whole team doesn't think or communicate like any one of you, sharing it with them in a way that works best for you alone will be limited in success. I suggest we look at how to meld these ideas together to make sure that our message is successfully communicated to each individual on the whole team."

"Does that mean we have to do a skit, John?" Tom asked.

"Not necessarily. What do you think, Ingrid?" John asked. Ingrid was fine not to do the skit; in fact, she already had three ideas of ways they could meld the key points from everyone's approach together.

Although you've never been in a meeting with Frank, Tom, Danielle, Ingrid, and John, you likely recognize the people in the story. You also probably found yourself agreeing or identifying a bit more with one of the characters than the rest. This brief story serves to introduce the concepts of communication and thinking styles. There are many competing assessments and training programs to help people understand their behavioral, communications, thinking, and personality styles.

 For a listing of some of these products and programs, download this Bonus Byte at www.RLBonus.com using the keyword "styles."

Rather than using any particular assessment, I will generalize four classic communication styles, represented in the story by Tom, Frank, Danielle, and Ingrid: they are, respectively, thinker, feeler, doer, and imaginer. You will learn to recognize these styles and determine ways to communicate and connect more successfully with people who communicate with that style.

The Four Classic Communication Styles

Danielle, the doer, wants to get results. Her focus is in the present because there is much to be done. In general, doers value action, achievement, and progress. They see a team's task as a straightforward, goal-oriented process and think the simplest, most straightforward approach will work best. Given this, it is no surprise that Danielle was the first to speak. (She'll also likely be the one who will drive the team to some conclusion and an action plan.)

Frank, the feeler, is the person most connected to the emotions and thoughts of others (which may not be surprising given his role in HR). He sees the organization as a community—a family—and believes that communication should always take that into account. If we continued in the story, he might suggest breakout groups or other ways to help people contribute. Generally feelers are motivated by the sense of contribution and think others will be too.

Tom, the thinker, loves the data, the logic, and a structured problem-solving process. Notice that he wasn't the first to speak and that he came to the meeting well prepared. Thinkers have this strength: they think things through and love a procedure or a process. Because they value the details and the background, they often communicate those things at length and ask for them if they aren't provided. Don't be surprised if Tom refers back to the way it was done last year, his reasoning being that if that works, why not replicate that process?

Ingrid, the imaginer, relies on her imagination and ability to envision the big picture of something. While Tom (the thinker) will be great at the details, the imaginers of the world focus on the future and the overall context. Imaginers revel in unstructured, creative tasks and keep asking, "Why?" They are future focused and love concepts, ideology, and discovery. Because of their focus on new ideas and the future, they often are the person with "one more idea" and the last person ready to make a decision. From their perspective, there is always one more way to consider when doing anything—from communicating strategies, to planning a party, to buying a new car.

Communicating with Each Style

If powerful communication is about building a connection, then what John describes near the end of our story is the answer: connections are built when we communicate with others in the way *they* wish to be communicated with. Your ability to communicate powerfully requires that you communicate not in the way that feels most comfortable to you, but in the way that will most quickly connect with the other person. Let's take a look at a few strategies for communicating successfully with each style.

When communicating with doers, be prepared, and be ready to move quickly. In an e-mail, send the executive summary, not ten paragraphs. Don't be surprised if the doer is assertive and interrupts or disagrees. Remember that his or her focus is on taking action and making progress. Conversation is a means to that end, and so you can help by getting to the bottom line (doers love the bottom line) as quickly as possible. Be confident and enthusiastic.

Feelers enjoy and appreciate a more informal, open, and personalized approach. In e-mails, adding a sentence or two of personal greeting or information is valued. They also respond to thoughts of collaboration and teamwork. Feelers likely want to spend a little more time getting to know you, so be willing to share why your ideas are personally important to you.

Think of thinkers as Joe Friday of *Dragnet* or Grissom of *CSI*. They want the facts and the details. They will be appreciative if you are prepared, share the plan with them, have details, and back up your points. Be ready to show where your idea has worked before and prove why you think it will work now. Speak slowly, and give thinkers time to soak up and reflect on what you have said. Encourage them to weigh the approaches and ideas you have shared verbally. This will help you understand where they are and what they consider important as they weigh the facts.

The imaginer wants to hear concepts and big picture ideas. They also want to contribute to the big picture vividly, so make sure to get their options and ideas on the table early. Discuss those ideas within the context of the conversation and help the imaginer see how the thoughts are connected to the long-term plan. Most of all, be willing to use your ideas as the starting point of a brainstorming or idea consideration process. Imaginers appreciate this approach and are more agreeable when they know that lots of options have been considered.

If you employ all of these ideas successfully, your effectiveness as a communicator will skyrocket. Then you can invest time to learn more in-depth strategies and approaches for communicating with the different styles.

One More Thing

To help you make some sense of these styles, I have associated each with a single person. But real life is much messier than that. None of us matches any one of these styles 100 percent. We all possess a unique blend of the four that develops into our own personal style. But this shouldn't be a deterrent to applying this information. Instead, it is a useful reminder to avoid labeling people or using a label to excuse or blame a person's behavior. This information and these approaches will be most useful to you if you employ them situationally: the person who is normally a thinker may seem to be more focused on results at the time, so try communicating with him or her as a doer because at that moment, if your diagnosis is correct, that person *is* a doer, not a thinker. This is a good reminder that all parts of the communication process will be more successful when we focus on the other person.

Your Now Steps

There are one-day (sometimes two-day or longer) workshops devoted to nothing but behavior and communication styles where participants strive to learn every detail and component of each style. All of that information is great, and having an implementation plan for the information is even better. These Now Steps will help you apply what you just learned, and you can start immediately:

1. Think of a person with whom you often have trouble communicating.

2. Using the information in this section, try to recognize that person's natural style.

3. Use that insight to develop a new communication strategy for that person.

4. Try it out as soon as possible.

 Remarkable leaders communicate with others in the way that is best for the other person.

Stories

While I was a Chevron employee (and after I began my company), I had the opportunity to train many people from the Cedar Bayou Chemical Plant near Baytown, Texas, to be more effective trainers. (This facility is now owned by ChevronPhillips Chemical Company.)

One day while on-site, I walked into the office of Pat Minsterman, a long-time training professional and past participant in a train-the-trainer workshop I had facilitated. I noticed that both the certificate and picture from her workshop were hanging on the office wall. I mentioned it and commented that it was still on her wall even after several years. She said, "Train the Trainer was a tremendous experience. Do you remember when... ?" She shared one and then two stories from the workshop—things that had happened during that week several years before. Not long into our conversation, another past participant walked into Pat's office. Greg had attended at a different time but added stories of his class to the conversation. The most gratifying part of this experience for me was not just that the stories were told, but that they reinforced the training they had received. The next day Greg commented to me that because of those stories, he felt as if he had had a complete review of the workshop all while standing in Pat's office.

Stories are powerful. In that short story about stories, you just experienced three things: an example of storytelling, an example of how stories are a natural part of our conversation, and an example of how helpful they can be in remembering things. Beyond those powerful lessons, this story also shows how stories create connections.

Greg and Pat extended their relationship and community in that brief conversation by sharing their stories with each other. If we want to create connections, stories are among our most powerful tools.

Stories are many things: a fable, a parable, a myth, a novel, a movie, a legend, folklore, hearsay, personal experience, gossip. All of these are stories, and they are among the most compelling forms of communication. A well-told story (and even a particularly good or relevant story not well told) piques our interest, gains and holds our attention, and causes us to listen. Jesus taught in parables, and his lessons are remembered and applied more than two thousand years later. The fables credited to Aesop, a slave and storyteller who lived in Greece more than five hundred years before the birth of Christ, have been told and retold and translated around the world. In fact, if stories weren't so powerful, why else would, according to Screenvision (2007), 1.4 billion movie tickets be sold in 2005 in the United States alone?

A story helps us understand things in a new way. Have you ever watched a movie and found correlations to a current or past life experience of your own? Has watching that movie or reading a novel helped you understand something in your life better? Has the story experience created conversation with others about those lessons and ideas?

Stories also connect us to the teller. Think about the tracking and following of movie and television stars, and the telling of their off-screen stories, a multibillion-dollar business.

For all of these reasons, mastering storytelling can make you a remarkable leader.

Types of Stories

In his book *Tell Me a Story: A New Look at Real and Artificial Memory* (1991), Roger Schank lists five basic story types: official, invented, firsthand experiential, secondhand, and culturally common.

OFFICIAL STORIES. Official stories are those that have been sanitized for public or organizational consumption. They are the stories typically told by institutions, the government, schools, and, not coincidently, bosses. When a public relations firm is involved, it is helping to create the official story. The term *spin* has become a part of our vernacular to define the official story. Leaders often make the mistake of waiting for the official story before communicating anything and then hiding behind it when that story has been shared. You will build stronger connections and communicate more powerfully when you desanitize the story and make it real. Even if the story is 100 percent real, it might be seen as spin because you, the leader, are sharing it. Keep this fact in mind, and you'll make your stories, even if they are the official version, more useful and valuable by telling them in your own language and unique way.

INVENTED OR ADAPTED STORIES. The stories that people often make up are actually adapted from other experiences and stories more than they are created from scratch. Adapted stories don't always have a point, but if you are using one as a leader, it should have a point that your audience can easily recognize. Typically these stories become richer and more detailed over multiple tellings. Fables, for example, fall into this category. Although no one believes the hare and the tortoise had a real conversation, the story has power and use. As a leader, if you are adapting a story to make your point, the more you practice telling it, the more effective it will become (perhaps more so than any of the other types).

FIRSTHAND EXPERIENTIAL STORIES. The story that opens this chapter is a firsthand story. These are the stories we tell about things that have actually happened to us. They are particularly powerful for leaders because they are often in a position to coach and mentor others. Using your personal experiences can be powerful in this situation. The best stories are of experiences that are out of the ordinary because they will be more instructive and more memorable. (Telling about your Friday pizza delivery won't be memorable or instructive unless something unusual happened.)

SECONDHAND STORIES. When you tell the stories of others, you are creating a secondhand story. These are often easier to tell because they mostly rely on your ability to recall facts in the correct order rather than creating all the details. The detail and richness of a firsthand story is often lost, so these stories tend to be brief and focused on the points to be made. In fact, it is the points themselves that typically create the structure of this type of story.

CULTURALLY COMMON STORIES. According to Schank, "The culturally common story is not as obvious a category as the other four. We get culturally common stories from our environment. No one tells them, and no one makes them up. They are pervasive nonetheless" (1991, p. 37). These are the stories that define 'the way things are done around here,' and they are especially important to leaders. When you become aware of these cultural norms, they give clues about an organization and its beliefs. As an external consultant, I can often learn much about an organization by listening for and observing these stories. These culturally common stories are part of the fabric of the organization itself. When you can connect your new messages and stories to these touchstones (when they are positive at least), you will multiply your communication success.

Making Your Stories Powerful

As a leader, your story likely will have one or more of the following goals: illustrating a point, transferring some specific information, helping the listener feel something, mentally moving the listener to another place (like the vision of a desired future discussed in the previous chapter), or summarizing or debriefing specific events. Your stories will be more powerful when you are clear on which of these goals you want to achieve.

Here are four specific ways to make your stories powerful:

○ *Be brief.* Stories should be long enough to cover the subject but short enough to be interesting. Do you know people who tell stories that go on and on and on? Have you ever thought, "Get to the point!"? Listen to your own advice when telling stories: get to the point! Remember that even if it's short, it should still be a story. Some details and description are important, but creating your verbal version of *War and Peace* is not necessary.

○ *Be vivid.* Use descriptive language to create word pictures. When you tell the story, draw on as many senses as possible. Don't just talk about the poor quality, for example; describe it. Listen to golfers tell about their favorite hole or their best day on the course. Instead of saying something like, "I shot a 62," they give details: "I hit a gorgeous pitch shot from about thirty yards that rolled within an inch of the hole!" Put more adjectives and pertinent details into your story to make it more memorable.

○ *Include action.* There is a reason that action films are consistently among the top in box office receipts: many movie-goers love stories with action. Even in "nonaction" movies, a common complaint is that they are "too slow" or that "nothing happens." To be compelling, your story must include action.

○ *Stories must make a point or create dialogue.* Your story's point may be right out front and obvious. Perhaps, though, you want your story to be discussed and considered. If that is your goal, conceal your point just a bit. Then when the point is discovered during dialogue, people will own the point *and* the story.

For a longer list of tips on creating powerful stories, request this Bonus Byte at www.RLBonus.com using the keywords "story tip."

Your Now Steps

The best way to use stories is, not surprisingly, to use stories. Your Now Steps will get you started:

1. Think of a message you need to communicate now or in the near future. Write down the message and the key points in your journal.
2. Think of a story that relates to this message directly or indirectly. Write your story ideas in your journal.
3. Pick a story line, and practice telling the story to a peer or colleague.
4. After you tell it, get feedback on the way you told it, the details you included, and whether the messages you wanted to stress were evident.

Once you have practiced the story, try it out as a part of your communication plan.

 Stories are powerful ways to create connections and common understanding.

Presentations

Leaders have to make presentations; it comes with the territory. Some leaders love it, and some loath it, but the fact is that presentations are an important part of the leader's work. Whether your presentations are in front of five or five thousand people, there are principles you can use to make them more effective and you more confident.

First, slow down and build a plan. Before deciding what stories to tell or creating your first PowerPoint slide, you must determine the desired outcome of the presentation, written from the perspective of the audience. You might have the desire to complete the talk without mumbling, have people see you as a strong presenter, or finish without leaving out a key point; those are all fine outcomes, but they aren't audience focused. *The presentation is not about you; it is about the audience.* Your presentation can't approach perfection unless the focus is properly placed on the audience.

Your desired outcome should answer one or all of these questions: What do you want them to know? What do you want them to feel? And, most important, what do you want them to do as a result of your presentation? Do you want people to back your approach? Buy your idea? Stop doing something or start doing something else? The best presentations end with a clear call to action that people take in part because of the power of the presentation. Therefore, before you start, make sure you are clear about audience-centered desired outcomes, and write them down.

WIIFM: The Golden Key

Once you have your focus clearly on the audience, you will realize that they need to see the benefits for taking your suggested actions. Remember that all of your listeners will be asking some version of this question as you speak: "So what? How do I benefit? What's in it for me?" For years presenters and trainers have codified these questions into the acronym WIIFM? (What's in it for me?). If you want to have a powerful presentation, you must be able to answer this question and provide that answer (or answers) to your audience during your talk. Otherwise your presentation won't be as effective as it could have been.

The answers to this question might be obvious, so you assume they are obvious to your audience too. Don't fall into this trap. As the expert on your topic, you don't see the issues and outcomes that your audience does. You've thought far more about this topic than they have, so providing the benefits to them in clear terms will make a huge difference to your success. Think about the perspective of the audience, and determine their benefits. While you want to identify the benefits as best you can, recognize that you can ask the group to share their thoughts during your presentation too. Identifying the benefits for themselves intensifies the group's attention and interest.

For a tool to help you think through the WIIFM question, download this Bonus Byte at www.RLBonus.com using the keyword "WIIFM."

Open with Impact

The opening of your presentation is critical to your success. In the opening, you want to get people's attention and prepare them to listen. If you don't get their attention and interest now, when will you? And if you do happen to earn it later, they will have missed important information that you will have already shared. The opening is worthy of significant planning and practice. The most successful presenters know this and spend a seemingly inordinate amount of time planning their opening.

Your openings will be most successful when they:

- *Set the context.* Your opening should answer the question, "What is the big picture?" Make sure people see how your objective and this presentation relate to the workplace or real life. Connect this information to what the group already knows. By providing a context, you are giving people a mental framework for learning from you.

- *State your objective.* Let people know what your goal or intent is for this talk, and let them see your picture of success (your desired outcome).

- *Provide a WIIFM.* Help people see why this topic will be compelling to them. Help them discern both the organizational and personal benefits they can derive from your presentation. When they understand how they will be affected, you will have earned their attention.

There are many approaches to starting a presentation successfully. You can follow your past successes, assuming you are including all three of the points above, or you can use one of the approaches in the sidebar.

WAYS TO OPEN A PRESENTATION SUCCESSFULLY

- Ask thought-provoking questions.
- Use a timely quote.
- State a startling statistic.
- Offer a personal example.
- Use a story to build a visual image in the listeners' minds.
- Use an analogy or a metaphor.
- Use a rhyme or a poem.
- Use music or an unusual sound.
- Show benefits by stating a promise: "When you leave, you will be able to..."
- Use a prop—something out of its usual context.
- Provide a historical reference to relate your situation to the past.
- Define a word or phrase.

○ Quote appropriate song lyrics.

○ Use humor, though not likely a joke. (Why? Because telling a joke well is difficult. If you don't have the skill mastered, your attempt may hinder rather than help your opening.)

Close with Action

Second in importance only to the opening is how you close your presentation. In the closing, you summarize your key points, cement your desired outcomes, create a compelling call to action, and leave the group with a memorable finish. You can use your opening as a template to help construct your summary or conclusion: remind your audience of the benefits or WIIFMs, or remind them or tie them back to the opening story or example you might have used. Repeat the three or four main points for emphasis and memory retention.

All of these points—connecting back to the opening, reminding of benefits, and creating repetition through a short, clear summary—are important because they take advantage of how the human mind works using repetition. Repetition is important to helping people remember, so use the closing to reinforce your points. In addition, our minds like to be able to organize what we hear and learn. When we begin to get a summary and know the message is ending, our brains begin to organize and file the material more effectively. A summary is critical to your audience's understanding and remembering of your key messages.

Your conclusion also serves a purpose beyond this important one: it is your chance to make sure you reach your desired outcome. Now is the chance to give (or repeat) your call to action. You've reminded people of the benefits they will achieve; you have outlined your key points; now you point them to the logical next step. Done correctly, using the tools discussed, you have created the energy and momentum needed for people to take action. Take advantage of it.

There are two critical mistakes people make in their conclusions that drastically hamper the impact, memorability, and action that will be taken because of their presentations:

- Putting new information in the conclusion
- Ending the presentation with a question-and-answer period

These mistakes are made far too often— so often that you likely will recognize them and may even think one of them is a good idea.

People often add new information in their conclusion because they suddenly remember something that they left out. If you realize as you are summarizing that you left out one of your key points (point number three of four points, for instance) and you can't leave it out (it is important and must be covered), then you must mentally take people back into your presentation—for example, "There is a key point I omitted. Let me step back and share this with you." In this way, you have literally moved people's minds from your closing and back into the body of your presentation. Do this in a matter-of-fact way, and don't be overly apologetic. You are doing this to aid the memory, understanding, and acceptance of the audience. If you get near the end and realize you left that point out, but still have people ready to take action, you may not need to worry about the point right now anyway. Make this decisions based on the specifics of your message and the needs of the audience.

However, if you forgot to tell your planned story to make a particular point, it is too late once you are summarizing your points: you have prepared your audiences' minds for the close. Going back now confuses and frustrates their minds. If you left out your story or favorite example, let it go, and remind yourself to be better prepared the next time. Again, think about things from the audience's perspective.

Often a presentation ends with a question-and-answer session. *Avoid this convention at all costs.* You have likely experienced a presentation that was powerful but then ended with the kiss-of-death question: "Any questions?" There are only two possible responses to this question: there will be none (in which case the effectiveness of the presentation has been compromised or could even be questioned), or the questions that do come are not about the most important or compelling parts of the presentation. If the talk ends on these trivial or overly detailed questions, the power of the presentation is severely affected.

Don't get me wrong: you should definitely invite questions (in fact, when the situation allows, questions should be encouraged at any point in the presentation), but questions should not be the last thing. Invite questions right before your closing. That allows you to answer them and still have control of the key messages and call to action in your closing. If, out of habit, people ask you a question after your close, go back and do a condensed close again, making sure you end with the most motivating and compelling messages that you can.

The Body of the Presentation

Much time could be spent on the body of the presentation—on how to craft your visual aids and make your points. Is all of this important? Of course. This is why people typically spend the most time preparing for this part of the talk. You need your data, research, background, reasoning, and logic. No one can present without knowing the meat of their message.

Even so, the message is about more than just this meat. You aren't presenting because of this meat; you are presenting to reach a desired outcome. The facts, figures, and details help you get to the desired outcome, but remarkable leaders know that the initial planning, opening, and closing are what make presentations remarkably powerful. That is why they focus their attention on those areas first and why I have spent much more time on them here.

 There are thousands of great resources on how to develop presentations. For specific tips on how to use (and not use) PowerPoint or other visual aids in your presentation, download this Bonus Byte at www.RLBonus.com using the keywords "visual aid." For additional help on creating the body of your presentation, download the Bonus Byte at www.RLBonus.com using the keyword "presentation."

Your Now Steps

Apply these Now Steps when developing your next presentation. If that presentation is soon, great! If you don't have an imminent presentation, apply the second set of Now Steps to the next presentation you attend. Apply both sets of steps and benefit even further.

Steps as a Presenter

1. Start by writing your desired outcomes. Avoid doing any other work, preparation, or data gathering until you have this identified.

2. Identify the WIIFMs for the audience.

3. Take as much time as you can to follow the rest of the steps described in this section. If time is of the essence, proceed with your preparation as you normally would. But if you have time, incorporate all of the advice above. Take on as much as you can now.

4. After giving your presentation, reflect on its relative success, considering how your new approaches aided in your success.

Steps as an Audience Member

1. When you are attending your next presentation, take notes on the speaker's desired outcomes and the WIIFMs that are identified for you.

2. Assess how successfully the presenter did these two things.

3. Determine what the presenter could have done differently to make the presentation more successful by doing these two things more effectively.

4. Apply those lessons to your next presentation.

 The most effective presentations are focused on the audience and their needs and desires.

 Go to remarkableleadershipbook.com/resources for more information, writing, tools, and other highly recommended resources to help you become a more confident and effective communicator.

7

REMARKABLE LEADERS BUILD RELATIONSHIPS

THROUGH A VARIETY of exercises in workshops, I have often asked people to tell me the keys to building better working relationships. Many of the same items or suggestions show up regularly:

- Listen.
- Put yourself in the other person's shoes.
- Learn more about the other person.
- Be willing to help.
- Teach them what they need to know.
- Smile.
- Be friendly.
- Make time for the other person.
- Be trustworthy.
- Be honest.

After they create this list, I ask them why better relationships at work are important. That list includes some items instructive to you as a remarkable leader:

- Improved productivity
- Reduced turnover
- Improved safety
- Improved quality
- Heightened morale
- Improved attitudes

In this chapter, we explore four skills that will help you build better relationships. In doing these things, you will be doing more than simply building relationships for yourself. As a leader, I believe it is your responsibility to model relationship-building behaviors that will lead to these highly desired organizational outcomes. When you model this, you will be teaching others how to do it and creating the expectation that better relationships matter in your organization.

 Strong working relationships are an indicator of organizational health and strength.

Self-Assessment

Here is a quick assessment to help you think about your skills as a relationship builder. Use the following scale of 1 to 7 on each question:

1. Almost never

2. Rarely or seldom

3. Occasionally

4. Sometimes

5. Usually

6. Frequently

7. Almost always

People like me. _____

I listen actively. _____

I am friendly. _____

I am trustworthy. _____

I trust others. _____

I expand my network, both inside and outside the organization. _____

Likeability

The gate agents were harried as they looked at the long line of tired and upset travelers they had to help. A big November snowstorm was making travel out of Denver a challenge on this Friday evening. As I stood in line, I watched the people in front of me—how they reacted and how the agents responded to them. The gentleman in front of me seemed especially upset and unloaded his frustration and disdain for the situation and the airline on the agent. The agent listened carefully and explained the options to the traveler, all of which included an overnight stay. As I listened, my heart sank: I was heading to the same destination. The person stomped off muttering words I won't share here.

As I stepped forward, I smiled at the agent and told her I didn't envy her and her colleagues on a day like this and with customers like the last one. She looked up at me and smiled. I told her my destination as I handed her my boarding pass. I told her that I had heard the word *tomorrow* in her last conversation. She looked at me and said, "You know, there might be another option. Give me just a second." She typed quickly, and I noticed a bit of a smile on her face.

"There!" she said. She outlined a creative option for me that would get me home that evening. Elated, I began to thank her. Then after typing just a little bit more, she proudly handed me a new boarding pass. "You'll have to go down about fifteen gates, but I hope you enjoy your first-class seat." I smiled and thanked her again. As I walked away, she said, "No, thank *you*!"

What was the difference between my exchange (and itinerary) and that of the gentleman in front of me? Nothing more than my choosing to be likeable.

Tim Sanders literally wrote the book on likeability: *The Likeability Factor*. In it he defines *likeability* as "an ability to create positive attitudes in other people through the delivery of emotional and physical benefits" (2005, p. 33). When I think of likeability, I think of attractiveness: likeable people attract others. People like being around and interacting with likeable people. Having this ability creates several benefits for you as a leader:

- It gives you followers. If you lead and no one follows, are you really a leader?
- It helps you give feedback, mentor, and coach. (These are discussed in the next chapter.)
- It helps you persuade. People are more readily persuaded by people they like.
- It helps you get better results. You can't do it alone. Since you need a team, your likeability can drastically increase your effectiveness.

These are all good reasons; in fact, likeability plays a contributing role in your effectiveness with every one of the remarkable leadership competencies. I'll let you judge that for yourself in the coming chapters, but let's look at the chapters you have read so far.

Likeability helps you as a learner because you know that your learning will be accelerated when you can learn from and with others. Your attractiveness to others will significantly influence their willingness to help you learn. Likeability helps you champion and lead change because people will be more open to your ideas and listen to your case for change when they like you. Likeability helps you create a personal connection and is an important part of successful communication. It also is the logical place to begin this chapter because it is the precursor to the other skills we explore: listening, trust building, and networking.

Likeability, according to Sanders, has four major components: being friendly, relevant, empathetic, and real. While these four components are described in some detail in his book, for you as a leader I am going to adapt his ideas slightly.

Be Friendly

How much time do you choose to spend with people you don't consider friendly? I'm guessing not much. If you aren't friendly, how much time will people want to spend with you? The answer is the same. So think about this more personal question: How much time do those you lead choose to spend with you? I'm guessing they come to meetings and scheduled events. But how much time do they spend with you when they don't have to? How often do they drop by your office for no particular reason? Do you get invited regularly to participate in team activities outside work?

Think about the people you think are friendly. The words you would use to describe them likely include *open, welcoming,* and *warm.* Now think about how people would describe you. Your level of friendliness will be reflected back to you like a mirror: how open, warm, and welcoming are people to you?

Consider friendliness as the foundation of your house of likeability. Without a foundation, you can't build a house. And without friendliness, people generally won't build any lasting relationship.

Be Relevant

There are millions of friendly people in the world, but until I know them and have the chance to interact with them or until they are related to me in some way, their friendliness doesn't matter. As a leader, you already have an initial precursor to relevance: you are in regular contact with people. Relevance, however, is about more than proximity or position. It is built when you have mutual interests with people. It is your opportunity and responsibility to find areas of mutual interest with those you lead—or at a minimum, become interested in things that matter to them.

Think about the leaders with whom you have worked and have had something in common. Did that make a difference in your relationship? Conversely, I'm sure you have experienced leaders (or know people who have) who seemed aloof and never made any effort to find common ground with you. Which of these leaders was more effective in leading you?

Be Caring

There is an old quotation I've seen attributed to many people: "People don't care how much you know until they know how much you care about them." If you want to be more likeable, care about people. Care about their situation; care about how they feel; care about whether they reach their goals. I once had a boss who thought highly of me and was very personable. But he had a vision for my career that was different from mine. He knew my goals, yet he continued to push me in the direction that he saw as better. Because of that, I never felt that this boss truly cared about me. Remarkable leaders care about people—their circumstances, situations, feelings, and goals.

Be Genuine

As I finished writing this book, President Gerald R. Ford passed away. As I listened to the comments made by his staff, the journalists covering him, and the colleagues he served with throughout the government, the most prevalent comment was that President Ford was *real*. He was described as uncomplicated, straightforward, and genuine and lauded for his willingness to share and live his values with everyone.

If you tell people that meeting customer needs is the highest priority and then cut the customer service budget, they will justifiably wonder about your sincerity. If you espouse the value of honesty and then lie when it is convenient, your genuineness will be questioned. Being genuine relates to trustworthiness, a concept discussed at some length later in this chapter. If you are seen as friendly, relevant, and caring, being genuine is the pinnacle of likeability.

WAYS TO MAKE PEOPLE LIKE YOU

Dale Carnegie, in his classic book *How to Win Friends and Influence People* (1998), outlined six ways to make people like you:

- Become genuinely interested in other people.
- Smile.
- Remember that a person's name is to that person the sweetest and most important sound in any language.
- Be a good listener. Encourage others to talk about themselves.
- Talk in terms of the other person's interests.
- Make the other person feel important and do it sincerely.

It is hard to state these principles any more clearly or effectively than this.

You might be wondering if likeability means that your goal should be to make everyone like you or to do and say things to please people (telling them what they want to hear, for example). You will certainly get further faster when you have become genuinely attractive to others, but that doesn't necessarily mean that every person will love you or that that should be your first goal. When you are genuine in the desire to be likeable, friendly, and attractive, you will have success without being fake or false.

Your Now Steps

Working on your likeability should start with being friendlier:

1. Look in the "friendliness mirror" today.
2. Notice how friendly people are to you, and recognize that they are in most cases reflecting what you are projecting.
3. Resolve to be friendlier today. Smile, and be open to building your relationships.
4. Review the results of your efforts.
5. Make notes, observations, and lessons learned in your journal.

 Remarkable leaders are likeable leaders.

Listening

The International Listening Association defines listening on its Web site (www.listen.org) as "the process of receiving, constructing meaning from, and responding to spoken and/or nonverbal messages" (1996). This is a beautiful textbook definition, but it feels a bit academic to me. Many people would define listening as understanding and remembering what was said. This too is a useful definition. However, remembering our goal in communication—to connect or make common—leads to a somewhat broader definition of listening. As we think about communicating powerfully through listening, consider a good listener as someone who has the ability to:

○ Receive spoken words and interpret the whole message (including intonation, rate of speech, gestures, and facial expressions) in an unbiased way.

○ Remember or retain the information for use in the future.

○ Maintain attention on the speaker.

○ Leave the speaker feeling heard and feeling good about the communication process.

While I was debriefing a recent workshop exercise on listening, one participant said the exercise was useful because "I never really stop to think about listening." This person's insight is instructive and, I believe, common. In reality, many people think of listening as a chance to take a break from talking. It should be exceedingly clear that to become a highly effective listener requires going beyond "taking a break" or "waiting for our next chance to talk."

More than once I have attended an event with the intention of practicing my listening skills. Rather than choosing to speak, I chose to be an active listener and engage in conversation with others by primarily listening—by getting (or letting) others do the talking. Every time I have done this, I have left having been complimented on being "very interesting," and on more than one occasion, I have been told that I was a great conversationalist. Interestingly enough, I had said very little, yet the perception was that I was a great communicator (and the by-product of this exercise is that I learned much more than I would have if I had spoken more).

Near the end of Carnegie's chapter on the principle of listening, he makes a critical comment for you to consider as a leader: "The people you are talking to are one hundred times more interested in themselves and their wants and problems than they are in you and your problems"

(1998, p. 93). This single sentence summarizes the importance of listening to building a connection, and it exposes a vital truth: connection is defined by the other person.

Proof Positive of Your Listening Skills

The best news about listening is that all of us already have the skills of a highly effective, active listener. We all are capable of doing this successfully. How do I know? Even though I haven't met you, I can cite a situation that I know proves you can listen in a highly effective manner.

Think back to about your second or third date with someone you really liked. You were probably sitting across from him or her in a restaurant, or maybe in some other quiet place, and you were really listening. You were truly interested, asking about experiences and opinions. You wanted to know more. You wanted to understand. You asked for clarification and paraphrased what you heard to make sure you understood and to make sure he or she knew you did. You made eye contact (if that is appropriate for your cultural norms), you leaned forward, and you used open and encouraging gestures. You smiled. And you did all of these things naturally for one reason: you cared.

Unfortunately for many of us, after our relationships grow stronger and deeper, we forget to practice those skills that served us so well early in a relationship. It is not that we forget the skills or suddenly don't know how to listen in that way; rather, we now take those skills and that person for granted.

Leaders can make that same mistake, and it is a grave one. You have the skills to be a great listener; you just need to be reminded of them and of their importance. That is the purpose of the rest of this section.

Key Techniques of Active Listening

I already have mentioned most of the key techniques, and you already know and can do them. Let this list serve as a reminder and a chance for you to recommit to using these skills starting today:

1. *Face the speaker.* Your body language shows your attentiveness. Sit up straight or lean forward slightly while facing the speaker.

2. *Maintain eye contact.* In most cultures, eye contact shows respect and interest. If you are listening to someone from a culture where this isn't the case, focus on the face, not the eyes. Use the comfort of the other person as your guide.

3. *Minimize external distractions.* Forward your calls, and turn off the cell phone. Close the e-mail, turn off the music, and eliminate anything else that keeps you from focusing on the speaker and the message.

4. *Minimize internal distractions.* You can think far faster than anyone can speak, so you may have thoughts (including what you want to say next) distracting you. When you become aware of those thoughts, let them go, and refocus your attention on the speaker and the message.

5. *Keep an open mind.* Wait until the speaker is finished before deciding if you disagree. Try not to make assumptions about what the speaker is thinking. Listen for understanding rather than for ammunition for your next comment.

6. *Show that you understand.* Nodding and other positive facial expressions are useful. Verbal cues like "uh-huh" and m-hmm" are helpful as well.

7. *Ask questions to deepen your understanding.* Remember that listening is about connecting. In order to connect, we must truly understand what the other person means, which can be much more than the words being said. Ask questions to probe, reflect, generalize, or get more specific. There are all sorts of questions you can put in your listening tool kit.

 For a list of twelve great listening questions to use, request this Bonus Byte at www.RLBonus.com using the keyword "questions."

8. *Pause before responding.* When you speak immediately after the other person finishes, two things can happen: you may accidentally interrupt because he or she wasn't quite done, or you may be seen as simply waiting for your turn to talk. When the speaker finishes speaking, take a breath, and collect your thoughts before you speak. This avoids these pitfalls and shows respect for the speaker.

9. *Observe nonverbal behavior.* Much of what is being said isn't being spoken. To more deeply understand the speaker, use the clues of body language, gestures, facial expression, and vocal inflection. These clues will provide more context for the words being said.

10. *Let the speaker finish.* Interrupting is something many people do, and it is a detriment not only to our ability to listen but also to the perception that we are in fact listening. When you let the speaker

finish, you likely will be seen as polite, and the speaker will feel as though his or her point has been made.

 For a list of seven ways to hold your tongue and stop interrupting, request this Bonus Byte at www.RLBonus.com using the keyword "interrupt."

11. *Summarize what you heard.* This ensures that you understand, and the speaker will appreciate that you are making this effort. This summarization sometimes helps him or her crystallize the message too.

Beyond Techniques

Techniques are important and are valuable—to a point. We could dissect many different listening techniques for many pages; in fact, books have been written solely on listening techniques. But there is no escaping that when you are focused on the technique, you aren't listening.

If you learn some approaches for not interrupting and practice them, you likely will get better at holding your tongue. Unfortunately, while you are consciously practicing the skill, you are having a negative effect on your listening as you practice. The good news is that after you have internalized the technique and it becomes a habit, it will happen subconsciously, allowing you to use the technique as a way to listen more intently and effectively.

Does that mean you shouldn't try new approaches? Of course not! But it does mean that you should be aware of this phenomenon. Consider this guideline to help you through this mental predicament: be mindful of your conscious thoughts as you listen because in that moment, your thoughts are having a negative impact on your listening skills.

Part of the remedy is to decide before the conversation what you are trying to improve. For example, if you decide at the beginning of the day or week to work on one skill (summarizing what the speaker says, for example), you will be more successful because you'll be focused. You won't be distracted during a conversation as you try to mentally work on two or three techniques at once. In addition, by focusing on one thing at a time, you will turn that skill into a habit much more quickly.

And finally, aside from all the techniques, the real key to listening more effectively is being interested in the topic and caring about the speaker.

Create a higher level of interest and caring, and your natural listening habits will take you far toward your listening goals.

Your Now Steps

These Now Steps will help you get past the problems that techniques can cause you:

1. Pick a relationship that could improve if you were a better listener with that person.
2. Resolve to be more attentive by being more interested in the messages you are hearing.
3. Remind yourself of this resolution before your next conversation with that person.
4. Review your results after each of your next five conversations.
5. Note your observations and lessons learned in your journal.

 Effective listening isn't about techniques. It comes from caring about the speaker and the message.

Building Trust

I haven't come across many who don't think trust, like motherhood and apple pie, is a good thing. Because of this practically universal belief, people don't spend much time thinking about the nature of trust and how to develop it. But if you think about it, we tend to have the best relationships with those we trust most highly. Since we have already identified the benefits of improved relationships and know that trust is an important part of relationship building, it shouldn't surprise you that most employee opinion surveys have at least one question exploring trust levels.

Beyond our intuitive "more trust is good" belief, most trust-related research positions trust as a variable with direct effect on work group performance. In other words, according to Kirk T. Dirks and Donald Ferrin (2002), when trust is increased, more collaboration and higher performance will occur. This idea isn't new. Ralph Waldo Emerson expressed it in reverse when he said, "Our distrust is very expensive."

These points reinforce the need for you as a remarkable leader to evaluate the components of trust so that you can better understand it and do all you can to build trust in all of your relationships.

Trust has four factors: believability, dependability, emotional closeness, and selflessness. The first three of these factors are additive, meaning trust can exist in one component independent of the others. The last component, selflessness, can multiply the effects of the other three when a person's motives are seen to be pure and genuine. While trust can exist with only one or two of these components in play, the highest levels of trust require high marks in all four areas. This should be your goal, your standard as a remarkable leader. Let's examine each component.

Believability

The first level of trust is believability. Believability relates to words: what people say. I trust you when I believe what you say. This level of trust has two parts: logical and emotional. On the logical level, I can believe you if I know you have expertise and credentials.

When I am introduced to a group as a speaker or trainer, my introduction is meant to grant me this first level of trust: the logical belief that I know what I am talking about. (Did you read the biographical information or testimonials on the cover and inside this book before selecting it? That is one process of determining your logical belief in my expertise.) The emotional half of believability relates to honesty: I trust you when I believe you are honest—that you don't lie. This requires direct experience and takes some time to be built. It can't be bestowed on a person by testimonial alone.

 For a list of seven ways to build your believability in the eyes of others, request this Bonus Byte at www.RLBonus.com using the keyword "believable."

Dependability

Liam got feedback from his team that he never made time to understand their personal concerns related to the impending change. Although he was seen as dependable because he made time in his calendar to listen to people's concerns, he would have scored higher marks in the minds of the team if he had done so in a way that felt as if he was doing more than going through the motions. It is one thing to make that issue an agenda item in a meeting. It is another thing entirely to take notes, ask probing questions about concerns, and search for actions to alleviate those concerns. This exposes the two different parts of dependability.

As we spend time with people, we begin to see how their actions line up with their words. The second component of trust is dependability: how you act and what you do. Dependability is judged on the linkage between promises and actions—for example, getting people the resources you promised or being prepared for the meeting after you committed you would—and also by performing in a way consistent with what we like (that is, meeting our expectations).

Emotional Closeness

There is an emotional component to trust. The most trusting relationships are those in which you can talk about a wide range of topics comfortably. You can have high scores on trust in the believability and dependability areas and yet never have any sort of emotional bond. Although this is still a trusting relationship, there is more depth. Some leaders would disagree, saying that business is business and that emotions are best left outside work. Remarkable leaders realize this is shortsighted and incorrect.

You build deeper trust when you are willing to open yourself up to talk about beliefs and values. Have you ever started to talk about a particular topic with someone, not sure if he or she really wanted to discuss something that personal with you? The risk that you felt in that moment is important to remember. Until someone is willing to step out and test whether those more personal topics can be discussed, this level of trust can't be developed. Be responsible for taking that risk.

Leaders who are open to having these sorts of conversations will be seen as more genuine and will have the opportunity to build even deeper levels of trust. Trust at the dependability and believability levels is relatively easy to build and maintain. Building emotional closeness is more difficult to develop but takes trust to a different and deeper plane.

Selflessness

I recently met with someone who has a clear belief that all salespeople are devious and disingenuous because "they'll say anything to make a sale." How easily will a salesperson build trust with this person? Even if she believes the car salesperson is stating facts about the model she's considering and even if the salesperson does everything she says she will, it's not going to matter. If the woman I recently met feels the salesperson is operating based only on a selfish agenda to sell a car, her level of trust will remain low. People will always withhold some trust based on what they see as the motives of the other person.

I see this play out in organizations all the time. People may trust an individual manager but distrust "management." They aren't sure they trust the motives of management based on either personal experience or organizational norms. The concept of servant leadership can serve all leaders well here. When you see your role as a leader as one of serving others, your selfishness naturally decreases and you will be seen as selfless. These examples show that selflessness is a multiplier: the trust bestowed in the other three categories grows or is supported when your motives are transparent and not self-centered.

You Are Responsible

Everyone has a "trust thermostat." That thermostat, which looks something like Figure 7.1, is a reading on the trust level you assign to people when you first meet them.

Figure 7.1. Trust Thermostat

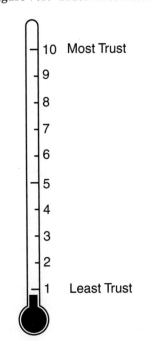

Your thermostat setting may vary in different situations (your starting trust level might be different in your personal life than in your professional life, or different with salespeople than neighbors), but you do have a set point on the 1 to 10 scale.

People with a set point closer to 1 believe that trust is all about the other person. Their motto is, "I'll trust them as soon as they prove to be trustworthy." This position is often justified by statements like, "I can't take the risk of trusting too much at first. I don't want to get burned." How does this approach look organizationally? Consider how many policies you have in place (for either employee dealings or customer dealings) that relate to a lack of trust.

RESPECT, TRUST, AND THE LOCKED BATHROOM

There is a public restroom at the retail pharmacy where my wife is a pharmacist, and it is locked. If I need to (or my daughter needs to) use the restroom at the store, I must ask if I can use the bathroom (which always reminds me, not so fondly, of kindergarten).

This bathroom door is locked with a keypad, and so you might expect that once I embarrass myself to ask to use the bathroom, I would be discreetly given the code. That expectation would be wrong. Rather, the policy is for an employee to stop what he or she is doing and unlock the door for the customer.

Physically this bathroom is near the pharmacy, and there is a back door from the pharmacy to the hallway where the bathroom is located. Given this proximity, pharmacy staff are most often asked to unlock the door. This wouldn't be too big of a problem if the staff were allowed to use this back door to meet the customer at the bathroom, but they're not: that door is off-limits. It is always locked and never used.

I surmise these policies flow from these beliefs:

o We can't leave the bathroom door open because customers might steal something (or use a personal product from the store while in the bathroom).

o We are not going to give customers the code because it might help them steal in the future because they can remember the code and give it to their friends.

o We better keep the back pharmacy door locked because the staff might try to steal something too. (Never mind that they are entrusted with thousands of dollars' worth of drugs and with counseling customers on the use of these drugs.)

What would be the impact or result of trusting your customers and employees more in this case? With more trust, would these policies be needed? What is the risk in changing these policies? Is the risk worth it in terms of the positive impact on customer service, employee time, and mindset?

 If you are thinking this is a company policy and therefore outside the store manager's control, think again: these aren't company policies, they are store policies. Someone locally is responsible. What policies like this do you have? What statements are those policies making about your organization?

People whose initial trust setting is closer to 10 begin every new relationship by treating others with trust, reducing their level of trust only if the situation warrants it. This starting point leads to much different behaviors and expectations.

You could argue which thermostat setting is correct, but it is hard to argue with which setting is most effective in relationship building. People tend to rise or fall to the level of your expectations for them, including expectations about trust. A set point closer to 10 can be riskier, but it also will unleash people's best selves and create higher levels of productivity and job satisfaction. Jim O'Toole, the author of *Leading Change*, said, "What creates trust in the end is the leader's manifest respect for the followers" (1996, p. 9). When you respect people, you treat them with higher levels of trust, and they reflect that back to you.

You are responsible for the level of trust in all of your relationships. You are responsible not only for your actions but also for your expectations and the amount of trust you bestow. Hear this message clearly: if you want greater trust in an individual relationship or across an organization, begin by trusting. Gandhi said it best: "We must be the changes we want to see in the world." If you want more trust, be more trusting.

Your Now Steps

You are responsible for the trust in each of your relationships. Although you can't control the other person's behaviors, you can control your willingness to be trusting and to exhibit trusting behaviors. Your Now

Steps address both of these choices:

1. Examine your overall trust level with your team. Unless you are sitting at 10 with every team member, resolve to raise your level now.

2. Ask the team what policy or procedure gets in their way.

When possible, eliminate or change that policy, procedure, or way of doing things.

 Trust is the currency of relationships. Remarkable leaders work to build trust every day.

Networking

Everyone—the people you know and those who know you—has a network. We tap into this network all the time to get information or knowledge, an opinion, advice, or something else. We also give help and receive help; our network is our circle of influence. While everyone has a network, many people don't like the term *networking,* which to them brings to mind being in uncomfortable situations, meeting new people, and trying to hand out as many business cards as possible. Unless you are in marketing or sales, you may not see the relevance of networking or even consider it to be a part of your job.

In reality, the value of networking for leaders is significant. Just as you use your personal network in a variety of ways, you can consciously build a professional network that can provide tremendous value to you and serve those you lead as well.

About the time I started writing this chapter, I had a cup of tea with a friend. Hazel Walker is a businessperson who, among other things, owns the central Indiana franchise for BNI (Business Networking International), the largest business networking organization in the world. During our conversation, we were talking about the book, and I mentioned there would be a section on networking. Because of her interest in and marvelous skills at networking, I thought she'd be interested. She was more than interested.

She suggested that I talk to Ivan Misner, the founder of BNI and a best-selling author in the area of networking. She said that it might be a great way to shed light on the topic, and I completely agreed. I had been introduced to Ivan previously by Hazel, via e-mail, after I recommended one of his books in our newsletter. That led to a short series of e-mails between him and me. As she mentioned her idea, I began thinking about how I could contact him, but my thoughts were interrupted by Hazel, who said, "Let me contact him, and we'll get an interview set up." And that is exactly how it happened.

I had been introduced to Hazel by a mutual friend at a networking event. Since then, we have become good friends and do everything we can to help each other reach our goals. Having Hazel in my network changed this chapter for the better. Hazel also introduced me to the person who eventually led to this book being published by Jossey-Bass. Networking works!

Networking isn't necessarily about handing out business cards and getting your name out. It is about creating mutually beneficial relationships that help everyone reach their goals more quickly and easily. As a leader, you have the opportunity to help those you lead move toward their goals and objectives. In addition, I'm sure you have some goals of your own that you would like to reach, so there also are personal benefits for you when you expand your network.

Ivan shared a story with me as we talked. He said in 1981 he was hired to be an assistant to the new president of an organization. This was a new position at a manager level working for this new president.

"On my first day on the job, the president's secretary showed me my office, told me that to make a call I needed to dial 9 for an outside line, and told me that the president was out for three days. There was no job description, and neither I nor his secretary knew what I was supposed to do. On top of that, in 1981 you didn't just call someone on their cell phone or drop them an e-mail. I knew I wouldn't hear from the boss for at least a couple of days."

"I wasn't going to sit around with nothing to do for two days, so I went from department to department talking to directors and their managers. As I sat down in their offices, I could tell they didn't quite know what to expect. Here was this new guy working for a new president. I'm sure they were wondering if I was the president's henchman! I opened each conversation by asking questions. I wanted to learn about their departments. I said, 'I'm new. Tell me about what you do and how I can help you.' Once people saw that I was earnestly listening, they opened up."

"I learned a lot in those three days! I had a grasp on the business and the challenges everyone was facing. More important, I had ideas on how to help improve things. I had asked how I could help, and then I helped. The most important thing that happened was that I had built trust with these people, and they became a part of my network."

Ivan went on to tell me that in a very short period of time, largely because of this network he had built and the way he built it, he was promoted several times and given a variety of opportunities that otherwise wouldn't have occurred.

BNI teaches networking as a three-step process: visibility, credibility, and profitability. Since most of its members are small business owners, marketers, and salespeople, you can see the lure of the profitability piece. Let's look at how these three things connect for us as leaders:

○ *Visibility.* If you want to expand your network inside or outside your company, you must find ways to meet people. You will be most successful at this when you are proactive.

○ *Credibility.* People aren't going to welcome you into their inner circle if you aren't credible. You can use the skills and ideas discussed in this chapter to help you here.

○ *Profitability.* If you are networking to build your business, the word *profitability* makes sense. But it works perfectly for other leaders too. This step is really about results. The end result of your network-building efforts is that you are able to receive help, advice, connections, referrals, and more while providing that for others as well.

Ivan cautioned, "Some people try to skip the credibility step. They think once people know them, they should refer them or help them or whatever the case might be. If they think and act this way, they will never be successful networkers."

People who don't see network building as relationship building won't be successful.

The Law of Reciprocity

I asked Ivan what his single biggest piece of advice would be to leaders who wanted to build their networking skills. He answered, "Clearly it would be to understand and use the law of reciprocity."

The law of reciprocity can be stated as, "You reap what you sow," that is, you will get back what you give. Ivan offered to help his new coworkers, and good things came to him as a result. When you smile and are pleasant to people all day long, blessings come back to you. Although the benefits may not be direct or immediate, you can trust that they will come, but *you* must start the process for the Law to work.

How does that relate to networking? Focus on helping the other person first. Give him or her a connection or an idea, or offer a helping hand. Be willing to help someone out with a presentation or fill in for him or her or do something else to assist that person. As you do this, your credibility is increased: people begin to trust you more and want to help you in return. The law of reciprocity isn't about keeping score. In fact, if you try to keep score, you are missing the point. Just as farmers know they must plant a seed before they will get a harvest, you must trust the law of reciprocity. Give to others, look for ways to help and be of service, and trust that more will come back to you.

Nurturing Your Network

Have you done a good job of staying in touch with all of your friends from high school or college or a past area where you lived? If you haven't, you know why nurturing your network is so important. Few people will automatically stay in your circle of influence if you don't stay connected and stay relevant in their lives. Because of this fact, you must proactively nurture your network, and one of the best ways to do that is to follow up and stay in touch.

 For a list of ten ways to nurture your network, request this Bonus Byte at www.RLBonus.com using the keyword "nurture."

Your Now Steps

This section was designed to expand your view of networking. These Now Steps will help you put that view into practice:

- Identify an event or opportunity to meet some new people inside or outside your organization (whichever makes more sense for you).
- Attend that event with the goal of getting to know people and what their needs are and looking for ways that you can help them.
- By using your listening skills and offering to be helpful, you will quickly begin to build these relationships.

 Remarkable leaders achieve their goals faster through the help of their ever expanding network.

Final Thoughts

The April 2006 issue of *Fast Company* magazine had an article by J. Bryan about Dan Mintz, an American who has become a successful businessperson in China. Early in the article, a Chinese word is introduced: *guanxi* (pronounced gwan-she). According to the article, it is literally translated as "relationship building," but in practice it means "carefully cultivated clout, a culturally calibrated measure of respect, influence, and honor." The article goes on to say that it is a personal as well as political form of capital. *Guanxi* is a word that expands my thoughts about relationship building. Relationship building is important to you as a leader, but it also is important in every other part of your life.

Here is a question for you: In the relationships you are working to build right now, how would the components of guanxi—respect, influence, and honor—influence your behaviors and choices? Asking and answering this question will help you become a remarkable relationship builder.

Build relationships by putting other people first: respect them at higher levels, influence them not for your gain but for theirs, and honor them highly.

Go to remarkableleadershipbook.com/resources for more information, writing, tools, and other highly recommended resources to help you build more and better relationships.

8

REMARKABLE LEADERS DEVELOP OTHERS

AT THE START OF MY PROFESSIONAL career at Chevron, I was blessed with two wonderful role models as my first two supervisors. Among their many wonderful leadership characteristics, Bob Strawn and Steve Furbacher agreed that their job was to train their replacements, and both shared this with me within days of my starting to work for them. Imagine how that made me feel as a twenty-three-year-old new employee to hear Bob, a district sales manager, say that he wanted me to have his job! Bob and Steve were positive role models for me as leaders who strive to help others grow. They both knew what all remarkable leaders know: an important part of a leader's responsibility is to develop others.

I've met few leaders who wouldn't say that, but I've met many who didn't behave as if they believed it. Have you ever experienced a leader who withheld information? Who wouldn't delegate important work? Who didn't share decision making in meaningful ways? Who took the hard work of others (perhaps even yours) and claimed the credit? All of these behaviors run counter to the belief that the leader's role is to help others grow and succeed at higher levels.

Imagine that you had these three employees on your team: Joey, Lisa, and Charles. Joey is an average performer at best—on his best days. You've worked with him in the past to improve his performance but have given up. He has long hair, and you've heard he plays in a band on weekends. All of this information contributes to your belief that at least at work, he's pretty much a slacker just trying to get by. Lisa is steady and efficient, but you feel from her performance that she has pretty much maxed out her capacity. She is a valued employee, but you don't see much growth for her. Her lead will soon be promoted, and Lisa could be seen as a replacement, but you don't think she has it in her. Charles is a different story altogether. Charles is your rising star. You had your eye on him when he was in the other division, and you couldn't wait to get him on your team. He continues to surprise you with his creativity and intuition.

Now that you have these three imaginary people on your team, which one you are going to work hardest to develop? I'm pretty sure your answer is that you will work hardest to support and provide development opportunities and coaching for Charles, primarily because of your beliefs about his potential. Your belief in Charles and his potential will motivate you to help him succeed.

But where does that leave Joey and Lisa? How can you be so sure that your perceptions are correct—that Joey lives to play in a band and therefore doesn't care to be a star performer, or that Lisa truly is maxing out her potential? The only real difference among Charles, Joey, and Lisa is your belief in, and expectations of, them. With similar beliefs and expectations, would you give more support, feedback, and coaching and mentoring to Joey or Lisa, or both? And if you did, how would their performance and capacity be affected?

There has been much research on the correlation between expectations and achievement in the educational system. In one study, educational writer Kathleen Cotton looked at forty-six studies and found "that teacher expectations can and do affect students' achievement" (1989). Based on our example above, we can be confident the same is true in the leader-follower realm as well.

In this chapter we explore four specific behaviors you can use to help you more effectively develop others: support, feedback, mentoring, and coaching.

 Your belief in someone's potential is the first and most important step toward helping him or her develop more fully and more rapidly.

Self-Assessment

Here is a quick assessment to help you think about your behaviors as a relationship builder. Use the following scale of 1 to 7 on each question:

1. Almost never
2. Rarely or seldom
3. Occasionally
4. Sometimes
5. Usually
6. Frequently
7. Almost always

I am consistently supportive and encouraging.   _____

I help people grow in their jobs.   _____

I express confidence in people's abilities.   _____

I ask for feedback on how I can better support
others' development.   _____

I look for opportunities to mentor others   _____

I provide effective coaching for the people I supervise
and lead.   _____

Supportive Behaviors

Imagine that you find yourself in the enviable position of being offered two new job opportunities within your organization. They are equal in every way: both are important to the mission of the organization, both have high visibility, both give you the opportunity for significant growth and development, and both are promotions. The only difference seems to be the immediate supervisor in each case. To help you determine which job to take, you do some investigation into these two vice presidents.

Torrance has been a vice president for five years. In talking with those who report to and work with him, you learn that he provides people the space and opportunity to do their job; in addition, he is very encouraging and creates a positive and supportive working environment. Not only that, but he encourages his managers to use this same approach within their portion of the organization. Andrew has been a vice president for several years and is known for being a hands-off manager. In all of your conversations with those familiar with him, the term *hands-off* comes up consistently. Andrew leaves you to do your work, but by all accounts provides little (if any) support, encouragement, or coaching.

Since everything else is equal, would you choose to work with Torrance or Andrew? My guess is you would choose Torrance because of his support and encouragement. Consider these facts from Gallup research (Rath and Clifton, 2004):

- The number 1 reason people leave their jobs is that they don't feel appreciated.
- At least 22 million American workers are extremely negative or actively disengaged. This loss of productivity is estimated to be worth between $250 and $300 billion annually.
- Sixty-one percent of Americans received no praise in the workplace last year.

All of these facts can be reversed or eliminated in your organization when you recognize the importance of, and continually practice, being more supportive. (Actually this isn't just a role of leaders. Being supportive is something everyone in the organization can do.) Do a cost-benefit analysis on the investment in supportive behaviors: showing appreciation and giving praise are activities that cost you nothing yet pay huge dividends (this analysis will make the accountant in you drool).

What are the things that your colleagues and team members will view as being supportive? Certainly some of the topics discussed in the previous chapter on developing relationships are supportive behaviors, chief among them being listening. Other topics are being genuine and caring about others and their needs. Beyond those, here are ten other incredibly valuable actions you can take:

- *Be flexible.* There is always more than one way to complete a task. Allow people to try a way that is different (slightly or significantly) from how you would do it. Provide them an opportunity to learn by trying it a new way.
- *Collaborate.* People feel supported when they have the chance to be involved, so give them more chances to be involved. Sharing your responsibilities with others is a great way to be supportive of them and their development.
- *Help out.* Have a team on a tight deadline? Roll up your sleeves, and get to work with them. If you don't know how to do the work yourself or are afraid you'll be in their way, ask them how you can be of assistance, or just go buy the coffee or pizza and provide moral support.

- *Be of service.* One of your most important roles as leader is to remove obstacles for people. You are a great service and provide tremendous support when you serve people in this way.

- *Value the person (always).* People may not always perform in the most appropriate way, they will make mistakes, and behaviors will need to be corrected. Nevertheless, remember that the performer is not the performance. You will be supportive when you separate the person from the performance. Value the person always, even if the performance needs correction.

- *Recognize and support their goals.* Do you know the goals of all the people on your team? Have you thought about how you and the organization can help them reach those goals? If the answer is no to either question, you have some work to do. Having clear answers to these questions and then supporting their goals in any way that you can (even if it means they eventually will leave your organization) is among the most supportive things you can do.

- *Encourage effort.* Results may not always be stellar, but we can always encourage effort. With the skills of feedback, mentoring, and coaching still to be explored, you will be able to help people improve results. Support them by encouraging and praising effort, regardless of the results.

- *Praise success.* When success occurs and goals are reached, give people praise. Leaders who feel praise isn't necessary because "that's their job" don't get it. We examine this in the section on feedback, but for now recognize that sincere and specific praise is always welcome and always deemed supportive.

 For more specific ideas on how to use praise more effectively and comfortably, request this Bonus Byte at www.RLBonus.com using the keyword "praise."

- *Celebrate!* Celebrate with individuals; celebrate with teams. Celebrate effort, and celebrate results. And make the celebration sincere. (Sincere is much more valued than elaborate.)

- *Be accountable.* As a leader, you have a role to play in others' success. When you are accountable for how you can help (including many of the points above), you are showing your support in a very tangible way.

Your Now Steps

Your Now Steps for this section are easy, and you can start immediately:

1. Pick one of the ten supportive behaviors just listed.
2. Practice that behavior at least three times today and three more times tomorrow.
3. Make notes in your journal about your results and lessons learned.

Remarkable leaders serve others and their development by supporting and encouraging their efforts. They realize they can develop others in every interaction, not just in a review or other formal conversation.

Feedback

At some point, we all want to improve at something. In addition, we all find ourselves at some point in the position to help others improve. One of the tools that aids in all of this improvement is feedback. Giving feedback is an important part of developing others. Being open to both giving and receiving feedback are two of the most important skills you can learn, or improve, if you want to maximize your productivity and the success of your team.

There are many useful techniques and guidelines for giving and receiving feedback. However, since feedback is such a central skill, we need to understand more than just the how-to's; we need to go underneath all the techniques and guidelines to the source of feedback.

The Source of All Feedback

There are three sources of all advice and feedback, and there is just one factor that will dictate how successful any of the feedback will be, regardless of the source. All the techniques and approaches you have previously read, learned, and used come from these three pieces of information. When we understand feedback at its deepest roots, we can transcend the techniques and use them as truths rather than as fill-in-the-blank formulas.

All feedback, whether requested (and received) or given (or offered), comes from one, or some combination, of these sources:

○ *Expertise/experience.* Often we are in a position to provide feedback or coaching to someone who isn't as expert or experienced in something as we are. Because of our experience and knowledge, we are in a great position to give wise counsel. When you really want to learn something new, one local strategy is to find an expert—a person with true subject matter expertise, from inside or outside the organization, is invaluable to the learning process. When you can get advice and feedback from a true expert, you will be open to what this person has to say because you value the information and perspective dearly. Remarkable leaders recognize when and how to give feedback from this perspective and are honest when they don't have an expertise others might assume they have.

○ *Relationship and caring.* People turn to the people they like and trust to give them advice. How often have you turned to a trusted adviser or friend to give you advice on something that he or she had no experience on? A trusted neighbor may know nothing about your business or organizational politics, and yet you turn to her for a perspective anyway. You are asking for counsel and feedback because you know she cares about your best interests. The fact that she cares and you trust her is reason enough. Sometimes we give advice and coaching just because we care about the other person. A strong relationship can make us more willing to give feedback, and that same strong relationship will make us much more open to receiving it.

○ *Power and position.* At work this is where feedback and coaching typically come from. The position of power could be the boss, supervisor, or manager; you are likely in a position of power for many others. (It also could come from a member of clergy, a teacher, or a parent.) We all have received feedback from people in a position of power. Because of your role, you know that you are expected to provide feedback from this perspective.

It is clear that some feedback may come from more than one of these sources. For example, someone may ask you for feedback both as his supervisor and because of your expertise in a particular area. If you are the boss, are seen as being an expert, and have a strong relationship with the person, you have a situation where the feedback has the best chance for success. The stronger the connection is to more of these sources, the more welcome (and therefore more easily received) the feedback will be.

The Master Key to Successful Feedback

If you want to be more successful in helping others succeed, regardless of the source of the feedback, you need to clearly understand and use this master key. If you want to take advantage of and be open to any coaching or feedback you receive, you must understand this key as well. The master key that unlocks successful feedback is intent.

Stated simply, when your intent is clear and pure and you are giving feedback and coaching with the very best for the other person in mind, it will be the most successful. With good intent, you will work harder to make the feedback successful, and the receiver will be more open to the feedback, even if he or she doesn't like the entire message. Conversely, if your underlying purposes are vindictive, punitive, meant to "fix" someone, or come from frustration or anger, your feedback will be less effectively delivered and will encounter more opposition and disagreement.

You have received much coaching and feedback in your life, so you know this is true. When you sense the feedback you are receiving is valuable and comes from a perspective of truly wanting to help you improve, you are more open to hearing and applying it. Isn't that what you want when you give advice, coaching, or feedback—to be heard and to have that feedback applied?

As much sense as this makes, it isn't the way it always happens. The truth is that feedback says as much about the giver as it does about the receiver. Here is an example. When I train and coach trainers and leaders on their presentation skills, I have the opportunity to give them feedback. I work hard to do that in a way that is balanced in terms of encouragement and corrective advice. I want them to feel supported and excited about their opportunity to improve and have some tangible ways to do that. But even when that intent is pure, my feedback is skewed by my perspective. If I have recently read an article about the use of voice in speaking I will notice, consciously or not, more vocal things and give more feedback in that area. If I have recently been working on improving the way I open or close a session, you can bet that I will have plenty of feedback for people regarding those components of their presentation.

Although none of this is really bad or off the mark, we all need to make sure we are providing balanced feedback based on what the other person needs, not what is most relevant or topical for us. In other words, coaching shouldn't be about us; it should always be about the other person and their success.

How do you practice this to give more effective feedback? Recognize it on a conscious level to help you balance the feedback. Or tell people up front this is where your focus has been. It will help them understand why you gave a disproportionate amount of feedback in one particular area.

How to Use This Knowledge

When you are coaching others, always have a clear goal or intention for that coaching in mind, and make sure that you communicate this intent in your words and your behavior. Also recognize the sources from which your feedback comes, and provide feedback from the most valuable perspective in that situation. Help the other person see where it is coming from and why it is important.

Before you pick up a book (and there are many) on specific tactics or skills to make feedback more effective and accepted, remember that your coaching will be much more successful when you start by thinking about the three sources of feedback rather than following any model or prescription perfectly. It won't matter if you muff up your words a little bit. When you focus on a clear intent and a solid foundation on the sources, any techniques and approaches will work much better.

 To explore a few techniques of feedback and how to apply them more effectively, request this Bonus Byte at www.RLBonus.com using the keyword "feedback."

If you are receiving feedback and truly want to improve, assume the other person's intent is pure and take the feedback as a useful gift (even if it doesn't feel like that at the moment). Remember that not everyone understands this concept like you do now. If once you have received the feedback you determine that the intent wasn't clear or was even counterproductive to your success, you can then decide what you will do with the advice and counsel you received.

Two More Things

Any conversation I've ever had about feedback in a meeting or workshop always includes discussion about positive feedback versus negative feedback. Some people say positive feedback isn't necessary, but I've never met anyone who didn't want to receive it, if done properly. Some people think negative feedback can be a demotivator, but everyone has received advice on how to improve something that they both appreciated and applied. The key to making feedback valued and used, whether positive or negative, is to make it specific, relevant, and timely.

 To learn more about positive versus negative feedback and how to balance them effectively, request this Bonus Byte at www.RLBonus.com using the keywords "balanced feedback."

Finally, feedback is typically delivered from the perspective of the word itself. We *feed* people information *backward*: the conversation is about something they have already done. Although information about past performance is important, what is often more important is information about future performance, or feedforward. By giving people advice about what to do now, you are giving them help for the next time. Given your experience and expertise, perhaps the next step is logical and obvious so the feedback should sufficiently lead to the obvious next step, but this isn't always the case for those we are advising. When we give feedforward, we are helping people map out a strategy for better future performance. After all, the only performance we can alter is the performance that has not yet occurred.

 For information on a process to help you apply the concept of feedforward more successfully, request this Bonus Byte at www.RLBonus.com using the keyword "feedforward."

Your Now Steps

Use your new perspectives on feedback to complete these Now Steps:

1. Consider the most recent feedback you gave to someone.
2. Review how successfully you felt you gave the feedback and how well it was received.
3. Think about which sources it came from.
4. Based on the sources, consider what you might do differently to make the feedback more successful the next time.
5. Make any notes, observations, and lessons learned in your journal.

Feedback is important, but when it is combined with feedforward, people will improve faster and more successfully.

Mentoring

The word *mentor* comes from Greek mythology; Mentor was the person whom Odysseus asked to counsel and instruct his son on being king while Odysseus went off to fight the Trojan War. This background for the word is important because it gives us context for how we use the word today. Mentors are typically seen as older, wiser people who provide their expertise to less experienced individuals to help them reach their goals. While *mentoring* is generally applied more broadly than "older people helping younger people," the concept of the mentor as a trusted person who helps, aids, instructs, and facilitates learning remains the same.

Mentoring programs are often set up by organizations to take advantage of this transfer of expertise and knowledge. Because of this, many people see mentors coming from the feedback source of knowledge and expertise; after all, that is why a person has been identified as a potential mentor. Although this is a necessary prerequisite for a mentor, great mentors work from the source of relationships and caring about the protégé at least as much as from the position of their experience and knowledge.

The best mentoring is really a partnership for learning. Mentors love facilitating learning, but not necessarily the role of teacher. Their focus is on sharing and helping their protégé succeed through learning. The most successful mentors are people who, like their original namesake, create a legacy through their efforts. Chip Bell, in his book *Managers as Mentors*, says that "great mentors are not only devoted fans of their protégés, they are loyal fans of the dream of what the protégé can become with their guidance" (1996, p. 8).

Mentoring Versus Coaching

The difference between coaching and mentoring for the purposes of this discussion is that in an organizational setting, coaching typically includes a supervisory and performance evaluation and management component. Stated from the perspective of the sources of feedback, coaches have a position of power due to their role in relation to the one being coached. In the discussion here, a mentor is someone whose focus is solely on helping the protégé reach his or her goals, regardless of the organizational context.

What Great Mentors Aren't

Great mentors avoid some serious pitfalls that other mentors fall prey to. Here are four attitudes (and the behaviors that accompany them) to avoid:

- *The fount of all knowledge.* People have come to you and asked for your help. They look to you as a person experienced in a particular area. This feeling of knowledge can become a bit intoxicating, and when it pervades your thinking, you are no longer mentoring for the right reason and likely are not mentoring very effectively. Beware the feeling that you have all the answers. A quick reminder that you don't have all the answers is to check with a close friend, spouse, or significant other. That person will surely remind you that you don't know everything. Your job as a mentor is to create learning for the other person, not to feel better about yourself.

- *The legend (in their own mind).* You've heard of the athlete or politician who has spent too much time reading his own press clippings and begins to believe he or she can do no wrong. If you have been helpful to your protégé, that person is going to thank you and attribute some of his or her success to you. This feels good, and it is probably true—to some point. If you find yourself falling into this trap, ask yourself why you chose to be a mentor. Was it to help someone else, or for your own personal reasons?

- *The indispensable one.* Sometimes mentors began to feel that they are solely responsible for the success of their protégé. They begin to feel that their protégé couldn't do it without them, that they are truly indispensable. When you feel this way, you are creating a dependent relationship when the goal really is to create strength and independence. If you find your protégé reluctant to meet with you or you find yourself more eager to meet than the protégé does, the relationship may be a bit too dependent. The best mentors realize that their role may well end. Just as children outgrow a favorite pair of shoes, your protégé may outgrow the need for you. This doesn't mean your contribution was not valuable; it just means you have helped create a success.

○ *Too helpful.* You become a mentor to be helpful. Right? This is certainly true, but we can take our helpfulness too far. Think of the parents of a child beginning college who do everything for their child, trying to make the experience as easy as possible (these parents even have a name: helicopter parents, because they hover over their son or daughter). At some point, the parents' good intentions are misguided because the student clearly needs to try some things and solve some problems without help from home. So it is with us as mentors. In your zeal to help your protégé be successful, remember that he or she has to try and fail just as you did. You must learn when it is appropriate to "save" the protégé. When you keep your protégé's learning as your guide, you'll do fine.

What Great Mentors Do

This list of skills and behaviors of great mentors is divided into two parts: concepts we have already explored in this book and ideas being introduced for the first time now. First, we'll look at the familiar skills and behaviors:

○ *Build rapport.* Great mentors know that the best results from mentoring come when the relationship is strong. Look for opportunities and ways to build a connection with your protégé. You aren't, and don't want to be, your protégé's best friend, but you do want a relationship that will foster the greatest possible learning and results to occur.

○ *Listen.* One of the most important ways to build rapport is to listen. A mentoring relationship is not based on one-way communication from you, the expert, to the protégé (see the "fount of all knowledge" pitfall above). Listen for understanding and intent. Listen to understand your protégé's goals. Listen for the underlying messages and challenges and experiences. Listen to your protégé carefully and completely.

○ *Build trust.* The more trust your protégé has in you, the more successful the mentoring relationship will be. Use the tools described in Chapter Seven to build your trust with your protégé.

○ *Make other connections.* As the more experienced person in the relationship, you likely know people who can be of additional benefit to your protégé. As you understand your protégé's goals, introduce others who might help in specific ways. Make your network available as a way to help your protégé reach his or her goals and find additional mentors in specific skill areas.

And now for the rest of the list. Great mentors:

○ *Maintain focus.* A mentoring relationship should always have a clear direction—the direction of the protégé's goals. Great mentors keep this direction clear for both themselves and the protégé. One of the most important things you can do for your protégé is to keep him or her focused on goal achievement.

○ *Remember the purpose of the relationship.* This relationship is for mentoring—for helping the protégé reach goals. Great mentors remember the purpose for the relationship and don't use it as a chance to create a new buddy or, worse, another pair of hands for achieving the mentor's goals.

○ *Offer advice.* As a mentor, you will have the opportunity to offer advice, counsel, and feedback to your protégé. This is one of the reasons for the relationship. Great mentors always remember that their role is to offer advice, not determine the protégé's next move. It is the protégé's role and prerogative to determine which advice to follow and which advice to defer or discard.

○ *Ask questions.* One of the best things you can do as a facilitator of learning for your protégé is ask a well-phrased, well-timed question. Knowing this, great mentors collect and plan the questions they will use in a given situation with the protégé. Be thoughtful not only with your advice but with the questions that you ask. Questions that generate reflective thought and discovery learning for the protégé are the most valuable ones you can ask.

○ *Look for teachable moments.* If you are a parent, you understand the concept of the teachable moment. You can tell your child something fifty times, to no avail, but at the time when the child most needs the advice, counsel, or perspective, she will listen. So it is with a protégé. The teachable moment is the intersection of the learner's readiness to learn, your ability to help, and her ability to apply the lessons. Be alert for these opportunities.

○ *Make themselves available.* In order to find the intersection between readiness to learn and your ability to help, you must be available. You are busy, and so are great protégés. Nevertheless, the best mentors make their mentoring relationships enough of a priority to be available, even if for only a quick phone call to chat or the timely return of an e-mail.

○ *Create dialogue.* The best mentoring relationships are successful because the two parties work together in collaboration. For this to happen, the conversation cannot be one-way. As a great mentor, you need to create dialogue. Do you have some advice to offer? Position it not as "the right answer" but as a spur for conversation. Do you want to ask a question? Pose it as an inquisitive open-ended question that stimulates thinking and conversation. Make your conversation reflect the relationship you want to create: a partnership aimed at the protégé's success.

○ *Are role models.* Model the behavior you offer your protégé. Your protégé will learn more from your actions than your words, so let your behaviors speak loudly, clearly, and consistently.

Being Mentored

Mentoring doesn't have to be junior person mentored by a more senior person. Think of mentoring in smaller niches. If you are a younger person, you may be in a position to mentor in a technology area or some other area where you are more expert (or if you are more senior, you might look to a younger person for similar help). Bust the mentoring paradigm for everyone's benefit.

 For a matrix of ideas for and uses of nontraditional mentoring approaches, request this Bonus Byte at www.RLBonus.com using the keyword "nontraditional."

Perhaps more important to you, one of the best ways you can accelerate your progress toward becoming a remarkable leader (or the achievement of any other skill or goal) is to find a mentor yourself. Seek out people with expertise, knowledge, and experience that you would benefit from. When you are selecting that mentor, think about the characteristics and attributes you've just read. Consider finding a mentor who embodies both the technical and mentoring skills to make the relationship most effective for you.

Your Now Steps

These Now Steps don't necessarily build on each other. You can pick any one of the three, and do just it. Of course, doing all of them will move you that much closer to remarkable more quickly:

1. If you are a mentor, look at the four pitfalls, and reflect on whether you find yourself falling for them now (or ever). If so, take some action to get out of that trap.

2. If you are a mentor, pick one of the skills outlined, and resolve to get better in that area immediately.

3. Identify a mentor to help you reach one or more of your goals. (You can use what you have learned here to create the best possible relationship with that person.)

 Great mentors facilitate learning for those they mentor.

Coaching

Coaching long ago left the athletic realm and even the realm of the supervisor. There are life coaches, finance coaches, dream coaches, personal coaches, business coaches, and coaches for leaders and even executives. There are clinics, university programs, and companies ready to help people learn these coaching skills (many of which you are learning in the various competencies in this book). Coaching, in fact, has never been a hotter topic. All of those roles certainly are coaching, but the coaching role outlined here is the one most important to you as a leader: your role as a performance coach for those who work with you.

Coaching in Most Organizations

Coaching in most organizations is the job of supervisors, and typically that means preparing the performance review. You know the annual dance: you are reminded when you get the notice from human resources with evaluation deadlines. HR sends you copies of the forms and may even give you some refresher information on how to use the forms or conduct the reviews effectively. And every few years the process will change—in either a small administrative way or some more substantial way (at least from the perspective of those revising the process). But to you, the supervisor or manager, it is all the same: once a year you have to have a performance conversation with your direct reports.

Although the employees don't get the memo from HR, they know the time is coming too: at some point they'll get an e-mail from you, or the topic will come up in a staff meeting: "Performance reviews will be soon. Look at your calendars, and let's find a time to do this," you'll say.

And so goes the dance: supervisors do performance reviews because they are expected to; employees participate because they must. Occasionally this conversation leads to meaningful changes in performance, either helping a high performer become a star or helping a person with some performance challenges make significant improvements. Of course, these are the goals of the performance review: to provide people with feedback on performance, compare that performance to the expectations of the job, and provide an opportunity for conversation on how to improve regardless of the current level of performance.

These goals are wonderful. Unfortunately, in almost all cases, a performance review won't achieve those goals, no matter how well it is done and no matter what the intentions of the participants or the skill of the supervisor. You do performance reviews because these goals are valid and because "everyone does them." Then when they don't reap the desired results, organizations look to update the forms, improve the feedback skills of the supervisors, or otherwise improve the process.

Here is the best way to improve the process: *Eliminate the performance review*.

Remarkable leaders know that the performance review might actually get in the way of successful coaching, and they'd prefer the results of successful coaching to the beauty (and I use that term very loosely) found in a stack of perfectly completed forms.

Key Components for Successful Coaching

Imagine that a dancer had a personal coach. That dancer would expect the coach to provide a clear picture of what excellent performance looked like, offer ongoing encouragement, and give positive feedback when appropriate and correction when needed. The dancer wouldn't be very happy if the coach watched only sporadically throughout the year during occasional performances or practices and then scheduled an annual meeting to discuss progress. Similarly, a golfer would want a coach to provide feedback.

We read these examples and nod our heads in agreement. Then we go to work and do exactly the opposite.

In the most fundamental ways, your work is no different from the dancer or golfer: you and those you work with perform or "do work" all the time. In order for people to benefit from coaching, it needs to be in context and in the flow of their work. Unfortunately, since most coaching is so closely tied to the performance review process, it (unnecessarily) tends to look at work as a snapshot rather than a running video recording.

But you can use your current performance review process and still make it work significantly better. Everything I suggest next is within your control and won't violate any of the tenets of your existing organizational process:

1. *Stop thinking of the annual event.* You may have to do the forms each year, but you can meet and discuss performance as often as you want.
2. *Turn it into a process.* Regular conversation, perhaps informal, leads to a much better outcome.
3. *Remember the key purposes of the review.* Your coaching process should include clear expectations, a discussion of progress, and feedback for continual improvement. This makes the conversations more useful to you and the person you are coaching.
4. *Explain the change.* Let your people know what you are doing and why. Once they know why you are making coaching an ongoing process, they likely will embrace it.
5. *Improve your skills.* You can get better at giving feedback, building rapport, and all of those other things effective coaches do. When you are having regular conversations, you will get better faster.
6. *Use your review process as a culmination.* You can fill out the forms and paperwork anytime. And if you are having ongoing conversations, it should be quite simple!

Since performance is ongoing, so should the conversation about it.

A Coaching Process

For many things, having a model, a template, or a process can make life easier. It doesn't reduce your need to know things but gives you a reminder, a checklist, and a flow. Coaching is no different. Figure 8.1 shows a model that you can use.

Beyond the steps themselves, there are two important components to this model: its circular nature and the fact that it sits on top of support. We've already discussed supportive behaviors, and this reinforces how important they are. Every step of the coaching process will work better if it is done in a supportive manner. Coaching is meant to be an ongoing process related to ongoing performance. To consider coaching as a

Figure 8.1. A Coaching Model

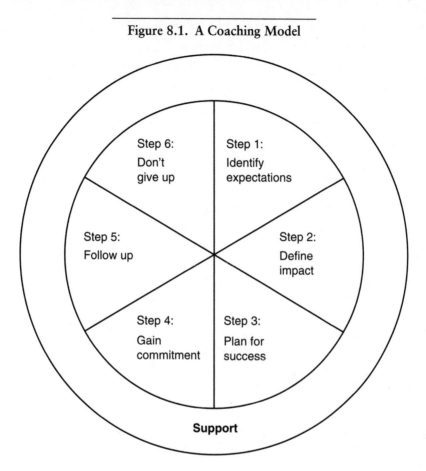

straight-line process doesn't make any sense. Think about the process as a continual loop that creates an upward spiral of performance.

Now let's examine each step of the process.

STEP 1: IDENTIFY EXPECTATIONS. The most important step to improve your coaching is to identify expectations with the person you are coaching. Until you each know exactly what is expected, how can you be held accountable for any of those expectations? In conversation with those you are coaching, you must discuss the expectations of the work product and their behavior and approaches. Here are some tips for identifying and creating agreement on expectations:

○ Be focused on one expectation at a time.
○ Get the input of those to whom you are coaching.

○ Acknowledge their feelings and perspective.

○ Be specific, descriptive, and nonhostile.

○ Give them airtime to help them understand the expectations.

○ Restate and clarify the expectations.

○ Use "I" language as a way to communicate expectations more clearly.

To learn more about "I" language, request this Bonus Byte at www.RLBonus.com using the keyword "I language." For more detailed thoughts on developing clear expectations, request this Bonus Byte at www.RLBonus.com using the keyword "expectations."

STEP 2: DEFINE IMPACT. People do things for their reasons, not yours (and not the organizational reasons either). To help them move forward and improve their performance (whether their current performance is below standards or you want to bump them up to the next level), they need to know their personal benefits. We talked about WIIFM in Chapter Six in the context of a presentation. The purpose of defining the impact in a coaching situation is exactly the same: people need to know the positives and negatives of reaching or not reaching their goals and expectations.

STEP 3: PLAN FOR SUCCESS. Get the other person involved in building the action plan to improve performance further. By now, you have expectations and goals, as well as the impacts of reaching them. Take these two pieces of information, and create an action plan to reach those goals. The best plan will be one that is co-created with the person being coached because it is harder to resist or defer a plan he helped create. Going one step further, I encourage you to have him lead the planning discussion, with you helping rather than you laying out a plan and saying, "What do you think?" The former will be more accurately viewed as his plan, while the latter may not be seen that way at all. (Much more about goal setting is discussed in Chapter Sixteen.)

STEP 4: GAIN COMMITMENT. This step begins with a question like, "Now that we have a plan, how do you feel about it?" and is followed closely by the commitment question: "How committed are you to this plan?" or "What do we need to adjust in this plan in order to deepen your commitment to achieving it?" Your actual questions will be personalized, of course, but these examples give the idea. Your goal is to create a commitment that he states to you. This step is important because it crystallizes the communication and removes all ambiguity about responsibility and accountability. It moves people from acknowledging that they can do something to committing that they will do it.

All of the steps in the process are important, but you could make a persuasive argument that this is the most important. Regardless of who created the expectations or built the plan, if someone is committed to implementing the plan and gaining the results, that is huge.

STEP 5: FOLLOW UP. Coaching, like performance, is a process: once a plan is in place and there is commitment to implementing it, it is your responsibility to stay connected and observe how things are going. This is your chance to check in, provide resources that the person needs to continue moving forward, and provide encouragement and reinforcement. It also is your chance to confront excuses and overcome resistance. Your follow-up conversations are the perfect time to talk about progress to date and the current next steps. Additional coaching or counsel might be required to adjust or modify the plan based on current progress or new information.

STEP 6: DON'T GIVE UP. People may start to lose momentum or hope. Their attention or focus might get diverted (though if you are following this process consistently that likely won't be a problem). To keep people on track, remind them of the WIIFMs and emphasize the positive consequences of their successful completion of their plan. This step is about more than a meeting. Coaching requires patience and courage. Stick with people, and believe in their success longer than they think you will. This commitment will prove your compassion and caring and provide you with relationship benefits as well as helping the person reach his or her performance goals.

Coaching on Performance Problems

Leaders often equate coaching with "dealing with performance problems." Although this is one purpose for coaching, it is a limited view. The coaching model is just as applicable when working with a high performer as it is when working with a person who is struggling in some way.

Even so, it is appropriate to discuss the specific challenges of coaching on performance problems specifically.

Again, the coaching model gives the basics for coaching performance problems. If you think about each of these steps from that perspective, you will see that the process will work if you work the process.

The approach of this section, then, is to look at some of the root causes of performance problems. Although not every performance problem you encounter will have started from one of these causes, many will, and by considering these potential root causes, you give yourself a significant head start in helping others move past these challenges. Consider the list that follows as a checklist to help you diagnose the causes of performance problems:

- Root cause 1: The employee doesn't understand what is expected (duties or performance levels).
- Root cause 2: The employee doesn't know how to perform the duties.
- Root cause 3: The employee doesn't know expectations aren't being met.
- Root cause 4: The employee doesn't receive any performance feedback.
- Root cause 5: The employee isn't committed to the work.
- Root cause 6: The employee doesn't see the importance of the work.
- Root cause 7: The employee is bored.
- Root cause 8: There are no consequences or rewards related to work expectations.
- Root cause 9: The employee doesn't have the proper tools, equipment, or supplies.
- Root cause 10: Your expectations aren't achievable (in reality or in the employee's mind).
- Root cause 11: Your expectations are too low.
- Root cause 12: The work process itself is the cause.
- Root cause 13: The employee has issues with you.
- Root cause 14: The employee has personal issues that are affecting his or her work performance.

The root cause might be with the employee, the organization, or you. Regardless of the nature of these causes, you have the tools you need in your toolbox to help the employee address these challenges. Use these skills, along with the coaching model, and you will have great success.

 For more specific ideas on how to deal with each of these root causes in conjunction with the coaching model, request this Bonus Byte at www.RLBonus.com using the keywords "performance problem."

As a final point in this area of performance problems, remember the power of expectations. One of the best ways you can help people overcome performance problems is to believe that they are capable of doing so. Your belief and expectations of their potential success will have a major impact on the energy and passion that you use in working with them. And that expectation is subconsciously transferred to them.

> **WHERE IS THE POTENTIAL?**
> Extraordinary potential exists in all of us. With the right environment, resources, skills, and knowledge, ordinary people can achieve extraordinary results.

Your Now Steps

Since coaching should be an ongoing process, it shouldn't be hard to find an opportunity to get started. Here are some steps to help:

1. Identify a person to coach.
2. Review the steps in the coaching model.
3. Schedule a time with that person to begin coaching using the model.
4. Start by having a conversation about expectations—both yours and theirs.

 The best coaches help people reach their potential in the context of organizational success.

Go to remarkableleadershipbook.com/resources for more information, writing, tools, and other highly recommended resources to help you develop those around you more successfully.

9

REMARKABLE LEADERS FOCUS ON CUSTOMERS

In preparing for the 150th Indiana State Fair, Cindy Hoye, the fair's executive director, asked me to help her team improve its focus on customers and provide training skills to support that focus. A large part of the audience was the temporary employees: those who would park cars, take tickets, and provide basic security functions. These employees were especially important because they had the greatest potential impact on customers' overall experience at the fair.

During each of two sessions, I asked, "How would you treat each customer if you knew that their full six-dollar ticket price was going into your pocket?" In one session, I heard, "I'd say thank you. Thank you VERY much. And please come again!" In another, I heard, "I'd treat them like *gold*."

There it is. That's pretty much everything you need to know about customer service: thank them, value their business, and treat them like gold. Cindy knew that a customer service culture and focus starts with leaders. It is your job to help people see the importance of the customer and create an environment where those behaviors can prosper.

Your employees know from experience that it is easy to treat "nice" and "pleasant" customers well. As a leader, it is your job to create that expectation and provide the skills so all customers are treated well (even when the customer is mean, grumpy, and irrational). An individual employee may not get the full six-dollar ticket fee (or your equivalent), but without the customer, no one gets any paycheck at all.

If you started reading this chapter thinking it doesn't apply to you because you don't have "customers," think again. You may not call them customers; you may call them clients, stakeholders, ticket holders, patients, students, users (heaven forbid!), or something else. When you read the word *customers,* see which of these synonyms applies to you and your work most directly. Regardless of your terminology, it is your job to create a customer-focused organization. Without it, neither you nor your organization can ever become truly remarkable.

 Your customers, regardless of what you call them, write your paycheck.

Self-Assessment

Here is a quick assessment to help you think about your skills as a relationship builder. Use the following scale of 1 to 7 on each question:

1. Almost never
2. Rarely or seldom
3. Occasionally
4. Sometimes
5. Usually
6. Frequently
7. Almost always

I focus on serving both internal and external customers. _____

I help others serve customers. _____

I know who my customers are. _____

I talk to my customers and understand their expectations. _____

I use mistakes as a way to improve customer relationships. _____

I find ways to partner with my customers. _____

Different Types of Customers

The concept of the customer for people who are parking cars or taking tickets makes sense. It's easy for them to see who the customer is because they are taking the customer's money or parking his or her car. However, if you work in an internal service group like human resources, finance, legal, or other groups removed from the paying customer, the idea of the customer may be fuzzier. Even if you don't have an interface with the external paying customer, you still have customers. You will help your group when you help expand your team's definition of "the customer" to include "whomever they deliver their work to or whoever uses their work output." With this broadened definition, everyone has customers for their work.

This may be different from how some people think about their customers. In the most traditional view, people think of their boss as the customer. And while it is true that the boss is one of your customers, nearly everyone has internal customers other than the boss. All of them are important because these internal customer and supplier relationships are an integral link in the chain that leads to satisfying the external paying customer (if you aren't serving the direct customer, you are serving someone who is).

As a remarkable leader, your job is to create the same expectations for internal customer service as a sales leader might create for satisfying external customers. The best news about this perspective is that when people begin to see their internal contacts as customers, they naturally create a more collaborative and supportive work environment. When they see how their work matters to both the people they deliver it to and ultimately the paying customer, it gives their work more meaning and helps them see the value their work generates. These factors can certainly help you foster greater teamwork and collaboration (see Chapter Twelve).

THE CYCLE OF MEDIOCRITY

Internal customer service often fails because of what Karl Albrecht, author of *The Only Thing That Matters*, calls the Cycle of Mediocrity:

> I can't,
> because he didn't,
> because she doesn't,
> because he won't,
> because they never . . .

In other words, blame and excuses typically are the source of most of our internal customer service challenges. (For more on blame see Chapter Fourteen.)

While the concept of customer is the same whether internal or external, there are clearly some differences in the strategies you might use to improve the service to each group. Here are six specific ways that you can use to help improve internal customer service:

○ *Model the value.* As a leader, you have internal customers too. You need to role-model the rest of the items on this list and focus on your internal customers and their needs. Remember that for some of your work outputs, your team is your customer. (Does thinking of your team as your customer put a new light on your role?)

○ *Understand their expectations.* Providing good customer service, regardless of who the customer is, requires understanding the customer's expectations. Create the time, space, and opportunity for people to think about and understand the expectations of their internal customers. How? By asking. A major barrier to internal customer satisfaction is familiarity; many people assume they already know what their internal customers want and need.

○ *Create dialogue.* Asking the question about expectations is the start of a dialogue, and that dialogue should be nurtured. Internal suppliers need to understand the internal customer's expectations. It is especially important to understand how the customer uses a work output. This understanding may help the supplier provide something new or different that the customer maybe hasn't even considered. By creating opportunities for internal customers and suppliers to have conversations, you are giving people a significant opportunity to improve.

○ *Innovate collaboratively.* Often the best way to improve the work process is to involve everyone participating in the work. Bring internal customers and suppliers together to define problems and identify opportunities for future growth. (Chapters Eleven and Fifteen explore both innovation and problem solving in more depth.)

○ *Foster cross-training.* One of the best ways to improve customer service is for people to empathize with their customers. That means putting yourself in others' shoes. When your customers are inside the organization, you can do this quite easily by offering cross-training opportunities. Encourage or mandate cross-training between people and their internal customers. Although cross-training is typically done to provide additional flexibility to handle peak demands for various departments, it also provides a chance for people to truly understand what their customers need by living in their shoes, even if only for a few hours or days.

○ *Celebrate more broadly.* Your group's success is a success or win for other groups as well. Remember this, and consider celebrating your successes more broadly. This will create a greater feeling of teamwork and provide other opportunities for dialogue between customers and suppliers.

While this section has been specifically focussed on the internal customer relationship, the rest of this chapter applies equally to both internal and external customers.

Your Now Steps

You can begin to improve internal customer service immediately. Here's one place to start:

1. Identify three or more of your internal customers (you can do this right now).
2. Schedule time to sit down with them to define and understand their expectations.
3. Build an action plan to help you better satisfy or exceed those expectations.
4. Capture any ideas, observations, and lessons learned in your journal.
5. Soon after completing this for yourself, lead this process for others on your team.

Internal customers are just as important as external customers. Remarkable leaders strive to satisfy their needs too—knowing this ultimately leads to success for external customers.

Instilling the Customer Mind-Set

Sam Walton said, "There is only one boss: the customer. And he can fire everybody in the company, from the chairman on down, simply by spending his money somewhere else" (n.d.). Getting this belief into the minds and hearts of everyone in the organization is the responsibility of the remarkable leader. However, this is not possible if the leader doesn't already have this mind-set. As a way to convince, or remind, you of the importance of the customer to your organization's health, here are some facts from *Extreme Management* by Mark Stevens (2002) (with some comments and questions from me):

○ It costs between five and six times more to attract a new customer than to keep an existing one. (Does this make you more interested in creating loyal customers?)

- Companies can boost profits anywhere from 25 to 125 percent by retaining 5 percent more existing customers. (That is a serious return on investment. What else could you do this year that would have as big an impact on your bottom line?)

- Only one out of twenty-five dissatisfied customers will express dissatisfaction. (So if you aren't hearing anything, that doesn't mean everyone is satisfied.)

- Happy customers tell four to five others about their positive experience. Dissatisfied customers tell nine to twelve how bad it was. (So the dissatisfied ones aren't telling you, but they are telling all of their friends and colleagues.)

- Sixty-six percent of customers do not feel valued by those serving them. (Create a feeling of value, and you will create loyal customers, retain those you have, and strengthen the bottom line significantly.)

What Is the Goal?

Most often people think customer satisfaction is the goal. After reading and reflecting on the statistics above, you can quickly see that satisfaction should not be the goal; satisfaction should be the floor, meaning anything at or below satisfaction is cause for great consternation. Customer satisfaction simply means people are lukewarm about your products and services. Satisfied customers don't have a compelling reason to stay with you and may well leave for someone they perceive as better in any way.

If not satisfaction, then what should the goal be? Consider Figure 9.1. Our minimum goal should be delight, because it is the path to customer loyalty. Consider those statistics again. Retaining customers will have a significant impact on the bottom line of your business. This thought is summed up in the title of Jeffrey Gitomer's book, *Customer Satisfaction Is Worthless, But Customer Loyalty Is Priceless* (1998).

Remarkable leaders recognize that the mind-set they create must go beyond simple customer satisfaction. If customers write the paycheck

Figure 9.1. Customer Service Continuum

Gone   Dissatisfaction   Satisfaction   Delight   Loyalty   Partnership

and you want them to continue to write the paycheck, you must do everything you can to create delighted and loyal customers.

Talk to Them!

In the late 1980s, I worked in Chevron Chemical's fertilizer business, a tough industry with tough economics. There was an opportunity to make a significant sale to a new customer who was located in Hawaii. As a part of the negotiation for this long-term supply of product, the customer wanted to meet with our general manager, Steve Furbacher.

Knowing this account was important and knowing the importance of sitting with the customer to build the relationship, Steve flew from San Francisco early one morning and met with the customer all day. He then went back to the airport and flew home on the red-eye.

He saved some money (no hotel stay, and reduced meal expense), which was an important consideration in our tough business climate. But the more important reason for his quick trip was that he wanted to lead by example. He told me later, "It was important for people to know that we will do what we need to do to build customer relationships and that I went for that business purpose, not for a mini-vacation."

We secured this important piece of business. Beyond that, Steve made a difference for those he led. Through his simple act, we were reminded of the importance of face-to-face customer relationships—of talking to people—and we were remotivated to find ways to improve the business and save money at the same time.

The single most important way to increase customer loyalty is to talk to your customers, face-to-face if possible.

Talking to people face-to-face gives you the chance to:

○ *Ask questions.* This helps you find out what their expectations are so you will be able to exceed expectations and delight customers. How can you do that without knowing those expectations?

For a "delicious dozen" questions to ask to better understand customer expectations and needs, download this Bonus Byte at www.RLBonus.com using the keyword "dozen."

○ *Build rapport.* Nothing builds rapport more than having a successful face-to-face conversation. If you have invested the time and money to bring people to the customer's location, they likely will see that as a positive sign of your desire to build a long-term relationship or even partnership.

○ *Build empathy.* When people have met their customers, seen their face, and (even better) been in the location where they may use your product, they will have an easier time building understanding of the customer's needs and perspective.

Don't take Steve's story too literally. There are times to send leaders and executives to meet with customers, and there are times when there is more value in sending people from throughout the organization for those visits (or to the trade shows or association meetings). The value of strong relationships, rapport, and empathy extends far beyond the executive suite and can pay incredible dividends (consider the value of relationships between your customers and your staff engineers or accountants, for example). Not only will the customer value that interchange, but the newly found knowledge and experience of your staff will be critical to building internal relationships as well. Once your team has spent time with customers, they should understand the needs and messages of your salespeople much more clearly, and those relationships will become more collaborative and less guarded.

There certainly are many things you can do, but here are two specific ideas you may never have considered that will help you create the customer mind-set you desire:

○ *Put the customer at the center of decisions.* Does this mean that every decision should be made to the customer's benefit and at the expense of the organization? Not at all. What it does mean is that all decisions should by made bearing in mind the customer's perspective, interests, well-being, and delight. Ask yourself how the customer will be affected by a decision and how he or she will react, or ask your customers directly. Using these ideas as a filter to pass your decisions through will firmly entrench the customer mind-set in your organization and help you create better decisions.

○ *Forget the script.* Nordstrom's employee manual says this about dealing with customers: "Use your own best judgment at all times." How do you feel about hearing a script when you call a customer service hot-line or when a salesperson is using a script? I bet you don't feel delighted or even satisfied in these situations. Certainly there is value in having some standardized messages, but that doesn't mean you have to have a follow-the-script approach. Your job is to create a customer mind-set and give people the skills and knowledge they need to succeed. When you do that, they won't need the script. Instead, you'll have a cadre of people who can talk to the customer and use their own best judgment.

Your Now Steps

These are really simple:

1. Get in front of your customers. (Use the phone if you must, but do this now.)
2. Ask them some questions about working with you and their expectations for your product or service.
3. Don't defend or rebut; be quiet, take notes, and listen.
4. Thank them for their time.
5. Put any ideas you glean into action as soon as possible.

 Serving customers is everyone's job.

Service Recovery

Despite your work to build the right customer service mind-set and even though you have built quality systems and processes to do everything right for the customer, and even when you have the most talented staff you could possibly imagine, mistakes will happen.

Mistakes, mix-ups, and errors: call them whatever you want, but when it comes to serving customers, any error is a problem. We collect data on customer complaints so we can identify which mistakes are significant problems. Nobody likes mistakes, especially when it comes to serving customers.

While this is true, consider this story.

After a full day of work at the office in Indianapolis, I boarded a plane to Denver. The flight was late but uneventful. I made my connection to San Francisco and then had the fastest cab ride from the airport to downtown that I have ever experienced. It was about 11:00 P.M. (2:00 A.M. at my home) when I walked into the lobby of the Hotel Rex.

Nicole Jackson, the front desk host, asked if she could help me, and I told her I was checking in. After a quick glance at her screen, she looked concerned. She informed me that my name wasn't on the reservations list until the following night, when the rest of the team I would be working with would be there. She then informed me she had no other rooms.

I was exhausted and suddenly homeless. Nicole quickly offered to find me a room in another hotel. When she made the call, she negotiated a better rate for me and, when making the reservation, told the person on the other end of the phone that I was pleasant. She then offered to store my bag full of workshop materials and get me a cab.

Since my new hotel was just five blocks away, I declined her offer of the cab and walked. During that five-block walk, I was no longer tired. Sure, I would have rather already been in my room, sliding into bed, but Nicole had taken my potentially (very) negative situation and made it right—and she called me pleasant to boot!

Nicole had turned a potentially bad service moment into a gem by her quick action and by going above and beyond the call of duty. She instinctively knew, or had been taught, the value of service recovery: the process of successfully fixing the error or removing the customer's frustration after a mistake has been made.

This story is instructive and makes several valuable points about service recovery:

- *Nicole didn't get defensive.* The first major roadblock to service recovery is a defensive response. Nicole calmly listened to my situation, researched it, and began looking for a solution.

- *She didn't assign blame.* The mistake wasn't hers; in fact, it's possible it wasn't even the hotel's (the client may have left my name off the list for the extra night), but that didn't stop Nicole from trying to solve the problem.

SERVICE RECOVERY AND FINDING FAULT

Finding fault is a major barrier to good service recovery. Too often, employees worry about who's at fault rather than solving the problem. Although it is important to determine how to keep the problem from reoccurring, the time for doing that is not when dealing with the customer. Successfully help the customer, and then concern yourself with process improvement.

According to Ron Zemke and Chip Bell in their book *Knock Your Socks Off Service Recovery,* (2000) there are four dimensions of fault or causation:

1. *We did it.* The organizational system or an individual in it caused the customer to be upset, hurt, or inconvenienced.

2. *The customer did it. It truly is the customer's fault.* The customer made a mistake, perhaps misusing or breaking the product, which led to the upset, hurt, or inconvenience.

3. *A third party did it.* A shipper, subcontractor, or some other third party did something to cause the customer's problem.

4. *An act of nature (greater forces) did it.* Tornadoes, floods, blizzards, or something else caused the problem that led to the customer's inconvenience.

Thinking about these causes will help in correcting the problem the next time—but only after you have successfully resolved the problem in the first place.

○ *She took action.* Nicole determined the problem and took action to get me out of her lobby happily. She used her best judgment to find a solution that would work.

○ *She solved the immediate problem.* In this case, she found me another place to sleep. Because she didn't start out by being defensive or trying to find fault, she was able to do this and be pleasant at the same time.

○ *She went above solving the immediate problem.* In reality, Nicole's only concern was finding me a place to sleep. In practice, she went above solving the basic problem by offering to pay for a cab, negotiating a better rate, and storing my training bag. Did she need to do any of these things? No. But these are the things that made for successful service recovery.

○ *She didn't give away the store.* Some people balk at thoughts of service recovery, thinking that the only way to make the customer happy is to give them their money back or in some way financially pacify them for the inconvenience. Sometimes this may be true, but I believe that's a rare situation. Nicole didn't give me a free night of lodging, but she did solve the problem in a successful (and economical) way.

○ *She left me with a positive story.* If Nicole had simply found me another hotel room five blocks away, I wouldn't feel the way I do. I wouldn't have told the story to the hotel manager the next day (which I hope benefited Nicole in some way), written about it in my blog, or told the training class the story. Had she not handled the situation with grace and aplomb, I might have told a very negative story to anyone who would listen.

○ *I'm still retelling the story.* Now, a couple of years later, I'm telling the story again, all because of how a bright employee solved a customer service problem—not to mention that I'm recommending the service at the Hotel Rex when people ask about where to stay in San Francisco.

Mistakes aren't always a bad thing. Not fixing them when you have the chance is the real problem.

If my room had been available that night, I'd likely have never given the Hotel Rex another thought. I stayed there for three nights, and it was fine—a good but generally predictable hotel experience—and I would have been satisfied. When I arrived and learned I had no room, one of two things could have occurred: I could have become dissatisfied with the Hotel Rex because of how the situation was handled, or I could become a delighted customer, telling others about my good experience with the Hotel Rex.

There was a mistake, yes, but due to an excellent service recovery, I'm happy, and I hope the hotel benefits long term. Interestingly, great recovery from a customer service problem can transform a customer from dissatisfied to delighted and loyal.

While the story offers some hints, here are six things that you can do to role-model brilliant service recovery in your organization:

○ *Start with the mind-set.* When you have created the mind-set discussed in this chapter, you have taken a huge step toward more successful service recovery. Help people recognize that when they do a better job of service recovery, they make their jobs easier. Once a customer is pleased with the outcome of a situation, there will be less complaining and friction. Elegant service recovery helps the customer, the organization, and the service provider.

○ *Take the customer's perspective.* If the customer has been inconvenienced or there is a problem, encourage people to start by taking the customer's perspective. There are two related questions to aid in gaining this perspective. If the customer is with you or on the phone, ask, "What would make this right for you?" or some variation of, "What can I do to make this better for you?" If you aren't able to speak with the customer at that moment, ask yourself what he or she would want.

○ *Think about your perspective.* Along with asking yourself what the customer would want, consider asking yourself what you would want if you were in the same situation. Although this question is not as powerful as the first, it can often help you get past your defensiveness and provide a clearer head to figure out how you might recover from the service bobble.

○ *Give people latitude.* The first questions are for understanding, but now is the time for action. Encourage people to ask themselves, "What would I do if this was my business or if this hurt my bank account?" "What if it was my mother who was the customer?" This gets people thinking about the action they will take now that they understand the situation from the customer's perspective. Identifying the actions makes the difference for the customer.

○ *Give people authority.* They must have more than latitude; they must have the ability to take the action they identify. Give people the authority to provide great service recovery. If you have set the mind-set correctly and taught people the questions to consider, they will make good choices. Remember Nordstrom's employee manual—"Use your own best judgment at all times"—and use it as your guide. Does this require trust? Of course it does. But if you don't trust your employees to interact with your customers, what does that say about your hiring or training process?

○ *Minimize policy.* You can't create a policy for every possible service mistake. Nicole didn't search through a book or an interactive Web site to determine the best response to my unavailable room situation. Certainly she may have had some other experience or some rough guidelines to follow, but she made a decision without consulting a policy. Think about how much better the experience will be for the customer when it is personalized rather than "policyized." Even if you wanted to, you'd never be able to come up with a guideline or policy for every possible mix-up anyway.

Imbue people with your mind-set: give them training, trust them, and allow them to delight customers. All of these are your responsibility as a leader. Taking these steps will create recovery experiences that your customers will remember and share.

Your Now Steps

These Now Steps will help you build a conversation about service recovery with your team:

1. Gather your whole team (or some segment of it) for a short meeting.

2. Share the concept of service recovery with them and why it is so important.

3. Take a recent customer complaint (or personal experience someone had with a customer problem) and talk about what could have been done or could still be done to recover with grace and create a loyal customer.

 A mistake is a great chance to improve a relationship with your customer.

Building Partnerships with Customers

Throughout this chapter in one way or another, we have examined building relationships with customers. I have said that the stronger the relationship is, the further you can move from mere satisfaction to delight and loyalty (see Figure 9.1). At the far end of the loyalty scale is the holy grail of customer retention: building partnerships with your customers. This is the logical extension of all we have discussed, and it is important because you as the leader must drive and lead this idea and the processes that support it.

We've already examined the number one bottom-line benefit to customer partnerships: a retained customer. But for a partnership to work, it must provide benefits to both parties. Your customers see many benefits: a strong partnership can lead to lower costs, higher quality, personalized or customized service, and other value beyond the direct value of the product or service they receive. You gain reduced costs and the opportunity to build your customer base from referrals. You certainly will invest money and resources into your customer partnerships, but likely not the same investment it would take to attract and retain new customers.

In addition to these significant benefits, there are more intangible benefits you may not have thought about. When you build a partnership with customers, many employees derive a greater sense of meaning in their work. It is one thing to process nameless and faceless invoices; it is quite another to do that for people they may have met or worked with to improve the process. It is one thing to work the logistics on customer shipments; it is quite another to work in collaboration with a customer to keep product at his or her site on a just-in-time basis (and that you understand the reasons for that system). Customer partnerships can engage employees in ways that many other programs, approaches, and methods cannot. This engagement occurs because people have a way to see how their specific work has an impact on others directly (their colleagues in the partner organization who they now care about) and indirectly (your employees also understand the end use of your products and services more fully).

In a partnership arrangement, work often gets simpler as both parties understand each other's systems and needs. This profound knowledge has an additive effect: work becomes simpler to accomplish, and even though communication gets easier (as relationships develop), many things no longer even need to be communicated, because everyone already has the information they need.

Developing the Partnership

Now that you see the various benefits of the customer partnership, your question might be, How do we make this happen?

Here are five steps to make partnerships a reality, no matter the size of your organization:

1. *Set expectations and objectives.* Like any other relationship, both parties should understand what they expect of each other in order to help reach the goals. Depending on the formality of your partnership, you also may want to develop some measurements of success that support the goals of both organizations.

2. *Consider new behaviors.* Would you bid work out that your partner could deliver? Probably not. Would you be more open to sharing your costs and strategies with a partner? Probably. These are just two examples of the kinds of behaviors that may need to shift as you build a customer partnership. The behaviors that need to change affect not only the interactions with the customer themselves but the relationships inside your organization as well.

3. *Make new commitments.* Partnerships are long-term, not quarter-to-quarter, events, so lead the partnership toward longer-term commitments and collaborations. Customer partnering frequently allows or requires communications that make the line between partners very fuzzy. According to Allan J. Magrath and K. G. Hardy (1994), "When communications become very tight, one partner can often take over a function formerly carried out by the other partner. For instance, 3M supplies diaper tape to Procter & Gamble's production lines for Pampers and Luvs. 3M has become so integrated into Procter & Gamble's ongoing quality teams that it has assumed an additional role for Procter & Gamble in developing supply or demand forecast for its own

tape production." This is certainly a level of commitment far beyond what most people would typically expect. Is 3M providing significant value for Procter & Gamble? You bet. And the partnership benefits 3M by providing it with a long-term customer for its materials.

4. *Consider creative alliances.* Strong partnerships may lead to new business ventures allowing the two partners to take advantage of new business opportunities. These kinds of alliances are not likely developed without the strong relationships built in a partnership.

5. *Share best practices across the organizations.* With strong partnerships, both organizations can create process improvements and quality benefits and share knowledge and resources for the benefit of each other.

Partnerships, Large and Small

You organization may not be large; your customers might be individuals (not departments or other organizations). In either case, some of what you've just learned might be a bit difficult to apply (though I encourage you to think of all the ways you can apply these ideas). But beyond partnerships, another way to build the long-term loyalty you desire is by building customer communities. Consider *Fast Company* magazine.

Fast Company is a business magazine that was first published in November 1995. In 1997, writer and editor Heath Row started a reader network called the Company of Friends (CoF). By 2002, there were more than forty-four thousand members in 165 groups in thirty-five countries. What is the Company of Friends? According to the Web site, it is "Fast Company magazine's readers' network. It is a global online and offline *community* of self-organizing groups of forward-thinking business leaders and innovators. Members help each other improve their careers, companies, and communities [italics added]." CoF members benefit from additional discussion of the topics in the magazine, networking opportunities with other members, the ability to network online, access to other events built for CoF members, and much more.

The cost for membership? Nothing. Is this part of the magazine business? Not in traditional terms, but it is a way for *Fast Company* to support and build its most loyal base of fans and become a more meaningful part of their lives. The lesson for you is that partnership doesn't have to be about big conglomerates. You can build partnerships and communities with customers regardless of the nature of your customers or the size of your organization. The only requirements are the desire and creativity to do so.

> **SOME WAYS TO BUILD YOUR CUSTOMER COMMUNITIES**
>
> - o Newsletters
> - o Live in-person events
> - o User groups
> - o E-mail discussion groups
> - o Customer Web sites, blogs, and other virtual communities
> - o Using customers in your marketing efforts

Your Now Steps

You can't create customer partnerships overnight, but you can start the process today:

1. Gather two or three people, and talk about the concept and benefits of customer partnerships.
2. Brainstorm a list of ideas that might help you create those partnerships.
3. Pick one that you could try immediately.
4. Get started.

Connect your customers, and watch your business grow.

Go to remarkableleadershipbook.com/resources for more information, writing, tools, and other highly recommended resources to help you make customers and their needs a more important part of your organization's focus.

10

REMARKABLE LEADERS INFLUENCE WITH IMPACT

OVER THE YEARS IN MY CONVERSATIONS about leadership, many people have described effective leaders as charismatic. I've noticed that when people talk about charisma they have a faraway, "I-wish-had-it" look in their eyes, as if charisma is reserved for a chosen few and unattainable by most. Certainly many successful leaders have been charismatic, but what does that actually mean, and how can a remarkable leader be more charismatic?

Various definitions of *charisma* include words instructive when thinking about what it means and how it can be developed. Consider these words: *attractiveness, influence,* and *inspire.* Charisma is an attractiveness that allows you to influence or inspire others. In this chapter, you will learn skills that will help you influence and inspire—and thereby build your charisma.

The skills of influence relate to many of the other remarkable leadership competencies: building relationships, championing change, and powerful communication, to name just three. Influencing skills, used wisely, will help you develop many of the other skills of a remarkable leader more quickly.

As a leader, you often have to sell an idea (not to mention a product or service), and although this chapter isn't really about sales techniques or processes, these are some of the foundational skills of highly effective salespeople and sales leaders.

Self-Assessment

Here is a quick assessment to help you think about your skills as a relationship builder. Use the following scale of 1 to 7 on each question:

1. Almost never

2. Rarely or seldom

3. Occasionally

4. Sometimes

5. Usually

6. Frequently

7. Almost always

I share and use my values at work.   _____

I consistently connect organizational values to the work
of my team.   _____

I am credible with others.   _____

I project a realistic positive attitude.   _____

I focus on the needs of others.   _____

I am empathetic.   _____

Your Values

Your values are those ideas, beliefs, and concepts that you hold most dear and guide your behavior daily. People with strong values that are clearly evident in their actions possess the sort of personal magnetism or attractiveness that defines charisma for many. This is not be confused with the sort of charisma an entertainer might exhibit—a wonderful stage presence or beautiful physical appearance, for example. The sort of attractiveness remarkable leaders aspire to emanates from their values.

SOME POWERFUL EXAMPLES

Here are some examples of strong leaders who lead (or led) from their values:

- Abraham Lincoln
- Billy Graham
- Eleanor Roosevelt
- Walt Disney
- Adolph Hitler
- Martin Luther King Jr.

○ Mother Teresa

○ Nelson Mandela

You may not agree with the closely held values of each of these leaders. That fact notwithstanding, it is hard to argue with their ability to influence with impact. Their strength, for good or evil, emanates (or emanated) from their strong beliefs. It, when combined with their other leadership skills, allows (or allowed) them to have tremendous influence.

As leaders, we use our influencing skills to help get things done through other people. Rosa Say, in her book *Managing with Aloha,* writes, "You will best get things done through others by incorporating the values you share with them, values that embrace collaboration and values that are also fundamental good practices in the business environment" (2004, p. 11).

The first step toward using your values to help you influence is to clearly define what your values are. You have values related to your work, leadership, your personal life, and all other realms of your life. Those most closely held values are those that would be most common across all the roles you play.

You have probably read a book or been to a workshop where you've been asked to define your personal values. This is a great exercise, and one that stymies many people as they look at the blank sheet of paper. You may be able to quickly list several of these values, or you may need a little help in getting past the writer's block. If so, don't worry: I have compiled a long list of values to help you with your process.

To get your starter list of values, download this Bonus Byte at www.RLBonus.com using the keyword "values."

Knowing your values is important, but it's only the first step. In order for these values to become helpful to you in leading and influencing, you must share them with those you lead. Look back at the list of leaders in the sidebar. Although Abraham Lincoln died more than 140 years ago and you may have only a grade-school knowledge of his life, you have a picture of some of his values, including the sanctity of country and human equality. These two values were the principal drivers of his ability to set the stage for a country that remained united even after a civil war.

Martin Luther King Jr. shared his values through his speeches and sermons, helping those he was leading to have a clear picture of how those values could lead to a better world. But his impact wasn't felt solely from his speeches, as powerful as they were. His message spread from more than the pulpit and lectern: it spread from his actions. He organized rallies and walked in marches, and he met with civic and political leaders. Your influence will be felt in the same way: through your actions.

What makes your actions more influential is alignment. When your actions are in alignment with the values you have shared, you are emulating King, Mother Teresa, and others. When people can see how passionately you believe in something, from both your words and our deeds, and they can see that the words and actions are anchored in your values (how else could you be so passionate?), magic occurs. The magic is that people are inspired to follow your lead and go where you are going, whether it is to lead a civil rights movement, care for the sick, or change the accounting software.

I share these well-known examples because they are well known, not because they are out of your reach. You are a remarkable leader who can change the world, even if that piece of the world is small. You know that you can't change it by yourself, which is why leadership is so important: the changes you envision require others. Your ability to influence from the passion that comes from your foundational values can create that change.

Organizational Values

Your personal values are vitally important to your ability to be a remarkable leader. However, if you are leading from inside an organization, whether as a volunteer Scout leader, a first-line supervisor, a vice president, or the CEO, you also must consider the values of the organization. If your values don't match those of your company or organization (whether they are stated or culturally embedded), you won't be happy or successful.

Have you ever had a job that many people felt was excellent and in a great company, yet something wasn't right? It wasn't that you were being mistreated or that the company was in trouble, and it wasn't that there was a specific problem with your job; still, you could sense that something wasn't right. There is a good chance that the source of this feeling was a mismatch in values. If the organization stands for something you truly don't believe in, the mismatch is drastic and probably obvious. If you are a vegan, you likely wouldn't be a successful leader at a national steakhouse chain, for example. Most of these mismatches aren't nearly that drastic. That is why you might just have a feeling that this isn't the place for you. To be a successful leader, your actions must align with your values, which must be in line with the organizational and cultural values of your organization. If your values don't closely match the organization's values, you will never lead in the most remarkable way that is possible for you.

Understanding this linkage has helped many people understand why they weren't succeeding in one place and then became a star in another environment while seemingly doing very little different. If you want to influence with the greatest impact, you must lead from your values, and your values must be in alignment with your organization's values.

Your Now Steps

Clearly defining your values is the foundational point in your ability to influence others. These Now Steps focus on just that:

1. List your personal and leadership values. Brainstorm them, or draw from the list in the Bonus Byte to help you.

2. If your list is long, trim it to those that are most important to you. Probably a list of fewer than fifteen will be most helpful.

3. Prioritize the list from most important to least important.

Keep this list in your journal and refer to it as you think about the rest of this chapter.

 Leading from your values is the foundation of your ability to influence.

Building Credibility

There are many ways to lead, and therefore many situations in which we need to be successful influencers. Regardless of our role, rank, or seniority and no matter what our job, we all can personally benefit and benefit others by being more influential. Enhancing your credibility is one of the best ways to become more influential.

People want to follow the advice and counsel of those with expertise, and you want to be one of those people. However, it is not enough to be an expert on a subject matter or a situation; you also must be perceived as an expert. That perception comes from how you carry yourself and interact with others on this subject and in every other way. Credibility is actually built by more than just expertise; credibility is a combination of expertise and trustworthiness.

In his book *The Science of Influence,* Kevin Hogan (2004) states this as a formula:

$$Credibility = Expertise + Trustworthiness$$

Very few people can maintain great influence without both parts of this equation. There certainly are situations where the expertise is so profound that idiosyncrasies and even rudeness will be tolerated because the person is so knowledgeable. This isn't the case often, however. If you lean on your expertise too much, you'll fall frequently.

But there are situations where you have likely trusted someone so much that she was credible to you on subjects where she might not have been a significant expert. As we discussed in Chapter Seven, people are far more open to listening to and believing us (and therefore being influenced by us) when trust is high. These cases too are isolated; leaning only on your trustworthiness won't work either. You need to work on both parts of this combination in order to become more influential.

Expertise

Expertise is a good place to start. If you are an information technology professional, you better know a router from a right click. If you are in finance, you better know a payment from a promissory note. That is basic expertise, but it is only a starting point. To greatly increase your influence through your credibility, you must develop your knowledge and expertise consistently and continuously far beyond the basics.

Ways to Increase Your Expertise
There are many traditional ways to do this—for example:

- Take a class or workshop.
- Read more in depth on the subject.
- Find a mentor, and learn from a master of that expertise.

And other ways you might not think of immediately—for example:

- Do the Now Steps in this book.
- Practice your skills in volunteer or community organizations.
- Start a study group of others who want to build the same expertise.

These are just some starting suggestions. You can determine the best ways to build your expertise.

Remember too that although having the expertise is important, being perceived as having it matters much more; this is a case where perception is everything. It might not be fair, but it is how the world works. Changing perceptions, especially of people you have worked with for a long time, won't happen overnight. But by consciously building your expertise and applying it whenever possible, your influence will grow.

Unveiling Your Expertise

However much expertise you have and however others perceive it, you must make it available and accessible to others for it to aid your credibility and therefore help you influence more successfully. Here are several things that can get in your way, along with suggestions on how to improve your success in having your expertise recognized and used.

IGNORANCE. Most people don't recognize how much they really know. After you have done something for a long time or read about an idea in many different places, you assume everyone knows that information. But that just isn't true. Your familiarity and deep understanding get in your way because you assume others already know. If you assume something is common knowledge or obvious, you won't make your expertise available to others.

The first key to getting your expertise used is to proclaim it to yourself. Recognize that what you know is significant and valuable. Without this recognition, you won't know what to share if asked or see the gap in knowledge that likely does exist.

ATTITUDE. Before you go too far down this "Man, I'm smart!" mental path, recognize that arrogance is the next stumbling block. Certainly you need to recognize your expertise and to value what you know. But none of this makes you better or smarter or above any other person.

My advice? Lose any budding arrogance. When you are arrogant about what you know, you tend to view offering advice as an opportunity to show what you know rather than a chance to genuinely help others. When you are confident, you can focus on the other person's or team's needs. Be confident in what you know, but you don't know it all, and you should always be willing to learn more.

Focus on being generous but helpful in your knowledge sharing. By remaining confident in your knowledge and keeping your focus on the other person's needs, you will have your attitude in the right place.

MEMORY. Often the challenge you will have in sharing your knowledge and expertise is that you don't really remember what it is like to be a beginner in the area. When you recognize what you know and its value, you may take short-cuts in explaining it to someone else by using jargon or skipping what seem to you to be obvious steps.

In order for you to transfer your knowledge or teach someone what you know, break the steps down and share each piece of information one step at a time. You have learned this information, and so can others. But you must teach them from their perspective, not yours. Remember what it felt like to be a beginner.

CONNECT THE DOTS. My daughter, Kelsey, loves to color and has many coloring and activity books. One of the activities in many of these books is a dot-to-dot puzzle, one for which you draw straight lines from point 1 to point 2 to point 3, and so on. When looking at the page before you start to connect the dots, you usually can't really tell what is going to be drawn. You may have some clues based on how many other lines and related pictures exist on the page, but until you complete the puzzle, you don't really know what you have.

Your expertise is like that. As a leader, you are asked to, or see the need to, share what you know with others for their benefit. Your job is to set a context and provide a bigger picture for them. Reviewing the steps, the procedure, or the technical components of something isn't enough. They need to know the situation, the environment, and the context. They need to understand the relative priority and importance of the various things you are teaching them. As the "expert," you help them complete their own mental puzzle by guiding them in connecting their own dots.

Making these connections is how you will be most successful in having your expertise valued and used by others. And you can connect these dots only when you have the other three barriers (ignorance, attitude, and memory) reduced or eliminated for yourself.

Trustworthiness

Trust is covered extensively in Chapter Seven, but here are three specific things that you can do, starting today, to build your trustworthiness and therefore your credibility:

- ○ *Build rapport.* In a situation where you want to influence others, don't rush to that goal too quickly. Build rapport by building your relationship with the other person. You know how to do this; just remember how important it is.
- ○ *Focus on others.* Be interested in them, and understand their issues and concerns. We all want to feel important, and we all want to be heard. By keeping your focus on the other person, you are serving yourself as well.
- ○ *Be consistent.* Build rapport in every situation. Be kind and thoughtful every day. Consistency in actions is a key trust component. We trust people when we know what to expect in their words and deeds.

Remember that in the end, this is about perception, which means you can't succeed by applying any of the above suggestions as a ploy or a technique. These strategies work when they are done with sincerity and honor, and they will backfire if people feel you are using them as a way to manipulate them or a situation. The good news is that by applying these approaches to build your trustworthiness, you likely will be building your perceived expertise as well.

Credibility is a combination of expertise and trustworthiness, which can be built simultaneously with conscious and consistent focus. With that conscious focus and determined actions, you can build your credibility—one of the keys to unlocking greater influence.

Your Now Steps

Credibility is the combination of expertise and trustworthiness. Since you have already examined trust in Chapter Seven, these Now Steps focus on the barriers to having your expertise valued:

1. Determine a current situation where your expertise could be well served.

2. Look at the barriers of ignorance, attitude, and memory, and determine which is your biggest barrier in this situation.

3. Build an action plan to reduce that barrier starting today.

4. Capture any thoughts, lessons, and ideas in your journal.

 Credibility is the key to influencing with impact. Without it, you are locked out.

The Importance of Your Attitude

Before any big game, coaches typically give their team a pep talk. Although different coaches have different styles and approaches to this talk, rest assured, they won't say anything like this: "Well, they are bigger, stronger, and faster than we are. Their coach is smarter, and their cheerleaders are more enthusiastic. I know we don't have much of a chance, so good luck."

Coaches know from experience that sharing enthusiasm and delivering positive messages prior to the start of the game will help the team perform better. Maybe the other team is bigger, stronger, and faster. The coach may share those facts during practice but would never include them as the focus of the final words to the team. Will a pep talk alone create a win? Probably not, but everything else being equal, it will help.

Think about it this way. At the far end of the "negative attitude scale" is helplessness: if the other team is so much bigger, stronger, and faster, how could we possibly win? There's no sense even in taking the court or field; we will simply be embarrassed. But the more expected pep talk provides hope—an opportunity to look at the world from the perspective of success and achievement. Some call this *optimism* or *enthusiasm* or *a positive mental attitude*. Whatever you call it, science increasingly shows it to be a powerful force. Science or not, our experience tells us this attitude is contagious.

Optimism

In their book *The EQ Edge: Emotional Intelligence and Your Success* (2006), Stephen J. Stein and Howard E. Book define optimism as "the ability to look at the brighter side of life and to maintain a positive attitude. Even in the face of adversity. Optimism assumes a measure of hope in one's approach to life. It is a positive approach to daily living. Optimism is the opposite of pessimism, which is a common symptom of depression" (p. 230).

Optimism is a misunderstood concept. It is not a belief that things will turn out for the best no matter what; it also is not a belief that affirmations or pep talks alone will solve all problems. True optimism is grounded in a realistic worldview and based on hope.

Martin Seligman, the father of the positive psychology movement and author of many books including *Learned Optimism* (1991), discovered three major attitudes that distinguish optimists from pessimists. First, optimists believe that any current misfortune is temporary in nature; it is darkest before the dawn, and the situation will turn around. Second, they see a problem or a downturn as specific and related only to the current situation, not an example of a continuing saga of problems. Because of this, they can look at a situation and determine what they can learn from it to keep it from reoccurring. Third, optimists don't really blame themselves. Although they know they have played a role in their situation, they consider outside sources as well when explaining and understanding the situation.

In the book, Seligman cites a number of scientific research studies that show that optimistic people have fewer illnesses and lower blood pressure, and they live longer. If being a remarkable leader isn't reason enough, perhaps these potential benefits will encourage you to be more optimistic.

Reasons for Reluctance

Many people consider themselves to be a "realist" and believe that realism is the opposite of optimism. (How many people do you know who consider themselves to be truly pessimistic?) If you discuss their approach with them, you will hear several reasons why they are reluctant to consider the value of a positive approach.

○ *Optimism is blind.* Many people see optimism as a blinding, Pollyanna view of the world that doesn't take into account any chance for something to go wrong. Instead, true optimists are realists who look for ways to find positives in negative situations. Joe Vitale, in his book *The Attraction Factor,* shares the following story: "I was at a meeting with my friend Mark Joyner, Internet pioneer and bestselling author. I overheard Mark talking to a man who had just gone through hell due to the FTC [Federal Trade Commission]. Mark listens to the man's sad story and then said, 'Turn it into something good'" (2006, p. 160). True optimists aren't in denial, but when things aren't perfect, they try to turn it into something good.

○ *Belief.* Some people are reluctant because they believe that if they think positive thoughts and those things don't occur, they are setting themselves up for disappointment. They believe they are better off having low or no expectations than to be disappointed when high expectations are not reached.

○ *They aren't a cheerleader.* These people associate optimism with waving pom-poms and cheering loudly. Since this isn't their style, they use being sincere and genuine as an excuse and dismiss optimism as "not them."

Beyond these reasons, the most pervasive is the one you will not hear: people aren't optimistic because it isn't their habit. Taking a positive viewpoint, approach, and attitude toward current and future events is a habit. The title of Seligman's book, *Learned Optimism,* says it all: optimism (a pervasive, positive outlook on the future) can be learned. Stated another way, optimism has nothing to do with what your circumstances are or have been, but what you do with and learn from those circumstances.

The Law of Attraction

If you've taken the Dale Carnegie course (and maybe even if you haven't) you'll be able to finish this statement: "Act enthusiastic, and . . . _____ ." (For those who aren't familiar with this, "Act enthusiastic and *you'll be enthusiastic.*") This simple (simply powerful) slogan mirrors a universal truth. When we act as if something will happen, our subconscious mind goes about helping us create that as truth. Charles Kettering, holder of more than three hundred patents, and the inventor of the all-electric starting ignition and lighting systems for automobiles, said, "Believe and act as if it were impossible to fail." I'm sure that although Kettering had massive success, he also failed often. How he saw those failures is what mattered. (Thomas Edison said he never failed at creating an electric light, but stated he had found thousands of ways that wouldn't work.)

This "as-if" approach, known as the law of attraction, states that like attracts like. The more you create the mental and emotional energy of already having something, the faster it will be attracted to you. Isn't this what the coach giving a pep talk is really doing? Isn't this what Carnegie's famous enthusiasm slogan is really suggesting?

Once you believe this principle as a leader and put it to use, it can be powerful. Imagine having your whole team in the state of attraction for the success that you all desire. Imagine harnessing the positive expectancy of an organization for the vision and strategies you have outlined. Remember that attitude, positive or negative, is contagious. As the leader, you have a tremendous opportunity and responsibility to spread an attitude virus that supports the results you want.

Can you see how applying the law of attraction can strengthen your ability to influence?

 For more details on the law of attraction and how it works, download this Bonus Byte at www.RLBonus.com using the keyword "attraction."

Turning These Ideas into Personal and Leadership Actions

It is one thing to believe in the power of a positive attitude. It is another to practice it daily, especially if it hasn't been your habit in the past. There are many ways to change your personal attitude habits; here I focus on three that have a direct impact on your ability to influence:

○ *Be proud of your team.* If you are already proud, show your pride more with the team and in conversations with others. If you aren't proud of them, start a personal campaign to find things to be proud of. Make a list, and share those points of pride.

○ *Say more nice things to everyone all the time.* Find reasons to make pleasant comments, and make them. Don't leave them unsaid. Set a goal for how many nice things you will say at work to your team each day (how about ten as a minimum goal?). Carry a small piece of paper in your pocket, and make a tick mark for each comment. Don't stop making these comments until you have reached your goal each day (actually, don't even stop then). If you haven't reached your goal by midafternoon, get going!

○ *Watch your language.* How much "loser language" are you using? Are you saying, "It's not my job," or "There's not room for that in my budget" (cue the whining tone), or are you saying, "What can we do?" or "How can we make it work?" The language you use is a window into your beliefs about yourself and your team. Remember that your team is listening and will emulate you.

And while I said I'd give only three, here is an important fourth one: count your blessings every day. This alone will make a huge impact on your attitude and your results.

For some ideas on counting your blessings and adding more gratitude to your life, download this Bonus Byte at www.RLBonus.com using the keyword "blessings."

Your Now Steps

I have already shared several specific things you can do to practice in this area. Your Now Steps will help you get started:

1. Do a personal attitude check. Ask five people (face to face or by e-mail) to honestly assess your attitude on a scale of 1 to 10 (1 is "in the dumpster" and 10 is "over the moon" or whatever other descriptors you want to use).

 For a cut-and-paste e-mail to use, download this Bonus Byte at www.RLBonus.com using the keyword "attitude e-mail."

2. If the results don't leave you feeling as if you are spreading the attitude you'd like, take actions to improve it immediately.

 Remarkable leaders know that attitude is contagious and choose one that they want to spread.

Being Other Focused

Author and speaker Zig Ziglar's most famous line might be, "You can get anything in life that you want, if you help enough other people get what they want" (2000). This line encapsulates a profound truth about life. It is directly applicable to you as you think about how to influence others because it gets to the critical point. Influencing others is about others. When you focus on others first, you can get what you want and need much faster and more easily.

Influence and Manipulation

In talking about this chapter on influencing with some people, I encountered some comments about influence and manipulation. "You aren't going to be helping managers manipulate the organization and the people in it, are you?" was one question I heard. My reaction at the time was to ask some probing questions, which led me to understand that that person's concerns were based on a confusion between the words *influence* and *manipulation*.

I think that many people confuse these two concepts, and if you as a leader are mixing them up, it will have a drastic impact on your ability to influence effectively.

You usually can get to the root of this type of confusion by looking at the definitions of the words. Dictionary.com defines the two words this way:

> *Manipulate:* To manage or influence skillfully, esp. in an unfair manner: *to manipulate people's feelings.*
>
> *Influence:* To exercise influence on; affect; sway, or to move or impel (a person) to some action.

See the difference? Manipulation brings gain only for the manipulator. Remarkable leaders aren't interested in manipulation. They see the advantages that are inherent in a situation and are interested in influencing people toward positive end results. As Ziglar says, "You can get anything you want if you help enough other people get what they want." Part of your job is to help people see how they can get something beneficial for themselves.

Being other focused means you are focused on results that will aid or support other people—whether that is the customer, the organization as a whole, the team, or individuals. This leads us directly back to the concept of WIIFM (What's in it for me?). Whether attempting to influence a group of people or one person across the table, we can't ultimately be successful unless we can help others see how they will benefit. This means that we either must already know how they will benefit or be willing to ask them what would motivate them.

What About Motivation?

It may seem odd to get almost through a chapter on influence and just now be reading the word *motivation*. Isn't it a leader's job to motivate? Is it just a literary oversight that I haven't used that word until now?

Not at all. It was completely on purpose.

I can't motivate you as a reader of this book to do anything or take any action (much as I wish I could), and you can't motivate someone else either. Motivation is an inside job. Helping people see the answer to the WIIFM question and that your intent is pure and that you really care will help them motivate themselves. We can't motivate others, but we can inspire them.

I hope that the examples, stories, and ideas in this book will inspire you (that is, influence you) to take the action outlined in the Your Now Steps at the end of each section, and I have designed and written this book to the best of my ability to do just that. But in the end, I don't own your behavior; you do.

In the end, you will either take action or not; you will decide. While you can't "make people" do anything as a leader any more than I can "make you" take action while reading this book, we both can come closer to our goal when we let go of our needs and focus on the needs of the team (in your case) or the reader (in mine).

Selflessness

I have learned, in sometimes painful ways, that I am often selfish. Everyone I know is selfish some of the time, but I have learned that I have been far too selfish far too often. Before I acknowledged the impacts of my actions, I would never have thought of myself in this way. Unfortunately, the people who have suffered the most from this selfishness have been those closest to me: my family. Since coming to this realization, I have found myself noticing how much better I feel about myself when I avoid my former selfish habits. As a not-so-inconsequential side benefit, I now have greater results as an influencer as well.

I share these insights for two reasons. First, when you begin to track the true intentions behind your actions, you will find times when you are being more selfish than is necessary. And second, sadly, the people who will be most affected are those we are most comfortable with and who are closest to us (our family and team).

We are more likely to be on our best behavior with customers or our bosses, but sometimes we let our guard down with those closest to us. You will be a better person, influence more successfully, and become a more remarkable leader the more you are aware of your selfish habits—even in what you may think of as the "little things," like not doing the dishes or keeping your reserved parking place.

Servant Leadership

Robert Greenleaf, the man who coined the phrase *servant leadership*, defines it this way:

The servant-leader is servant first.... It begins with the natural feeling that one wants to serve, to serve first. Then conscious choice brings one to aspire to lead. He or she is sharply different from the person who is leader first, perhaps because of the need to assuage an unusual power drive or to acquire material possessions. For such it will be a later choice to serve—after leadership is established. The leader-first and the servant-first are two extreme types. Between them there are shadings and blends that are part of the infinite variety of human nature.

The difference manifests itself in the care taken by the servant—first to make sure that other people's highest priority needs are being served. The best test, and most difficult to administer, is: do those served grow as persons; do they, while being served, become healthier, wiser, freer, more autonomous, more likely themselves to become servants? And, what is the effect on the least privileged in society; will they benefit, or, at least, will they not be further deprived (1970, p. 7)?

Although this definition begs questions beyond the scope of this chapter, it does highlight the crux of your ability to influence with impact: when you remain other focused, you are taking steps toward becoming a servant-leader first: one who leads to serve the needs of the communities you want to influence—your team, the organization, your customers, and perhaps—if even in a small way, the world.

Your Now Steps

Think about a new goal, objective, task, or initiative in front of you, and do the following:

1. Stop thinking about your goals until you can place them in a positive, beneficial context for others.
2. Write down those other-focused benefits before attempting to influence others.
3. Focus your attention and intention on these benefits for others, taking on faith that your objectives will be met as a result.

Remarkable leaders know they influence best when they serve the most.

 Go to remarkableleadershipbook.com/resources for more information, writing, tools, and other highly recommended resources to help you continue to influence with greater impact.

REMARKABLE LEADERS THINK AND ACT INNOVATIVELY

A FEW YEARS AGO MY SON, PARKER, WALKED into the room as I was looking for my wallet. When he asked me what I was doing, I replied, "I'm looking for my wallet."

"I'm sorry you lost your wallet, Dad."

"I didn't lose it, Parker. I had it this morning," I replied, as I continued to look.

I didn't have to look up to feel the sense of bewilderment my son was feeling. I'm sure he was thinking, "Dad must be crazy. If he can't find his wallet, it must be lost." But like a good son (and a smart one too) he didn't comment on my apparent craziness.

After a couple more minutes of searching, I said, "Found it, Parker."

He couldn't resist any longer: "I thought you hadn't lost it Dad."

"I hadn't lost it Parker. It was just misplaced," I replied somewhat matter-of-factly.

The wallet wasn't lost: I knew that I had had it earlier in the day. But it was misplaced because I couldn't locate it.

Author and speaker Brian Tracy (2007) cites on his blog a research study done with children aged two to four that found that 95 percent of them were rated as "highly creative." They assessed those same children at age seven and found that only 5 percent still tested as "highly creative." The number doesn't get any better as children turn into adults.

It seems that creativity and my wallet have something in common: neither was lost (the wallet was still in my house, and our creativity doesn't vanish), but both certainly were misplaced (I couldn't access my wallet, and we can't always access our creativity either).

What is creativity? In *The Social Psychology of Creativity,* Teresa Amabile defines creativity in part this way: "A product or response will be judged as creative to the extent that it is both a novel and appropriate, useful, correct or valuable response to the task at hand" (1983, p. 360).

All of us were born creative, and everyone on your team is creative, but like my wallet, their creativity (and yours) might be misplaced. Remarkable leaders know and deeply believe that everyone is creative and use that belief to support, draw out, and help people find their creativity again. When creativity is in play, great new ideas can be applied to the organization's challenges and opportunities.

Self-Assessment

Here is a quick assessment to help you think about your skills as a relationship builder. Use the following scale of 1 to 7 on each question:

1. Almost never
2. Rarely or seldom
3. Occasionally
4. Sometimes
5. Usually
6. Frequently
7. Almost always

I am open to new ideas. _____

I create an environment conducive to good brainstorming. _____

I am flexible. _____

I am creative. _____

I support new approaches and ideas. _____

I try new things regularly. _____

Supporting Creativity

Allyson, new to the team, was excited about the meeting. She knew that the team was going to work on some possible solutions to the nagging problem the marketing department was facing. As she ran the night before, she thought of a couple of ideas she believed could make a difference and walked into the room confident and prepared.

Once the meeting got going, the group began brainstorming on the problem she had been thinking about. Not wanting to be first, she waited as a couple of ideas were offered. They seemed okay to her but pretty safe—not blockbuster ideas. Then she shared one of her ideas. A couple of people looked at her, and one said, "Um, I know you are new, but that probably won't work here." A few minutes later, she offered her second idea. "Wow, that would be really expensive!" someone else offered.

She had a third idea as they continued to brainstorm but didn't see the point in offering it. Although her other two ideas were recorded on the flip chart page, she was disheartened and disappointed. If they didn't want her ideas, she didn't see why they even asked. She noticed that some other people seemed to be less willing to share after they got the same kinds of comments she had received.

She had walked into the meeting full of excitement and anticipation. She left with her excitement and passion doused by the comments and reactions. That's why I call these reactions and responses to new ideas "cold water comments."

EXAMPLES OF COLD WATER COMMENTS

- "That will never work."
- "We tried that once."
- "It's not in the budget."
- "It's too risky!"
- "That's crazy."
- "They'll never buy it."

Get the idea? I'm guessing you could quickly add to this list from your personal experience. Regardless of the words or whether it is body language that provides the cold water, they spell disaster for any new ideas and innovative approaches.

Have you ever watched this happen in a meeting? Has someone thrown cold water on any of your ideas? If so, how did you respond? Did hearing that kind of feedback make you want to come up with even more ideas? I doubt it.

These kinds of comments should be a warning sign for you as a remarkable leader: a warning that your environment isn't as conducive to idea creation as it could be.

To get a report to help you recognize and reduce the effects of cold water comments, download this Bonus Byte at www.RLBonus.com using the keyword "coldwater."

What Squelches Creativity

Beyond the opinions and cold water comments of others, there are other obstacles to creativity. Once you recognize them, you can take action to reduce their impact:

- *Thinking habits and personality types.* Some people are naturally more critical or tend to create by adapting existing ideas rather than creating something new. These thinking habits are helpful for modifying ideas once they exist, but they can be a hindrance during the idea generation phase. Help everyone realize there is a time and place for critical thinking; it just isn't when you are generating ideas for consideration.

- *Poor team functioning.* If your team is struggling in other ways, its ability to be creative will be inhibited. As your team improves, so will its ability to be creative. (See Chapter Twelve for more information.)

- *Organizational culture.* If your organization or team is generally conservative or relishes the status quo, creativity will be reduced. Allow the team to feel okay about risk and mistakes.

- *Too many closed questions.* The more open-ended questions your team asks, the more creative they will be. Help people by converting closed-ended questions (those that can be answered with a yes or no) into open-ended ones.

- *Time pressures.* Additional research from Teresa Amabile warns that unnecessary time constraints are one of the biggest killers of creativity. Look for ways to expand the time people have to brainstorm, even if meeting time itself is limited. (Ideas for solving this challenge are offered later in this chapter.)

- *Lack of a clear purpose or focus.* When people don't really know what they are trying to create or why it is important, they will be less successful. You can eliminate this obstacle by adding clarity. (More on this idea later in the chapter too.)

 For a list of personal creativity obstacles, download this Bonus Byte at www.RLBonus.com using the keyword "creativity obstacles."

How You Feel About Mistakes

Do you see mistakes as a problem? Do you view them as an opportunity to find fault or affix blame? Or is your view closer to that of Thomas J. Watson, CEO of IBM? He said, "Would you like me to give you a formula for . . . success? It's quite simple, really. Double your rate of failure. You're thinking of failure as the enemy of success. But it isn't at all. . . . You can be discouraged by failure, or you can learn from it. So go ahead and make mistakes. Make all you can. Because, remember that's where you'll find success. On the far side." (cited in Lewis, 2000, p. 167)

How close is this to your belief about failure? And just as important, how close is this to how others *think* you feel about failure?

Watson is widely reported to have continued his thoughts about mistakes: "Recently, I was asked if I was going to fire an employee who made a mistake that cost the company $600,000. No, I replied, I just spent $600,000 training him. Why would I want somebody to hire his experience?"

If you want to increase the level of creativity, you must allow (and even celebrate) failures and mistakes. Otherwise you are inhibiting the creativity of your team by implementing a new idea too risky. Many leaders encourage people to try new things. Remarkable leaders take the necessary next step and eliminate the risk of making the mistakes that will inevitably come as a result of trying new things.

 For specific suggestions on helping a team get past the fear of failure, download this Bonus Byte at www.RLBonus.com using the keyword "failure."

Your Now Steps

If you want more creativity, you must support creative behaviors and endeavors. Here are some ways to get started today on what will be a long-term effort:

1. Try something new yourself. It can be something little, but it needs to be visible. It will be best if you adjust something you are known to have "always done that way."

2. In your next meeting, encourage people to come up with more ideas before deciding on which ones to try. By creating a longer list of possible ideas, better ideas will emerge. Make sure to set the

expectation of no cold water comments during the brainstorming session.

 Remarkable leaders want more creative thinking, so they let people be creative.

Better Brainstorming

Think about the last five meetings you went to where brainstorming was on the agenda. You probably walked into a conference room with a long table. Nondescript chairs and standard corporate beige or gray walls greeted you, along with the requisite whiteboard or easel at one end. Depending on how big the room was, you might not have been able to see the board or easel very well. To call this environment sterile isn't too far from the truth.

The meeting began, and when it came time to brainstorm, someone (perhaps you) got up and with marker in hand said, "Okay, what do you think?" There was likely an initial smattering of ideas that the recorder dutifully wrote down. Some of these ideas encountered some cold water, and at least one comment led to an exploration of that particular idea—perhaps led by the idea generator trying to explain or justify their idea. Soon there was a brief lull in the flow of ideas, and then someone (again, perhaps you) said, "Does anyone have any more thoughts or suggestions?"

After this prompt, there might have been one or two more ideas that came forward, but the pause that followed this small flurry of suggestions signaled the end of the brainstorming session. If you were lucky, there were more than six ideas on the flip chart or whiteboard.

Have you attended meetings like that? Although I've probably never attended a meeting in your organization, I'm confident that some, if not all, of this story rings true for you. There are several problems with this experience, and the rest of this section explains those problems and offers help for avoiding them.

Environment

The first problem with the brainstorming process is the room. Beige or gray walls and perfectly ordered chairs and spaces are not stimulating. Creativity is a whole body process that is supported by a variety of stimuli. Since you probably can't remove the conference table or paint the walls (if you can do these things, I'd encourage it), consider some little ways to add some stimulation to your brainstorming efforts:

- *Add some tactile stimulation.* Bring some clay, Playdoh, a Slinky, or Nerf or Koosh balls to your meeting, and put them on the table. People will play with them, and that's good. Rather than being a distraction, they will help people be more divergent and open in their thinking.

- *Add some music.* Put a CD player in the room, or plug your MP3 player into some small speakers for some energizing music before the meeting and during breaks. Consider playing some classical music softly during the brainstorming session itself. Creativity can be stimulated in many ways, including with music.

- *Toss in some treats.* Throw a little candy on the table, or offer some fruit or another healthy snack. Hotels and conference centers do this. It isn't just a ploy to raise the fee for your meeting; having a little something to eat keeps our blood sugar up and helps people be more creative.

- *Have people move around.* If this is a long meeting, have everyone stand up and stretch before you begin brainstorming or consider having them move to a new seat before you begin. Getting even a little bit active before or during brainstorming can be stimulating. You can brainstorm standing up too.

- *Brainstorm somewhere else.* Get out of the conference room if you can. How about the cafeteria? The local coffee shop? Outside? If you have to stay in the conference room, how about gathering in different parts of the room? If you can pick a more stimulating, creative, or at least different environment, you will stimulate new thoughts and energy.

Getting Focused

Have you ever been brainstorming something in a group and partway through realized that not everyone was viewing the problem the same way—or even considering the same problem? In order to brainstorm anything effectively, we must know what we are brainstorming and why.

As the leader, make sure people have a clear and common statement of the situation they are trying to improve and that they all know why it is important. You can do this by sending out information on the issue and rationale before the meeting, and you can discuss it before you begin brainstorming.

Having a clearly stated goal and rationale will help people focus their creative energy correctly, and it is one of the best ways to create synergistic thoughts. After all, if you aren't all working on exactly the same thing, how can you create synergy?

Seven Ideas

After you have improved the environment and created a clear goal for your brainstorming session, here are seven other ways to generate vastly more ideas during a brainstorming session:

1. *Warm up*. Improvisational actors are people typically considered to be highly creative. Do you think they get out of their cars and walk on stage? Hardly. They warm up together with a variety of exercises meant to loosen them up and free their creativity. Do you stretch before you run or hit a bucket of balls before hitting the first tee? Although your brain isn't a muscle, warming it up is critical to generating more ideas.

 For a list of five ways to warm up your group (or yourself) for greater creativity, download this Bonus Byte at www.RLBonus.com using the keyword "creativity warmups."

2. *Set a goal*. Why be satisfied with a list of six to eight ideas? The process of brainstorming is meant to generate lots of ideas, so set a goal. When I brainstorm personally, I don't stop until I have at least 20 ideas. Depending on the size of your group, 20 might be a good starting point. When I was facilitating a group of 45 recently, I set the goal of 125 different ideas. They generated more than 140. Would they have created a good list without the goal? Sure, but it likely wouldn't have been more than 140. Not all 140 were good ideas, but some of them far down the list were implemented or adapted.

3. *Don't stop*. Although the first pause seems to drain the energy out of your brainstorming, it doesn't have to. Often the best ideas are sitting in people's minds, and they are trying to decide whether to share them (they are doing a bit of internal evaluation before even sharing the idea). Don't let the pause stop you. There are naturally going to be pauses during brainstorming. Rather than a signal to stop, they are a

signal to open up even further. If you are facilitating the process, use the pauses as a chance to ask some additional questions. The section on creative geniuses later in this chapter will help you think of some of those questions.

4. *Allow more time.* Time doesn't have to be a challenge. You can allow more time in the meeting, or you can pose the question at one meeting and brainstorm it at the next. You also can e-mail people before the meeting so they know what will be brainstormed. Consider ending the meeting with brainstorming, and then send out the list of ideas to the group after the meeting, explaining that you plan to continue or conclude at the start of the next meeting. This allows them to continue to brainstorm, if only subconsciously.

5. *Adapt, modify, and "steal."* Encourage people to adapt or modify the ideas already on the list. A new idea doesn't have to be completely original; it could be an adaptation or a combination of two or more of the ideas together.

6. *Save the evaluation and conversation.* Brainstorming is not the time for evaluation and conversation. You absolutely need to clarify and discuss the ideas, but not right now. If you do, you will slow the process unnecessarily and reduce the effectiveness of the idea generation process.

7. *Remember the rules.* There are some common ground rules for brainstorming to make them more effective. You probably know them, and your team may as well. Taking the time to remind people of these guidelines before you begin will help the ideas flow faster and longer.

SOME STANDARD BRAINSTORMING "RULES"
Although there really aren't any hard-and-fast rules, consider these suggestions to help your brainstorming process work better. Remind people of the rules of engagement before starting, and you will reap better results. Here are a few examples:

○ There are no wrong ideas.

○ Focus on quantity, not quality.

○ Don't stop to explain or evaluate.

○ Hitchhike on other ideas.

○ There are no bad ideas.

Methods for Brainstorming

Most of your brainstorming experiences probably are like the one I described earlier: an open forum of freewheeling brainstorming where everyone participates. While this is a great way to brainstorm, it isn't the only way. As a remarkable leader who supports and encourages creativity and innovation, it is important that you have as many tools in your tool kit as possible, and one of those tools is having multiple ways to brainstorm:

- ○ *Freewheeling.* This is the type of brainstorming you probably are most familiar with. The whole group collectively focuses on the problem together, and one person captures the ideas as they are randomly suggested.

- ○ *Round robin.* In round-robin brainstorming, you move consecutively around the room, collecting ideas. When it is your turn, you suggest one item to be added to the list. Someone who doesn't have a new idea on his or her turn passes. When it comes back around, that person has another chance to share an idea because passing once doesn't put someone out of the game. You continue until everyone passes. When using round-robin brainstorming, consider asking questions to spur more thoughts after everyone has passed. Then start the round-robin process again, or move to a freewheeling approach at that point.

- ○ *Slips or private brainstorming.* Rather than the hubbub that is created by the freewheeling or even the round-robin system, some people prefer to allow each individual to brainstorm on slips of paper or sticky notes. Once everyone has finished a personal brainstorming list, the slips or stickies are given to the facilitator to create a single list. When this approach is used, some time will be required to read the slips, reduce the duplicates, and generate a complete list. It may make sense to plan a break after everyone has written their slips.

- ○ *A hybrid.* From these three approaches, you can generate any number of hybrids to better meet your needs. One popular approach is to have people individually list their ideas prior to doing freewheeling or round-robin brainstorming. An approach that extends this idea is to send out the question to be brainstormed in advance of the meeting and encourage people to start their list before arriving.

○ *Small groups.* Often one of the best ways to increase creativity in a group setting is to brainstorm in smaller groups. If you have a group of more than eight to ten people, consider brainstorming the same question in two or more smaller groups. During the evaluation and discussion phases, consolidate the ideas into one list. Alternately, if you have several items to brainstorm, you can start the process by having each subteam brainstorm a separate question, and then add ideas from the full group when reviewing the individual group lists.

For a comparison of these various methods and the strengths and weaknesses of each, download this Bonus Byte at www.RLBonus.com using the keywords "brainstorming approaches."

Your Now Steps

This section has given you many ideas. Your job is to apply one now:

1. Pick one of the suggestions in this section, and apply it in your next brainstorming session.
2. Make notes in your journal of the results, your observations, and lessons learned.

To get better ideas, you must create more ideas. To get the best ideas, you must expect to get them.

Techniques of Creative Geniuses

If you want to be more creative (or find some of the creativity you have misplaced), it makes sense to model the skills and techniques of highly creative people. This section describes some approaches used by a wide variety of creative geniuses.

Generating more ideas through the brainstorming process makes sense because many people in an organizational setting equate creativity with brainstorming. Creative geniuses, however, recognize that creativity is a process that goes far beyond brainstorming.

Graham Wallas described a four-step process of creativity in his book *The Art of Thought* (1949) that is still used today. Updating the language a bit, here are his four steps:

1. *Preparation:* This step encompasses doing the research, gathering the facts, and getting the right people and resources together.

2. *Incubation:* During this part of the process, all of the resources collected are allowed to simmer so that people can gain a new perspective. This allows their conscious and subconscious minds to work on the data as they relate to the situation to be improved or created.

3. *Inspiration:* This is the actual "Aha!" moment that most people associate with creativity. Brainstorming is aimed at stimulating this stage.

4. *Evaluation:* Once ideas are generated, they are considered for relevance and applicability. The question of this step is, "Will it work?"

Consider these two questions: How often do your personal and organizational creative processes include all four of these steps? Or, more bluntly, how often is your creative process just the last two, smashed together into a fifteen-minute brainstorming session?

Creative geniuses (and remarkable leaders) recognize that creativity is a process, and they take advantage of all four steps. Putting this realization to work will improve your creative results significantly. Here are some other approaches you and your team can emulate:

○ *Look at problems in different ways.* You can improve your creative output by considering your creative challenge from a variety of perspectives. How would your customers solve it? How would your competitors solve it? How would your mother solve it? How would a twelve-year-old, a Nobel Prize winner, Britney Spears, Thomas Edison, or Fred Flintstone solve it? By thinking about the question from a completely different perspective, you give yourself a chance to find completely different solutions. You may choose some specific perspectives, like your customer or competitor, but you may also choose some random or silly ones, like your favorite superhero, world leader, or relative.

○ *Invite other opinions.* Since you are most often trying to stimulate creativity within a group, you also could invite a person from another department, another work group, your neighbor, a college student, or an actual customer to participate and offer perspective. In this way, your team won't have to simulate another perspective; you've provided it for them.

○ *Make novel combinations.* This is a step to take once you have your brainstormed list. Making novel combinations means considering your whole list as additional fodder rather than using your list to select one idea. What if you adopted ideas A and B? Or perhaps, more novel yet, what if you combined ideas C, D, and G?

o *Force relationships by thinking in metaphors.* One of the best ways to create new ideas is to force your brain to find connections. To facilitate this, provide people with random words, ideas, phrases, or pictures. Ask them to compare the problem with this random word or phrase. Ask them about the characteristics of these words or phrases and how that makes them think about the problem. Look for similarities between the problem and the word, and look for differences between the problem and the word. Once you offer this approach and a random word is selected, you must use that word or phrase. If you pick one and the group quickly dismisses it as not relevant, you won't get the value from this exercise. The value comes from forcing people to find the connections and relationships. Be patient. This may take some time, and people may think it's silly, but it will help you create new ideas. You also can provide each person, pair, or small group with a different random word as a way to spur even more ideas.

For a list of random words that you can use, download this Bonus Byte at www.RLBonus.com using the keyword "wordlist."

o *Make thoughts visible.* Everyone thinks in pictures; creative geniuses simply take advantage of that fact. Allow people to draw pictures to describe the problem or their solution. Give them big pieces of paper and colored markers, or let them work in smaller groups at the flip chart or whiteboard. Allowing this visual component will help spur many new ideas.

OUR MINDS AREN'T WORD PROCESSORS

Do this simple exercise. Immediately after you read the word below, close your eyes and think about the word. Then open your eyes and continue reading.

The word is: *Apple.*

Close your eyes.

Now what did you see?

In your mind's eye, did you see a red or green apple, an apple pie, an apple tree? Did you see an iPod? Did you immediately see a-p-p-l-e? Or did you see something else entirely?

Since we all know how to spell the word *apple,* eventually our thoughts will go to the actual word, but for more than 90 percent of people, the first thing they will see is a picture, not the word itself.

When you help people use their visual brain, you help them be more creative.

○ *Think in opposites.* Let's say your challenge is to double revenues this year. Consider asking the opposite question: "How could we halve revenues?" If you want to gain acceptance of a new idea, ask, "How could we make sure everyone hates this idea?" By turning the question around, you allow your brain to think about the situation in a new way. You'll be surprised at how many great ideas you can generate using this think-in-opposites approach.

○ *Prepare for chance.* Because creative geniuses recognize the creative process to be more than just brainstorming, they spend time on the first two steps: preparation and incubation. By gathering data, studying, and experimenting, they improve their chances for success. Pose a challenge to people, and give it time to incubate. Let them know that the new idea may come at any time, and help them be prepared to capture that fleeting thought when it does. Many creative geniuses have found the key to their solution in a dream or casual conversation. If you limit your creative output to the time allotted for brainstorming in a meeting, you never have the opportunity to take advantage of these chance encounters.

○ *Produce!* Creative geniuses create lots of ideas, and they stay in practice. They brainstorm for the thrill and experience of doing it, and they welcome the chance to help other people brainstorm their problems. If you want to have a more creative and innovative team, find ways to exercise its creativity regularly.

Your Now Steps

You again have plenty of ideas to choose from; the key is to get started:

1. Pick one of the suggestions in this section, and apply it in your next meeting.

2. Make notes in your journal of the results, your observations, and lessons learned.

Remarkable leaders want more creative ideas, so they use the techniques of creative geniuses.

Innovation

You might wonder why the title of this chapter mentions innovation and not creativity, especially since the whole focus has been on creativity until now. The decision was intentional. Creativity is important: it is necessary to generate lots of ideas to find great ones, but ideas by themselves have no value.

Think about it this way. Have you ever seen a new product advertised and thought to yourself, "I had that idea!"? If so, how much benefit did that idea bring you? None, of course. It isn't the idea that is valuable; action is what creates the value.

Innovation is the act of putting an idea (or ideas) into action. Until there is action, there is nothing. Remarkable leaders are creative and support the creative process in as many ways as they can, because they know creativity is a necessary step toward the ultimate goal of putting new ideas into action.

The question then becomes, How do you innovate? How do you put the ideas you have created into action?

The Six "Gets"

I have identified six actions to help you implement the great ideas that you and your team have created. Each of these suggestions is something you need to "get":

1. *Get aligned.* As a leader, you know the goals and objectives in front of you. Your job is to get the group in alignment with these goals and objectives. Make sure every problem or challenge you brainstorm is important to your goals and objectives. What are the most important things you are trying to accomplish? Having a good idea isn't enough. The idea must also be relevant and important to your goals. Ideas that don't pass this first test should be set aside.

2. *Get clarified.* Ideas in their infancy are fun and exciting, but they are seldom complete or crystal clear. Before taking action on them, make sure that everyone involved in both the creation and implementation of the idea truly understands what is meant by and involved in it. Make sure that people have a clear understanding of the results that are expected. This step is especially important for ideas that will be

implemented by a group because not everyone will have the same picture of the idea until it is clarified.

3. *Get organized.* If your idea has passed the first two tests, it is time to plan. Determine the implementation steps, and think about the time line. Put this idea into the larger scope of your efforts. Time spent in planning and organizing will always pay dividends.

4. *Get help.* Your team may not be able to turn its idea into reality by itself. Your planning should help the team see where it might need other experience, insight, or help. As a leader, you can provide those resources. Think about what resources you will need, and work on lining them up from the beginning. These steps will help your idea become real much more quickly.

5. *Get focused.* Once you have decided which idea to implement and have a plan, you have to make the time so that it will happen. Getting focused means creating the space and time to turn the idea into reality. It has to move from the idea stage into action. Focus your energy on making that happen. Since the team must be focused, you can provide significant assistance by setting expectations and removing other time obstacles that might impact implementation.

6. *Get over them.* You may have an idea (or many) that you love. But remember that there is a big difference between a good idea and the right idea. The team may generate many good ideas, but they probably can't implement them all right now and may not even want to. For some, the timing isn't right. Some of them aren't important enough. Some won't be completely aligned with your goals and objectives. That is okay. In order to implement our best ideas, sometimes we must be willing to let go of, or at least defer, some others. This is especially true of the ideas you have personally generated. Recognize that your ideas may not be the best and that you need to support the most effective ideas, not just your ideas. When you are willing to do this, you improve your chances of implementing the others you have chosen.

Each of these "gets" will help you share and prioritize ideas and will help your team to decide what to work on and who should be involved.

Change, Resistance, and Innovation

If innovation is the act of putting new ideas into action, then it is by definition a change phenomenon (which makes Chapter Five highly relevant here). In Chapter Five, we talked about one of the change levers being the risks or costs of change. It seems appropriate to expand on that a little bit more now.

There are two types of risk people see in a change or innovation: the emotional risks, including being blamed, feeling foolish, fearing making a mistake, and fearing negative feedback; and the rational or logical risks, such as that the idea might not actually work, it might cost too much, we might not be able to finish, or it might not solve the problem. Thinking about these two types of risks led me to adapt an idea from *The Innovator's Handbook* by Vincent Nolan (1989).

Let's look at each of the quadrants in Figure 11.1.

Quadrant D is the quadrant of lowest risk—both logical and emotional. Implementing innovations in this quadrant should be the easiest, although they might have the lowest payoff or benefit. There's nothing wrong with innovations in this quadrant, but if you limit yourself to these, you'll likely never create remarkable results.

Innovations in quadrant C have higher emotional risk for people, but the real logical risks are still relatively small. If you are nurturing a team, trying to build trust in the team, or attempting to make your culture more innovative, innovation of this type will be helpful because you can appeal to the lower risk of real failure and can then help to acclimate the team to taking more emotional risks. You still have to get people past their emotional concerns, but when you can do so, you should create some

Figure 11.1. Risk Quadrants

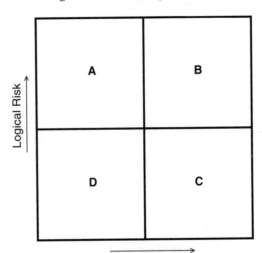

Logical Risk

A   B

D   C

Emotional Risk

tangible results relatively quickly and help them feel more comfortable with taking another risk in the future.

Innovations of the type in quadrant B are more of a gamble. Does this mean that you shouldn't support a team that wants to innovate in this way or personally innovate in this way? Not at all. You must just be aware of the heightened risks and therefore be ready to exercise your skills as a change champion more fully.

You will want to be aware of the types of innovations in quadrant A and the unique challenges they pose. Because these types of innovations feel safe to people (due to the low emotional risk), they may not stop to recognize the larger real risks involved. They may also tend to minimize the logical risks if they are confident due to a past track record of successful innovation.

Putting ideas (especially those viewed as quadrant B or C) into action may generate significant resistance from outside the team, inside the team, or both. Don't be surprised by the resistance; it is a natural occurrence. Review the material in Chapter Five to help you and your team consider the response to any resistance that occurs.

Machiavelli wrote, "There is nothing more difficult to carry out, nor more doubtful of success, nor more dangerous to handle, than to initiate a new order of things." Creating a new order of things is what you are doing as a remarkable leader when you think and act innovatively. With all due respect to Machiavelli, however, I believe that while change and innovation can be a challenge, you now have the tools to improve the likelihood of success and reduce the dangers inherent in these efforts.

Your Now Steps

Recognizing that your ultimate goal is action, take action on the Now Steps below:

1. Identify an idea that is stalled currently.
2. Review the "six gets" to determine why it is stalled.
3. Take the action suggested based on your diagnosis.
4. Capture the lessons or ideas in your journal.

Creative ideas alone aren't enough; you must translate those ideas into action.

Go to remarkableleadershipbook.com/resources for more information, writing, tools, and other highly recommended resources to help you continue to think and act more innovatively.

12

REMARKABLE LEADERS VALUE COLLABORATION AND TEAMWORK

TEAMS. EVERYONE VALUES THEM. Everyone "knows" they are important. And while we value individualism (especially in the United States), we still believe that teams are a good thing. Ask almost any leader, and you'll hear about the teams in her organization. Ask her in private, and she'll often tell you how much of a challenge teams are, with all manner of problems emanating from the collaborative efforts desired from working on teams.

Teams are formed to capture synergy: that magical event when the result is greater than the sum of the parts. Many leaders and organizations chase that synergy and never find it or don't find it nearly often enough. They won't openly reject the concept of teams, but they are disappointed in the results they have achieved.

Remarkable leaders desire synergy as well, and because they understand team dynamics and the components of team success, they help their teams achieve. This chapter gives you tools and models to help you create that successful collaboration and help your teams be more than teams in name only.

Self-Assessment

Here is a quick assessment to help you think about your skills as a relationship builder. Use the following scale of 1 to 7 on each question:

1. Almost never
2. Rarely or seldom

3. Occasionally

4. Sometimes

5. Usually

6. Frequently

7. Almost always

> I provide teams the resources they need to succeed.   _____
>
> I am successful in leading teams.   _____
>
> I help teams align their goals to the organizational goals.   _____
>
> I build relationships with people in the organization.   _____
>
> I work to break down interdepartmental barriers.   _____
>
> I participate in meetings appropriately as a leader.   _____
>
> I facilitate meetings effectively.   _____
>
> The teams I contribute to produce great results.   _____

A New Model for Team Success

When leaders want to improve the results of their teams, they often talk to their training or human resource department or call an outside consultant. They tell their selected expert that their team needs some help and typically request some team building. That request usually is followed by, "We just need to help people get along and get to know each other better." These leaders assume that once this happens, team performance will improve. It is true that relationships are an important part of the team building puzzle, but it is far from the only piece.

In this section we explore a model that will give you a broader perspective of factors that lead to highly effective teams. As you read about this model, think about how you can use it as a framework to better understand the gaps a team might be facing and how you might support them more successfully.

The CARB Model

CARB is an acrostic representing the four major dimensions ultimately responsible for a team's effectiveness:

> Commitment to the team and each other
>
> Alignment and goal agreement

Relationships among team members

Behaviors and skills

Let's evaluate each component (Figure 12.1).

Commitment to the Team and Each Other

Commitment is powerful; without it, the work of teams won't be as successful as possible. The reason is that people have many tasks and priorities. The work of the team will fall on that long list of priorities unless there is a reason to be truly committed to the team and its goals. With only so much focus and energy to spread around, team members won't be fully participative and effective on the team without commitment. And conversely, they won't be committed without feeling truly involved in the team.

There are two parts to this commitment: people must feel a commitment to the team and its purpose, and they must have some commitment to the individuals on the team—believing in them and the contributions they will make to the project.

Figure 12.1. The CARB Model

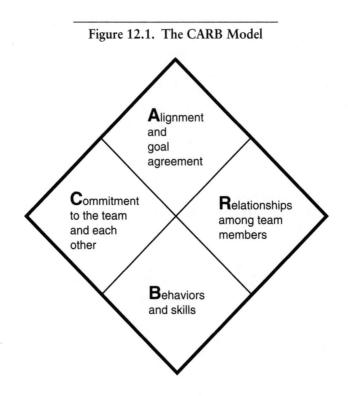

Commitment often needs to be built. It usually won't preexist when you put people on a team. Since team formation, development, and success are complex, several of the other CARB factors will aid in the development of this commitment. But recognizing its importance is a good first step.

COMMITMENT AND THE STAGES OF TEAM DEVELOPMENT

Bruce Tuckman created the most famous model for team development, stated in four stages (1965):

- ○ Forming
- ○ Storming
- ○ Norming
- ○ Performing

According to this model, teams move through these stages sequentially as they mature as a team (though advancement to the performing stage isn't assured). One of the key components of their ability to progress is their understanding of and commitment to the goals of the team. In fact, increasing any of the CARB factors will help a team move through these stages of development.

For a complete description of these four stages and how you can move a team through them, download this Bonus Byte at www.RLBonus.com using the keywords "team development." Or use your favorite search engine.

You will you know when you have built a level of commitment when high levels of commitment correlate with several factors:

- ○ *Belief.* People believe in each other. Individual motivations are clear and generally understood. When people are able to believe in their fellow team members, they start to develop a belief in the team as a whole and take pride in the work of the team. Team pride is an outgrowth of this belief.

- ○ *Agreements.* People have mutually agreed to a set of behaviors acceptable to the team. By building agreements on behavior, expected levels of performance, and "how things are done," productivity is greatly improved. Because effort and energy aren't spent on these distractions, effort can instead be directed to the work at hand.

o *Trust*. A major underpinning for team performance is trust in team members and leadership. Trust clearly is necessary for the high level of commitment required for high performing teams. (Review the keys to trust building in Chapter Seven.)

o *Support*. Support is a critical factor, but it also is a bellwether for the rest of these factors. If people are supporting team decisions, commitment is likely present. If they are supporting each other through tough parts of a team's life, they likely are committed.

It is possible for a team to get some results with low commitment, but you will never approach the results that can be achieved with people who are committed to the team and to each other.

As you survey the performance of your team, make sure to think about commitment. Depending on your level of direct involvement with the group, you may be able to learn much simply by observation. If the team works remotely or largely independent of you, ask questions to probe any commitment issues or challenges that might exist.

Of particular interest to you may be the agreements component. In my experience, one of the most valuable things a team can do is to create agreements that will guide team behavior on both the little annoyances and the big behavioral issues. This is done as a working dialogue facilitated by someone who can help the team identify its issues and help the members craft agreements that everyone will live with and abide by. While you as the leader likely wouldn't facilitate this exercise, you are the one who can recommend, support, and make it happen. This effort can have a positive impact on team performance.

Alignment and Goal Agreement

Teams can't succeed in a vacuum, but far too often that is what organizations expect them to do. There are three primary reasons for the vacuum:

o *Omission*. Leaders aren't thinking about or are "too busy" to set the context for team success. Ultimately, however, the leader's primary responsibility is to help establish the context for success. Without it, there is no basis for the team to be formed in the first place.

o *Optimism*. Leaders believe in their team members and their skills. They reason that they hired bright people, and those bright people will figure it all out. Assumptions like this can frustrate or burn out talented people and kill teams.

o *Lack of clarity.* Leaders do not provide clear organizational goals, objectives, or strategies. People (and teams) need to be able to connect their work to the important strategies of the organization. In my experience, lack of clarity is the most pervasive problem by far.

It takes effort to get a team in alignment with the organization's goals and strategies, and it is impossible if those goals and strategies don't exist. Chapter Sixteen deals with goal setting and will help you significantly in this area.

When strategies and goals exist and they may have been communicated, this is a good start, but it isn't enough. Teams can't gain the clear direction they need without conversation. A PowerPoint presentation may start the conversation, but it shouldn't be all there is. It is the responsibility of leadership to provide that opportunity for conversation. This conversation creates the understanding that teams need to clarify their goals and make the decisions about how they will deal with the opportunities and challenges that they inevitably will encounter as they do their work.

If you need to build stronger alignment between the team's work and the organization's goals, consider the following:

o *Start at the beginning.* Make sure the organization's goals and strategies are set. If they aren't, there isn't much chance that the team will be highly successful. At a minimum, the team needs to understand from the start why their work product matters in the bigger picture and how they can make a positive impact.

o *Generate conversation.* Make the time to have a conversation about overall organizational goals. The alignment team's need for great success must be deep, almost visceral. It is your job to engage the team in this type of conversation. Only the most mature and aware teams will ask you for it. Help individuals and the team develop meaning and purpose, and understand how they can create work that matters.

o *Get the team's help.* Get their input. Remember that you are trying to create alignment and agreement. When people help shape the goals of the team, they will have greater agreement with the goals.

o *Provide a connection.* Teams need someone in leadership above them who can provide support and resources—someone who can answer questions and keep them on track. Some people call this a team sponsor. The sponsor doesn't need to be on the team; rather, the sponsor needs to provide leadership, support, and connection. The sponsor keeps the team from feeling as if it is all alone. That person may be you; if it is not, you can help the team identify the right sponsor for the situation or project.

○ *Make the team accountable.* If the alignment is clear and the goals are set, the team needs to be held accountable for results. In organizations where accountability has been lax in the past, this may seem like a jolt, but it won't be long before this accountability not only drives results but improves team dynamics too. Accountability and how to create it in your organization are discussed at length in Chapter Fourteen.

It is easy to see how these steps will help a team succeed. But more than helping them deliver a desired result, the sense of clarity, meaning, and direction will help teams get over many other hurdles. People want to belong to something that matters; they want things to believe in. When we give them those things, collectively they will work through many personal issues and challenges, and they also will become more committed to the end product. Stronger alignment also reinforces and builds the commitment component of the CARB model.

It is important to recognize that providing teams with a traditional team-building event or training class won't likely address the issues of alignment. Training might highlight the need for alignment, but only if you know that is something you want people to discover and work with your consultant or trainer to make happen. Alignment can come only with your input; you can't pass this off to human resources or senior management. Those groups might communicate the organizational goals, but they won't create significant dialogue, and they shouldn't. It is your role as a remarkable leader to make that happen.

Relationships Among Team Members

As a consultant, I've heard it said many times: "We need people to get to know each other better. Once we have done that, we will be fine." This is a dangerously limiting view of teams. Relationships do matter, and this has long been the traditional realm of much team training: let's get people to know each other better and build a sense of camaraderie. And although that is important, it won't cause lasting improvement; it only sets the stage for that improvement. When teams with good relationships also have the other CARB factors in large amounts, team performance can soar.

Here are three specific things that can help build team relationships. Consider helping or encouraging your team members to:

○ *Learn each other's strengths.* Strong team members not only like each other; they know each other's strengths. They are collectively able to tap into every member's strengths and experiences—for example, strengths of knowledge, skill, experience, tendency, or interests.

○ *Find ways to capitalize on those strengths.* The best team-building activities give people a chance to be themselves without the structure and trappings of the workplace. And when people are themselves, others will see them in new and often flattering ways. This gives their strengths a chance to shine and helps others see how those strengths can be tapped by the team.

○ *Get comfortable with asking for help.* Highly effective team members are willing to ask for help regardless of their role on the team. Structure or encourage team-building activities that can help raise people's comfort with reaching out for help.

There are other factors about team relationships that matter that likely won't get addressed in traditional team building, but they are quite important. These factors require effort and time spent to develop processes for addressing. And they are your responsibility as a leader to create. These include:

○ *Integration processes.* How new team members are added to a team, how they become oriented and acquainted with other team members, and how they learn the norms and expectations of the team are all typically left to chance or a quick meet and greet. Leaders and organizations that develop processes and plans for these initiations have greater success with teams that change membership frequently.

○ *Role definition.* Team members need to understand their roles and where they fit into the team's structure. When new teams are started, there needs to be a format and plan for discussing team member roles and expectations.

Both of these suggestions can be supported by a strong team chartering process. If your organization doesn't have a process for helping teams get started (and get through the forming and storming stages more quickly), this is another opportunity for you to be remarkable.

To get a complete list of reasons that team charters will help you and a suggested process for creating a charter, download this Bonus Byte at www.RLBonus.com using the keywords "team charter."

As you can see, the relationship component of this CARB model is about more than just liking one another. Consider all of the factors set out here when diagnosing a team's situation and from that determine how you can best support the team's development.

Behaviors and Skills

Being a successful member of a team requires different behaviors and skills from those required of an individual contributor. Therefore, when you put people together on teams, they will perform more confidently and successfully if they have the right skills.

The list of skills and behaviors that support team success is long; here are a few to get you thinking about the types of behaviors and skills to look for when creating a team, or to develop in an existing team.

- *Strong technical skills and competence.* Having the subject matter knowledge, industry perspective, or specific skills the team needs is critical. Of course, not everyone should bring a set of skills, but it is important to identify the subject matter needs of the team and make sure that each team member contributes to one or more of these skills.

- *Able and willing to collaborate and share credit.* Working alone allows people to feel the spotlight and glory when things go well. It also means those individuals will be accountable when they aren't as successful. Highly effective team members recognize that the team success will reflect on them most when they focus on team success rather than individual accolades. The best team members are willing to collaborate.

- *Able to trust others.* Trust is critically important to team success and is developed among people over time. The most effective team members are willing to start from a position of basic trust in their teammates. Certainly this trust can deepen and grow, but teams that are willing to assume the best from the start will progress much faster. This behavior is more important when the makeup of individual teams changes more quickly.

○ *Able to participate and lead effective meetings.* Meetings are an important component of team success. Whether the team meets every day, is on periodic conference calls, or meets only quarterly, the ability to contribute ideas and insights, help the team move toward the desired results, provide feedback when needed, and stay focused are critical skills for effective teams.

○ *Comfortable and competent at group problem solving.* Some problems can be solved by individuals, sometimes a subteam will tackle a problem, and sometimes the entire team will be required. In every case, effective team members know how to work together to solve problems, listen to the ideas of others, and ask questions without being condescending. The best teams also make sure that the strengths, experiences, and insights of each team member are taken into account in the problem solving process. (Chapter Thirteen deals with problem solving from the leader's perspective in much more depth.)

○ *Willing to continuously learn.* Work today is more complex and demanding than it has ever been before. This means that for teams to succeed, each member needs to continuously improve his or her individual skills.

Your Now Steps

The CARB model gives you a comprehensive look at the factors that contribute to successful teams. Don't let that breadth of concepts dissuade you from putting it to use immediately. These steps will help you get started:

1. Look at the CARB model, and determine which components offer the greatest improvement opportunity for your team(s).
2. Once you have made that assessment, determine an immediate action you could take to help them.
3. Take that action.

 Remarkable leaders understand the components of team success and use them to help teams prosper.

Types of Teams

All sorts of teams exist in the world of work today: work teams, project teams, ad hoc teams, planning teams, leadership teams, shift teams, and departmental teams, to name just a few. With all of these types of teams (and many people belonging to several different teams), it is no surprise why there are so many people offering advice on how to make your team more successful.

With the CARB model, you now have a basis for diagnosis and growth of your teams. All teams need all of those components to be the most effective, and yet we recognize that not all teams are created equal. Different types of teams are ... different. Nevertheless, I believe there are only two types of teams, exemplified by basketball teams and track and field teams.

Basketball Teams

Basketball (or soccer or hockey) teams require that everyone play as a single unit. For these sports, the players are *interdependent*. In order to be successful at every moment of the game, the entire team needs to be working in harmony. The role of each player is designated by position, which usually takes into account innate strengths and acquired skills. However, the situation at any moment during the flow of the game may require any player to take any role.

On great basketball teams, all players are willing to be flexible, assist, change roles, and do what it takes. They take this approach because they know that without working together, they cannot achieve the goal of victory; they are interdependent for success.

Track and Field Teams

Players on track and field teams are not interdependent; they are *independent* (except in a few relay events). Shot putters have a skill set that is largely unrelated to the sprinters. The high jumpers can be personally skilled and successful without any tangible help or support from the distance runners.

At the end of the day (or meet), the team can win if enough of the individuals do well. The most successful of these teams have highly talented individual contributors, supporting each other to reach the common goal of winning. In this way, they are definitely a team. They may feel allegiance to the group, certainly can have pride in being a part of the group, and are supportive of each other because they want each other to be successful and because they all will be more successful when each individual is more successful. They can have a common goal (to win the meet or championship), but the fundamental relationship between the players isn't the same as it is on a basketball team.

What This Means to You as a Leader

Most organizations likely have both sorts of teams. You will have teams that work in a process flow or projects where the outputs of one person directly affect the work of the next: the work and the people are highly interdependent. In these cases, goal alignment will come more quickly because team members tend to sense the need to understand the connections and relationships among themselves.

You also have teams that look more like the independent track and field team. Since their work doesn't intersect in nearly the same ways as highly interdependent teams do, they may not initially see the connection. This is the source of much of the resistance you will experience when encouraging people to work in a team: their view of their work doesn't coincide with their view of a team. In the workplace, members of these teams may not see themselves as part of a team at all. Helping individuals see how they can support each other and create synergy is a key to success here. Recognize that these teams look much more like a group of individual contributors, and they may act that way until they see the value of thinking of themselves as a team.

You may really appreciate the value of an interdependent team, but it makes no more sense to force your team into that model than it would to force all the hurdlers to pole-vault and all the sprinters to throw the javelin. Your teams will work best when their team structure and expectations accurately reflect the nature of their work.

In my experience, this happens all the time. Leaders and team members tend to think that all teams "should" be interdependent because that is the way teams are "supposed to work." This classic classification leads people to have unrealistic and unnecessary expectations when the team is really independent in nature.

As you lead and form teams, you need to think about these distinctions. Does the work demand interdependence? Your answer to this question is critical to the team's formation and growth. Once you establish a clear distinction in your mind, talk about the implications with the team itself. For an existing team, introduce this model and get the team members' thoughts on how they see their team. For a forming team, you can use the discussion as a way to develop agreements on which type of team is the most appropriate.

Once there is agreement on the type of team it is (new or existing), you can begin to set the right kinds of expectations for team members and for yourself. You also can build more appropriate plans for training, development, and team building if necessary.

 To get a list of questions to help you determine which type of team you have (or need), download this Bonus Byte at www.RLBonus.com using the keywords "team type."

Your Now Steps

Ask yourself these questions as a starting point:

1. Look at the team(s) you lead.
2. Determine which type of teams they should be.
3. Look for mismatches between the way they should be structured and the way they actually operate.
4. Determine a next step for closing those gaps if they exist. (It likely involves talking with the team.)

 Remarkable leaders structure their teams based on the needs of the work, not their preconceived vision of great teams.

Leading Teams

This entire book provides ideas and skills that will help you in any leadership role, including leading a team; however, there are some specific ideas that become important when leading teams, especially interdependent ones.

- *Help the team identify its purpose.* You've read this before, but it is a critical component for every team's success. As a team leader, you must recognize the role you can play in helping this happen. The sooner a team is clear on its purpose, the faster it can become highly productive.
- *Set the scope and boundaries.* Teams need to know what they can and should tackle and what is too big or not their responsibility. They need your guidance in this area. Many times there are things

outside their decision-making realm. Unless you let them know where those boundaries are, they may spend unproductive time trying to work outside their scope. By helping teams manage the scope of their work, you will keep them focused and on target to reach goals more quickly.

○ *Show your belief.* If you don't believe in teams, it will show, and you won't effectively lead. If you do believe in both the team concept and the people on the teams, let them know through your actions and your work. Once they have purpose, goals, and your belief, they are on their way to success.

○ *Define your role.* Your role is to lead, not to do the work or make all of the decisions. Let the team know what your role is and what it isn't. You are relying on their experience, knowledge, and intellect in the completion of the team's work. Let them know how you can and will help and what you expect of them too.

○ *Be a team member too.* Often as a team leader, you also are a working member of the team. When this is the case, don't pass your work off on someone else, and don't hide behind your role as the leader. If you are a working member as well as the leader, keep those two roles clear and distinct. This will reduce your stress level and allow you to be far more productive and valued by the team.

○ *Be a supporter.* Support the team with your actions. Don't just delegate the work to the team and be gone. Teams will experience obstacles and roadblocks, and it is your job to remove those roadblocks, find additional resources, and provide needed support. It is like a hike. If you are in front of a group on a hike, you do your best to remove impediments that might slow or injure those who follow. That is your role in leading a team: check for obstacles, and be present enough to anticipate as many of them as possible.

○ *Keep your mouth shut.* Teams often look to leaders to make the final decisions or assume that the leader has veto power on any decision. If you really buy the team approach—that you want and need everyone's input—you have to keep quiet. If you are the first person to talk on a subject, the overall amount of discussion and idea flow will drop dramatically. Team members will subconsciously assume that your first word is the last word, whether they agree or not. Because of your position, you must abstain from the early part of a dialogue on any issue and share your thoughts near the end of the conversation.

Your Now Steps

Consider the tips above and do the following:

1. Identify which of the suggestions presented you could most benefit from implementing.
2. Make notes in your journal as to how you can improve in this area.
3. Take those actions at your next team meeting, if not sooner.

 Remarkable leaders don't lead just organizations or individuals; they lead teams.

The Leader as a Facilitator

One of the complaints I hear about organizations using many teams is that with teams come meetings; the more teams, the more meetings—and meetings don't always have the best reputation. According to Tom Terez in research cited in his book, *Twenty-Two Keys to Creating a Meaningful Workplace* (2002), meeting goers spend an average of nine hours per week in meetings, and nearly all attendees report that at least 20 percent of that time is unproductive. That's an average of at least 1.8 hours of unproductive time per employee per week.

How many employees do you lead? Multiply that number by 1.8, and then multiply that result by 50 weeks (assuming two weeks of vacation). How many total hours did you come up with? Now ask yourself how many ways you could put those hours to better use than to have people be unproductive in meetings. I'm guessing you can come up with a long list.

More collaboration and more teams clearly means more meetings, which then means that it's a critical productivity point to make meetings more productive and effective. As the leader, that is your responsibility. There are few things you can do to improve the productivity of your team more than learning how to facilitate those meetings more successfully.

Your role as facilitator is to make it easier for the group to progress toward its goals. Throughout this book, we have examined the leader's role of removing obstacles and providing resources to people. These efforts certainly make things easier for a group too, but there is a difference.

Leader Versus Facilitator

In a meeting, the leader is concerned about the content of the meeting; he or she is constantly thinking about what is being said, if ideas being discussed can be achieved, if they fit into the budget, and the implications of these ideas or actions across the organization or on other projects.

A true facilitator isn't concerned with these questions at all. Rather, the facilitator is concerned with the process of the meeting; he or she is constantly thinking about what is happening and how it works toward the successful achievement of the meeting's desired outcomes. The facilitator is also thinking about the group dynamics, how to get everyone to participate, and how to help the group clarify its problem.

The leader wants action items that can be accomplished given the current constraints of the organization (content). The facilitator makes sure the group forms action items and that each one is assigned (process). The leader cares about the desired outcomes in terms of the actual decisions (content). The facilitator is concerned only that decisions are reached (process). This division is quite clear and extremely helpful when there are two different people playing these roles. However, as a team leader, you often will be the one facilitating the meeting too, so you must balance these two roles.

Notice that I said you must balance these two roles, not pick one. If you put the facilitator hat on and never lead, the team might flounder looking for guidance. And if you keep your leader hat on entirely (assuming no one else is playing the facilitator role), the meeting may be less productive and more like thousands of other meetings team members have attended in the past.

To be most effective, even in a highly developed team, meetings need a facilitator. The facilitator does not have to be the leader (it could be an outside person or another team member with the necessary skills and experience). The leader is then responsible for making sure this role is covered, and in many cases, it will be the leader.

To become a remarkable leader, you must develop facilitation skills.

The Skills of a Great Leader-Facilitator

Here is a list of skills that will get you started on your path toward facilitation excellence. This list isn't complete, but it is focused on the specific skills that are most important if you are leading and facilitating:

    ○ *Recognize both roles.* Because you are balancing the roles of leader and facilitator, you must understand that they are two distinct roles and treat them as such. Let the group know you will be playing both roles. Generally you will be more effective when you stay in the facilitator role except when your leader role is needed. This gives more process ownership to the rest of the group and makes the meeting more collaborative. When your input is needed as a leader, you state to the group that you are changing roles and now acting as the leader—and when that role is no longer required, just as clearly return to the facilitator role.

○ *Listen.* We have examined the importance of listening to building relationships, developing others, championing change, and more. This skill is as important in your facilitator role as in your leader role.

○ *Provide a process structure.* Facilitators need to know ways to get everyone involved in a conversation, they need to know a variety of ways to help the group generate more ideas, and they need to know the problem-solving process. When dealing with the process dimension, the best leader-facilitators have a bag of process tools that they can use when the time is right.

○ *Provide process suggestions and feedback.* Facilitators must help a team in the midst of its group process to get unstuck, get back on track, and move past a tough issue. Facilitators are able to intervene gently to help these changes occur without inserting themselves into the process. This is a particularly challenging place for the leader. Balancing your roles in these situations, and not reverting to "here's how we are going to do it because I'm the leader," is important if your goal is to keep the group engaged and actively participating in the process.

○ *Observe without judgment.* Facilitators exist not to judge but to make things easier. Effective leader-facilitators are able to make observations and tell the group what they see without turning the comment into feedback or correction. By remaining in a process dimension, they help a team guide itself through difficulties and challenges while maintaining its sense of ownership.

○ *Keep quiet.* The best facilitators make meetings better without really being noticed; they aim for the lightest possible touch. They know that they have done their best work when the meeting was successful but no one can really say what the facilitator "did."

Other Keys to Improving Your Meetings

While the ideas that follow are not completely in the realm of the facilitator role, three things are the most important attributes of any

successful meeting: agendas, desired outcomes, and the meeting participants. Whether in your facilitator or leader role, make sure that these
three items are considered. When they are, the nonproductive time spent
in meetings will shrink rapidly and predictably.

○ *Agendas.* Make sure your meetings have agendas, preferably dis-
tributed ahead of the meeting to help everyone be prepared to participate and contribute. If an agenda wasn't prepared prior to the
meeting, the first order of business should be to create one.

 To get an agenda checklist and template, download
this Bonus Byte at www.RLBonus.com using the
keyword "agenda."

○ *Desired outcomes.* Desired outcomes are specific statements of what
will be accomplished. These statements go beyond listing a topic
on the agenda and provide specific guidance as to what successful completion of the meeting looks like. Just as goal alignment is
important to overall team success, having clearly stated desired outcomes is the single best way to improve your meeting and team
productivity.

 To get a process for creating and stating the desired
outcomes for any meeting, download this Bonus
Byte at www.RLBonus.com using the keywords
"desired outcomes."

○ *Those you invite.* One of the reasons people find meetings unproductive is that they don't know why they are there. Make sure only the
people who are critical to the desired outcomes are present and that
each of these people understands how he or she can contribute. In
my experience, far too many meetings have extra people involved,
adding complexities to the group dynamics and frustration because
they don't know how they can contribute.

 To get a tool to help you identify the critical people to
invite to your meetings, download this Bonus Byte at
www.RLBonus.com using the keyword "invite."

Your Now Steps

Take a first step toward facilitating more effective meetings by doing the following:

1. Resolve to create an agenda with desired outcomes for all of your meetings this week.

2. Commit to this resolution by rescheduling any meeting that you don't have an agenda for. (If the meeting is really important, you'll make the time to build the agenda.) If the meeting is urgent or impromptu, make creating a quick agenda the first item of business.

 Remarkable leaders facilitate meetings effectively.

 Go to remarkableleadershipbook.com/resources for more information, writing, tools, and other highly recommended resources to help you continue to build and lead teams more effectively.

13

REMARKABLE LEADERS SOLVE PROBLEMS AND MAKE DECISIONS

PROBLEMS ABOUND. How do we raise employee retention? Improve product quality? Reduce costs? Streamline a work process? Get more people to attend the company picnic? Market the new product? John Dulles, former U.S. secretary of state, said, "The measure of success is not whether you have a tough problem to deal with, but whether it is the same problem you had last year."

Problems are one of the reasons leaders have jobs. If there were no problems, you might not be needed (or at least fewer leaders would be needed). I don't say this to be negative or to spread a somber message; it is just the way it is. And even when it seems there are few problems, opportunities for improvement are ever present.

Problems, and their possible solutions, require some decisions and action. If you want to eliminate a problem's cause or improve your situation, you must make decisions. Making effective decisions is another part of the leader's role. In this chapter, we explore the ways leaders can best help and support problem solving for the maximum benefit of the organization. We also examine decision making, a necessary step when solving problems. While problem solving and decision making have always been leadership expectations, exploring *how* those problems are solved and *how* those decisions are made can be very enlightening. This chapter provides that exploration.

Self-Assessment

Here is a quick assessment to help you think about your skills as a relationship builder. Use the following scale of 1 to 7 on each question:

1. Almost never

2. Rarely or seldom

3. Occasionally

4. Sometimes

5. Usually

6. Frequently

7. Almost always

I ask questions effectively. _____

I use questions to help develop a full understanding of a problem. _____

I think of questioning as a leadership skill. _____

I support the decisions others make. _____

I challenge people to try new approaches. _____

I consider a wide range of factors when making decisions. _____

I am willing to take calculated risks. _____

I use a proven problem-solving methodology. _____

Asking Questions

The skill of asking questions is important to problem solving for obvious reasons: well-asked questions can help determine the nature and causes of a problem, as well as determine how people feel about the situation. Questions also aid in the decision-making process as a method for understanding the situation and exploring the implications of the decision.

Questions are a lot like listening (you can review the section on listening in Chapter Seven): because they are so prevalent and we "do it all the time," we take these skills for granted. It is precisely for that reason that I've included this section because remarkable leaders can't take asking well-crafted questions for granted. I also could have included a section on questions in several chapters because there is such a clear linkage in those chapters as well. Consider the connection between:

o Questioning and creativity

o Questioning and coaching and mentoring

○ Questioning and learning

○ Questioning and influence

○ Questioning and focusing on the customer

Perhaps noticing all of these connections is just another way of recognizing how important your questioning skills are. Improving your ability to phrase (the words) and ask (the tone, intonation, and timing) a question is a core skill for any remarkable leader.

The Key to Asking Great Questions

Like so many of the other skills in this book, the key to asking great questions starts with you and your intent. If you want to ask great questions, you must ask them for the right reasons. When you do this, your questions generally will be well received and successful, even if your wording isn't perfect.

If your intent is to use questions to intimidate, be clever, incite or fan an argument, delay a decision, show off, prove you are right, or get a reaction, you also will likely be successful. Questions can achieve all of these things. However, I encourage you to read this list again, because chances are you ask questions for more of these reasons regularly, whether you are consciously aware of it or not.

But if your intent is to solve a problem, make a decision, gather information, satisfy your curiosity, learn something, form an opinion, gather feedback, encourage someone, or foster participation and engagement, questions can do all of these things for you too. Get your intent straight before asking questions, and you will have greater success.

EXAMPLES OF DIFFERING INTENTS
Dorothy Leeds in her book *Smart Questions* (1988) calls questions with selfish or personal intent dumb and those with a more genuine intent smart. Here are some examples of how intent can change the wording and outcome of the question:

Smart: Can you tell me how many people have signed up for the session today, please?
Dumb: Have you looked at the roster for the session today?

Smart: Where have you been today?
Dumb: Where have you been all day?

> Smart: What types of marketing approaches have you tried?
>
> Dumb: Have you tried the new approach recommended by Dr. X in his latest book?
>
> Each of these pairs might garner the same answer (though that isn't guaranteed), but notice the difference in how you feel about receiving the question. The difference in intent might be more subtle than in these examples, but that doesn't change the results or impact. Intent can be heard through your question.

Types of Questions

There are two basic kinds of questions: open-ended (those that encourage more than a yes or no, either or, or short answer) and closed-ended (those that can be answered more succinctly). Both types of questions are valuable, but each is best when used appropriately.

Open questions create a conversational tone and eliminate any chance of the sense of interrogation that might be associated with closed questions. Some other advantages of open questions include:

○ Allowing people to think about their responses.

○ Gaining more than just facts. You learn about attitudes, emotions, and thoughts, all of which influence the person's opinion, behavior, or performance.

○ Providing an opportunity to gain any additional information the other person feels is relevant (even if you were unaware of that information or its connection to the question).

○ Creating dialogue and partnership rather than a one-way, data-retrieval exercise.

Closed questions can be used to tie up the loose ends of a conversation, build commitment, and drive for closure. They also can help you:

○ Bring a conversation to a close (or get someone off the phone or out of your office).

○ Paraphrase to check for understanding.

○ Get information in a hurry.

To get a tool to help you transform closed questions into open ones, download this Bonus Byte at www.RLBonus.com using the keywords "open questions."

A Question-Asking Process

Asking great questions is a process. Reflect on these seven steps to help you consistently ask better questions:

1. *Consider the purpose and intent of your question.* Knowing why you are asking will help you ask a better question.

2. *Consider the person you are asking.* You might ask a question of a person you just met differently than you would an old friend. Your question might be posed differently to a senior leader than to a peer.

3. *Formulate your question.* Based on the purpose, intent, and target, create a question that will help you reach your purpose.

4. *Listen to the response.* You have asked a question in order to get a response, so stop thinking about your next question, and listen carefully to the answer to this question.

5. *Probe for more information if needed.* Ask a follow-up question as required and desired.

6. *Be gracious.* Continue to listen and thank people for their help.

7. *Take action.* Now that you have the information or results you were looking for, it is time to take action.

Your Now Steps

Rather than focusing these Now Steps on technique, consider your intent:

1. Think of a time when you realize your intent wasn't focused correctly, and reflect on your results.

2. Reflect on the situation, and consider how you would have asked the question if your intent had been different—or if you would have even asked the question at all.

3. Make any notes and write lessons learned in your journal.

 Remarkable leaders ask great questions.

Problem-Solving Basics

Attend any problem-solving workshop, and you will learn a model or process for solving problems. That model might have anywhere from four to twelve steps; it might be very specific or very general. There are

Figure 13.1. PDCA Cycle

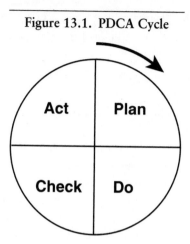

many things about all of these models that will differ, but all have two things in common: they focus a great deal on planning and follow a flow similar to the PDCA cycle, a cyclical four-stage improvement process: Plan-Do-Check-Act (Figure 13.1). It is a process that promotes problem solving and continuous improvement.

The Plan step encompasses identifying a problem, creating a problem statement, and gathering data on the current situation and past history. The Do stage is an experiment step where possible solutions are tested or piloted. In the Check step, the results of the solution's implementation are measured and the success of the solution in eliminating the initial problem is determined. And the Act step is used to adopt improvements or continue to use the solution if it was found to be successful. The model's circular nature is important; it suggests that problems can always be solved and then improved with successively better solutions.

The other common feature of all problem-solving models is the strong emphasis on planning. As an example, when I was a corporate trainer for Chevron, I taught a seven-step problem-solving model; four of the seven steps were planning steps. Rather than teaching you any particular model, let's review some of the keys at each step in the generic PDCA cycle.

Plan Step Considerations

During the Plan step you will:

○ Identify the problem using data.

○ Seek to understand the problem from different perspectives (customers, suppliers, and other stakeholders of the work).

o Clearly define the problem (by writing a problem statement).

o Identify the root causes of the problem by asking the Five Whys (see Chapter Four for details).

o Identify possible solutions (brainstorming possible solutions once the problem is clearly understood).

o Select a solution to implement (from the list that was created).

Of all of these steps, the one most likely to improve your problem-solving results is to clearly define the problem. Having a clear definition of what you are trying to solve is critical. Far too often people work diligently to solve problems, only to find out that they aren't all trying to solve exactly the same problem. This happens in part because there hasn't been enough investigation and conversation, and so they don't have a common or complete understanding of the problem. Many problem-solving processes have significant rigor included to help you use data to identify and clarify the problem.

CREATING PROBLEM CLARITY WITH A PROBLEM STATEMENT

A problem statement is a sentence that describes in specific terms what the gap or overall improvement need is, including how it will be measured. It clearly defines the purpose of the problem-solving activity. It should address the who (who is affected by the problem), what (what the actual problem is), when (when it occurs), and where (where it occurs) questions. It should not attempt to answer the why question because that implies that you know the causes of the problem, and at the stage of creating the problem statement, you haven't likely progressed that far in your problem-solving process yet.

Do Step Considerations

In the Do step, you are implementing your chosen solution, so several of your remarkable leadership skills come into play. The solution will inevitably cause some change (and potentially much change). In fact, all of Chapter Five is relevant here. To be successful, you need to communicate the solution, the problem it is meant to solve, the steps in the implementation plan, and more to all of those affected by the change.

Make sure your action plans include detail on the tasks, who is responsible, and when these tasks will be completed. The more specific these action plans are, the more successful they will be. Many problem-solving efforts have stalled at this point due to resistance or lack of follow-through. Remarkable leaders won't let either happen.

Check Step Considerations

In the Check step, you are checking to see if the planned solution achieved what was hoped for. The best way to do this is with measurements. An effective way to demonstrate results is by using measurements before and after the solution is implemented. Compare your measurements to both the root cause and the problem statement.

Act Step Considerations

If your solution was successful, it is time to celebrate. Also, if the problem you solved is related to an important work process, recognize that with all of the information and focus that has been given to this area, now might be a good time to try to improve even further. Consider what you have learned in the process to determine what other changes you might make. Look at your original list of potential solutions to see if any of them might provide further improvement now.

Your Now Steps

As you look at the work before you in the next few days, you undoubtedly see at least one problem that you need to work on. Your Now Steps will help you work on solving that problem:

1. Identify the problem, and write your problem statement.
2. Don't do anything else related to solving this problem until you have written (not just thought about) this problem statement.

 Remarkable leaders use proven processes to help solve problems.

Decision-Making Approaches and Strategies

There are two important things leaders need to consider relating to decisions: the decision itself and how the decision was reached. Remarkable leaders recognize that the latter is at least as important as the former. There are four basic decision-making approaches or strategies:

- Independent
- Consultative
- Collaborative
- Consensus

There is a time and place for each type of decision in even the most participative team-centric cultures. The leader's job is to understand these decision-making styles, select the right one in the right situation, and communicate the approaches being used.

Independent decisions are those reached by the leader (or someone else) alone. This is the best approach when the leader has all of the needed information, the decision is urgent, support is likely (regardless of what choice the leader makes), or the problem isn't or truly can't be shared.

Figure 13.2 demonstrates what the independent decision making looks like. The *leader* is responsible for the decision and then shares that decision with those who will be affected. If you were in a meeting and the fire alarm sounded, you wouldn't come to some sort of consensus about what to do next and where to go. In this urgent situation (and many others), people support the decision any knowledgeable person makes. Although this is extreme, it is a perfect example of independent decision-making being the right choice.

Some decisions require the input of others, and so the leader may seek and receive consultation: information, ideas, opinions, and more

Figure 13.2. Independent Decisions

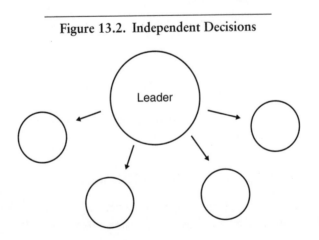

Figure 13.3. Consultative Decisions

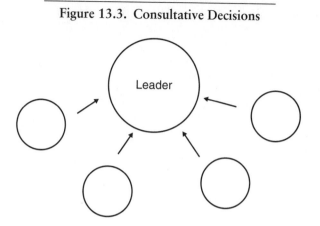

regarding the decision at hand. In this type of decision making, the decision still belongs to the leader (Figure 13.3).

Since input is being given, the decision can't be as urgent as a fire alarm; some time must be available for making the decision. These types of decisions sit on a sliding scale of time allowed and the amount of input needed, received, and used; with more time, more input might be sought. You also may want to gather ideas if you think the decision might be controversial. When people have a chance to be involved, they are more likely to accept the resulting decision.

The next approach to decision making is the *collaborative decision* (Figure 13.4). In this approach, the leader is letting go of more of the control and granting more of the decision-making power to others or the group. The group is now collaborating on the decision, and although the leader may make the ultimate decision, the group is deeply involved in the decision making process.

Consensus (Figure 13.5), considered by some as the holy grail of all decision making, is considered an anathema by others. Consensus is reached when all members of the group are able to say:

- "I believe that you understand my point of view."
- "I believe that I understand your point of view."
- "Whether or not I prefer this decision, I will support it because it was reached openly and fairly."

Consensus decisions are difficult to achieve and take the most time, but when they are truly reached, they lead to the highest levels of agreement

Figure 13.4. Collaborative Decisions

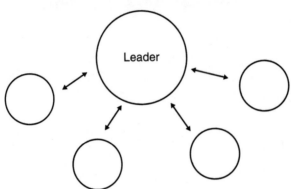

and engagement among team members. If you want the highest levels of buy-in, consensus may be worth striving for.

 To get a list of tips to help you reach consensus decisions, download this Bonus Byte at www.RLBonus.com using the keyword "consensus."

Figure 13.6 shows another way to look at these various decision-making types—plotting them comparing time required and engagement gained. This gives an accurate picture of the trade-offs among the

Figure 13.5. Consensus Decisions

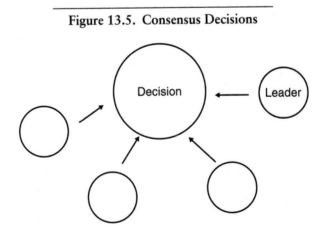

Figure 13.6. Decision Slope

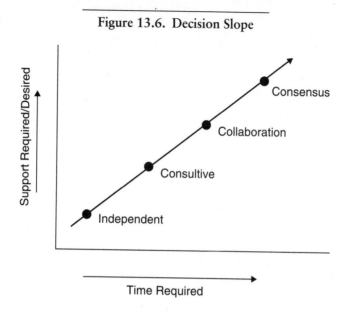

various decision-making approaches and will help you decide when to use each one. One important note: the slope of the line isn't necessarily at a 45-degree angle as shown. The slope of the line will be determined by the amount of trust that exists between the leader and the team. If there is more trust, the line gets steeper; in other words, it would take less time to get higher levels of engagement and agreement.

The Big Caveat

I have worked in and with many organizations trying to push decisions downward or get more participation in decision making. I support this approach 100 percent, and as a remarkable leader you will too. You'll find that this approach develops and empowers others and shares the responsibility and accountability more broadly in the organization.

This said, leaders often make a critical error in their zeal to get people involved. They ask for input on decisions they have already made (or are close to making). Do **not** ask for input if you are planning to make an independent decision. People will accept the independent decision more readily than they will accept anything else when they feel their input wasn't really valued or used. Ask for input, but only when you really want and need it.

Your Now Steps

Look at a decision you need to make soon and take the following steps:

1. Make a conscious choice about how you want to make that decision.
2. Communicate that choice, and take the necessary steps to make the decision in that way.

 How a decision is made is crucial to the decision's success.

Being Decisive

In *The 100 Absolutely Unbreakable Laws of Business Success*, Brian Tracy defines the law of decision as "every great leap forward in life is preceded by a clear decision and a commitment to action" (2002, p. 61).

Remarkable leaders believe in and follow this law. You can call this a bias for action, being decisive, or a willingness to try, but whatever you call it, it is a required skill of remarkable leaders.

Have you ever worked for someone who was wishy-washy or couldn't ever quite make up his mind? How closely did you want to follow him? How much did you want to emulate him? I'm guessing not much or not very likely.

Once we recognize that it is imperative to be decisive, we can begin to build the skill. There are several things that can help you in becoming more decisive:

- o *Realize the truth of waiting.* Not deciding is deciding. When you think of this, you might think that it is then okay to delay and not decide. If you were on a desert island with no one else around, that might work. You, however, are a leader, and others are relying on you to make decisions. If you have decided to delay or not to decide at all, tell people so they know. When you do this and communicate it, you have actually decided something, even if another decision will emerge after your delay.

- o *You can delegate.* As a leader, you don't have to make all the decisions. You can get your team involved or delegate the decision to them. When you do this, make sure that you set them up to succeed. Make your expectations clear, provide clear boundaries and the information they need, and then let them decide. When you delegate the decision, it no longer belongs to you.

○ *Apply decision criteria.* If you have a complex decision, assign some criteria to help you decide. If there are three factors that you want to consider in making the decision, look at your decisions through the lens of each of these factors.

To get a tool to help you apply criteria to any decision, download this Bonus Byte at www.RLBonus.com using the keyword "criteria."

○ *Asking the decision question.* The decision question helps you assess your risk and gets you moving. The question is, "What is the worst thing that could happen?" Usually people don't decide or defer because they are afraid of what might go wrong. By asking this question (and perhaps gathering some input or opinions from others), you can quantify the risks; even if those risks are just fears. Taking the next step of writing down your answers will further help you determine the worst-case scenarios. Once you ask the question, if you figure that you could live with the worst case, make the decision and get started.

○ *Connecting decision making to your values.* One of the most powerful ways to make decisions is to connect them to your strongest values. (See Chapter Six to think more about values.) Taking this step will lead to better decisions and lead you to feel more comfortable with those decisions.

○ *Use data.* Most business decisions can be made with data. Certainly if you have followed a problem-solving process, you should have some data to help you make a decision. Don't use data as a crutch, continually seeking more to justify your decisions. Use data to help you be more informed about the choice you ultimately make.

○ *Use your intuition.* While data are important, your intuition can be a valuable tool too. Recognize and use it as an input to your decisions.

Your Now Steps

Identify a decision that is in front of you or one you have been delaying and apply these steps:

1. Make a decision, and communicate it immediately.
2. Capture your thoughts in your journal after making the decision.

3. Review the results and your ongoing experience in your journal one to two weeks later.

Nothing happens until a decision is made. Remarkable leaders are decisive.

Go to remarkableleadershipbook.com/resources for more information, writing, tools, and other highly recommended resources to help you solve problems and make decisions more effectively.

14

REMARKABLE LEADERS TAKE RESPONSIBILITY AND ARE ACCOUNTABLE

THE LIST OF BUZZWORDS IN BUSINESS and industry grows by the day. In many cases, these words describe important concepts, yet with overuse or misuse, they begin to lose their power. Unfortunately, I think that *accountability* is one of those words.

According to various dictionary definitions, to be accountable is to be answerable, liable, or responsible. The media tell us that politicians and corporate executives need to be "held accountable" for their actions and their decisions, as well they should. But these statements are often made with an accusatory tone that implies that they are accountable only for things that have gone wrong or for poor choices. Because of this "accountable = liable for something wrong" definition, many people have lost their personal taste for this concept, or at least for this word.

Now that we have acknowledged the baggage that may come with this word, let's be clear: if you want to be a remarkable leader, you must take accountability seriously. If you want to lead people to highly productive and successful outcomes, they must feel accountable for their role, be invested in their team's success, and be engaged in making decisions that support that success. To do this, you must hold yourself accountable and model the behavior.

If you want others to be accountable, you must first be accountable yourself.

Self-Assessment

Here is a quick assessment to help you think about your skills as a relationship builder. Use the following scale of 1 to 7 on each question:

1. Almost never
2. Rarely or seldom
3. Occasionally
4. Sometimes
5. Usually
6. Frequently
7. Almost always

I take personal responsibility.   _____

I set an example of what I expect.   _____

I follow through on promises and commitments.   _____

I share work responsibilities with others.   _____

I empower others.   _____

Being Personally Accountable

I was once working with a senior leadership team doing strategic planning. As I listened to conversations throughout the day, I noticed one word being used more and more: *they*. It was "they this" and "they that." The group wasn't referring to other people in a specific way or talking about tasks that had been completed. In fact the conversation grew less productive the more often the word *they* was used. It became increasingly clear that this group of leaders was looking for others to blame for everything.

I have heard this sort of blaming before with people saying that "'they' just don't understand." In these cases the "they" could be senior management, the corporate office, the administrative assistants, or some other somewhat nebulous "they" off in the distance. But to hear that from this specific group of leaders who by any measure was ultimately responsible for the entire organization seemed very odd.

Finally, I walked to the flip chart and wrote the word *they* in big black letters, then circled it in red. Having the group's attention, I talked for a minute about what I had been hearing: about blame and a general lack of responsibility. I tried to share my thoughts as observations without passing judgment, but I'm sure they soon learned that I felt they were creating their own problems. After talking for a few minutes, I turned back to the flip chart and put a slash right through the word.

I turned to the group and said, "There is no they. *You* are *they*. Until you take personal and collective responsibility for what is in your control, you won't move this organization to where you want it to be." I can't say that that one short commentary changed everything in the organization, but it did create a new dynamic in the meeting, a more positive conversation, and new awareness that lasted far into the future.

The first step in creating greater accountability—in getting people to take ownership, in engaging people to be accountable—is taking ownership and being engaged yourself. There really is no they. It all starts with you.

When we talk about being responsible or accountable, what are we really saying? What are we talking about? Here are some of the things you can choose to be personally accountable for:

- Your beliefs and perspectives
- Your attitude
- Your choices
- Your behaviors
- The commitments and promises you make
- The things for which you are responsible
- Your work—the tasks on your list

I'm guessing that when it comes to accountability or responsibility, you were thinking about the last three things on the list, with little regard for the first four points. But looking at the picture more completely changes your perspective on responsibility and accountability. Being fully responsible and accountable means understanding how our beliefs and attitudes affect our choices and how those choices affect our behavior. It is from this stream of personal accountability that we build real accountability for our commitments and tasks.

What Gets in our Way

Two things in particular get in the way of personal accountability: blame and being the victim.

BLAME. When you reflect back on the senior leadership team story, you may see one of the major barriers to being more personally accountable.

When that group became focused on the actions of others, they immediately lost their sense of personal responsibility; they began to become victims because they began to blame others.

Of course, we don't always call it blame; we call it explaining, or commiserating, or understanding a situation. But in fact when we are focused on what *others did* in a situation, we are giving ourselves a mental "out" and releasing ourselves from personal accountability.

Am I saying that others never do anything to affect your results? Of course not. What I am saying is that when you focus your attention on explaining your results due to someone else's behaviors, you are releasing yourself from some responsibility.

Let me be clearer: blame is a waste of time.

 To learn more about the five truths of blame, download this Bonus Byte at www.RLBonus.com using the keyword "blame."

BEING THE VICTIM. Blame often leads to another crippling problem: being the victim. First, we blame others (or external factors) for our predicament, and then we begin to feel sorry for ourselves.

Have you ever said, "I would have finished except the ballgame went into overtime"? Or, "If they had provided their part on time, we would have met the deadline"? Or, "They are always doing that to us. The numbers aren't right and that puts us behind"? These statements aren't too far, in reality, from, "It's not my fault; the dog ate my homework." In each of these and many other similar situations, we can choose to be a victim or look for what is in our control and take responsibility for it. If you knew you were going to watch the game and were going to wait until it was over to finish the report, perhaps you could have done more of it before the game; maybe you were cutting it too short on time. The game isn't in your control, but when you do your work is. In most cases, there is work you can do on your tasks that can be done before someone else gives you the other portion. If you do what you can when you can rather than relying on others to give you their portion, perhaps you get the complete task done sooner. If the numbers you receive are always wrong, perhaps you can see what you could do to help improve the accuracy of the numbers or at least plan for the fact that changes will have to be made each month.

The victim mentality can't exist without blame. And blame goes away when we continually think about what is inside our sphere of influence.

To learn more about the victim-accountability choice, download this Bonus Byte at www.RLBonus.com using the keywords "victim choice."

Your Now Steps

Here are some things you can do right now to strengthen your personal accountability. These are actions you can take at any time to change your perspective and remind you that holding others accountable can come only with the foundation of personal accountability:

1. Think about the last person, group, or situation you blamed. Ask yourself what role you played in creating the situation.

2. Stop reading right now and say out loud, "I am responsible!" five times. Repeat this phrase again later in the day. Affirming your responsibility is one way to remind yourself and build your belief and resolve.

3. Decide to be accountable. There is likely one task or project in front of you now that has significant issues or challenges. Decide today to do what is in your power to make it work. Don't think about any of the obstacles other than to acknowledge and accept them. Don't give the problems power over you. Decide to make it happen.

 Remarkable leaders take personal responsibility.

Sharing Responsibility (Delegating)

You may have started reading this chapter thinking delegation is where I would, or even should, start. You might have been thinking, "What I really need to do is stimulate some accountability in others. I'm not all that worried about myself." I am going to discuss sharing responsibility now, but I hope you realize why I started where I did. It is critically important to start inside and work out rather than just focusing externally.

In fact, an external focus is what causes much delegation to go wrong and gives delegation a bad name. Simply put, most delegation doesn't create anything close to remarkable results. Contrary to what leaders say, the major reason people don't delegate has nothing to do with the tasks they would be delegating or to whom they would be delegating. The biggest barriers to effectively sharing responsibility and opportunities with others are their own personal beliefs, values, and habits—for example:

○ "I don't have time to show someone else right now."

○ "It's just faster to do it myself."

○ "No one can live up to my quality standards." (Also expressed as, "If you want something done right, do it yourself.")

○ The belief that there is one best right way to do a task. (And I know what that way is.)

○ The need to be indispensable.

○ The need to be the hero.

○ The desire to earn the mythical badge for being perpetually busy.

○ The desire to look smart.

This is not a complete list, and so it may not include all of your personal beliefs, but before you dismiss them as quickly as you read them, think about your own willingness and ability to delegate and reflect on the list again.

Now that you have reviewed the list, have you noticed that none of those things is really about anyone but *us*? If we are going to effectively delegate and share responsibility, we must first really *want* to share that responsibility.

On the flip side are the things we are more than happy to delegate— often busywork or tasks we don't like to do at all. But the reasons we make this choice have very little to do with the person who is receiving the tasks; we are simply trying to offload these tasks from our list. Again, our motives are about us.

If you ask people to do a word association on the word *delegation*, many of the resulting words will have a negative connotation. In my conversations, most people (when thinking about it with their nonleader hat on) think of delegation as something done to them—a way for their boss, supervisor, or leader to take things off his or her plate. Few of the comments I heard mention delegation being a growth opportunity for the person receiving the work.

As a leader, there are times that you do need to delegate tasks to others. It isn't appropriate for you to do everything that comes your way. But the major barrier that gets in the way of your effectively delegating is yourself.

Turning the Vicious Cycle Around

I've outlined the issues related to the choices we make about delegation. When all of these factors are put together, they often manifest as the vicious cycle of delegation:

1. I'm busy too busy to delegate, so I will try to get by.
2. I know I should delegate, but it is faster to do it myself.
3. I'm getting buried, so I better get Joe to do that.
4. I quickly hand off the task to Joe, not giving very clear direction or expectations, because I don't have time and he'll figure it out.
5. Joe realizes that he has been given work not because it will be challenging or further his goals; in fact, it may be clear to Joe that he has just been dumped on.
6. Joe's attitude about this task, given these observations, may not be the best. And although he'll get the job done, it might not be with the enthusiasm or final result that I hoped for. I may well get minimum performance levels.
7. Which leads me to hesitate in delegating again.

And the cycle just continues, spiraling downward with you less willing to delegate and Joe feeling worse every time you do.

Granted that description may be a bit cynical, but it is more accurate than any of us wish it were. The good news is that it does not have to go this way. To fix it, you start with *you* and a new view of delegating. But since words are so powerful, let's not start with delegating; let's start our new cycle by replacing "delegation" with "sharing responsibility."

Sharing responsibility need not be any different from delegation if the delegation is done successfully and correctly. But delegating often feels like dumping or simply giving or assigning tasks. Sharing responsibility is much less about you and your needs and much more about sharing with the other person—sharing, *not* assigning. When you share responsibility, rather than quickly and perhaps incompletely assigning tasks of delegating, you have a much better chance to stimulate people's commitment and accountability for the outcome.

When we change our motives for handing tasks to others, we can change the vicious cycle to a virtuous one—for example:

1. I'm too busy to delegate, but I know that I have talented people who can do this task at least as well as I can.

2. I choose to invest the time to share this task, and the responsibility for it, with Joe.

3. It is going to take some time, but it will be time that reduces rework and helps Joe succeed, so I outline the goals, expectations, and boundaries with Joe, asking for his thoughts, ideas, and questions.

4. Joe takes the responsibility and integrates it into his work. He knows what success looks like and how this task fits into our overall goals.

5. Joe realizes that he has been given work that matters (even if the task is relatively small, he still sees how it fits into the organization's overall success) and that it has been entrusted to him. While he might already be busy, he feels good about both the communication and the opportunity that has been presented to him.

6. Joe succeeds with the task, maybe the first time or maybe with some coaching, but he now owns the task. He also has built the skills necessary to do this task in the future and the confidence to succeed with other new challenges as well.

7. And this overall success, even if I had to invest some more time at the start, leads me to want to share more responsibilities with Joe and others.

And the cycle begins again, spiraling upward with you more willing to share and Joe feeling better and having greater skills each time.

Sharing responsibility must start by looking inward at our beliefs and our motives rather than at the tasks or the people we might give those tasks to. It is only from these beliefs and motives that actions that promote accountability will emanate.

Your Now Steps

Here are some things you can do right now to strengthen the accountability and commitment of others by shifting from delegating to sharing responsibility. These actions will help you move into the virtuous cycle of responsibility sharing:

1. Devote some time to thinking about your beliefs and habits around delegating and sharing responsibility. Ask yourself what your first (or maybe knee-jerk) reaction to the idea of sharing responsibility is.

2. List the tasks or responsibilities that you could share for the benefit of yourself and others within your organization, those whom you will share those tasks with, and when that transfer can take place.

3. Pick one of the items you listed, and consciously start the virtuous cycle with someone or a team today. Recognize that if this is a very different approach than you have taken in the past, you may want to explain your approach to those with whom you are sharing the responsibility. As you change habits, they will be changing their habits too.

Remarkable leaders don't delegate; they share responsibility.

Empowering Others

What is the difference between delegation and empowerment? I posed that question to some of my closest colleagues and clients while writing this chapter. Although I didn't get a completely consistent answer, the general message was clear and consistent with what we have already explored about delegation and sharing responsibility.

Delegation is done *to* people and is more tangible in nature: we give people a task or the responsibility for a specific outcome. Empowerment is done *with* the other person or group and the organization in mind. When we empower people, we give them boundaries, but also the latitude to be successful in their own way.

By adjusting your approach to delegation to one of sharing responsibility, you have taken a big step on the path toward empowering others. However, that in itself doesn't get you all the way there. Five of the major steps toward that destination are you (again), boundaries, resources, latitude, and the other person or group.

You

Empowerment, like sharing responsibility, starts with your own beliefs and values. You must be willing to let go of things at an even higher level than when you share responsibility. Until you have the clear intent to value, support, develop, and aid others in making increasingly meaningful contributions to the organization, you won't be successful in empowering them.

Beyond believing that empowering others is logical, smart, and the right thing to do, you must also have a deep belief in the potential of those you are empowering. Chapter One discussed *your* potential. You now need to build that same empowering belief in others. When you know others have great potential, you will be more willing to share with and empower them because you have a deep belief that they will ultimately succeed.

Boundaries

Empowerment requires clear boundaries. Leaders often tell me that they have empowered others and yet they are frustrated. On deeper diagnosis, it is clear that leaders think they have empowered people simply by proclaiming them empowered. But a proclamation doesn't empower anyone.

When we empower people, they need to know the size of their sandbox. I use the word *sandbox* purposefully. When people feel they have been truly empowered, they are ready to play. They are engaged, committed, and ready to succeed, even if they are a bit apprehensive or feel that they are going to be challenged by what you have given them. By letting them know what is inside their sphere of influence, by letting them know how far they can go and how much of the work process or project they can affect, you reduce their anxiety and ramp up their excitement.

People or teams need to know how their work fits into the strategies of the organization. They need to know what is valued in the final result, and they need to know what success looks like. Providing these boundaries is about more than just the mechanical things like signing authorities and deadlines. The boundaries provide a jumping-off point for building commitment, engagement, and ownership.

Resources

Once people have been given some boundaries—the limits of their playing field—you need to provide the resources needed to be successful. If you have successfully empowered others, they will know the scope of their work and will have the money, tools, people, and other resources they need to succeed. The resource limits (for example, money or staffing) can be tight or challenging, but they need to be believable. And while people appreciate knowing when and why resources are tight, engaged and committed people can create miracles—often with fewer resources than others might have thought possible.

Latitude

Henry Ford couldn't have empowered people inside his organization to determine the color of Model A's because he had already decided. His famous quotation, "We'll make them any color as long as they are black," says it all. And yet every day there are leaders empowering people with a sandbox so small or restrictive that they are actually doing the opposite of empowering people: they are frustrating them by telling them one thing but doing something entirely different (actions speak much louder than words).

If you have truly empowered others, they know what authority they have. If they believe you have given them a project but you already have a specific decision or approach in mind, you won't get the results you hope for. As a remarkable leader, you must first make sure you don't have a specific approach or decision in mind when you are empowering others. (If you do, simply share the necessary responsibilities needed to reach your very specific target.) You know instead that true empowerment provides people the latitude to get to the outcome through whatever means they decide.

The Other Person or Group

So far we have looked at what you need to do to empower others. All of this is important; in fact, you can't have true empowerment without these things. But you could do all of these things flawlessly and still not have effectively empowered people. Even if you give power to others, they must be willing to accept it. They too must feel and be willing to be personally responsible. People often have been conditioned by their experiences both inside and outside your organization to follow orders or place blame or act as a victim—all things that get in their own way.

Overcoming this challenge will engage many of the skills we are discussing in this book, but it can be done. You can help people come to a place of accepting personal responsibility for their work and their results. And one of the most important first steps is what behaviors you model in your words and actions and in the questions you ask.

Empowerment is played together: you can't empower people without their accepting it. But did you notice that even when the responsibility is theirs, you still have a role to play? This is the overriding lesson of this chapter: it all comes back to you. You are at the root of creating accountable and engaged people and teams.

What About the Organization at Large?

You may be wondering why I haven't mentioned the culture that you work in. If you aren't the CEO or otherwise in charge at a high level, you may not feel empowered to address culture issues or approach leadership in this way. We'll look at that in the next section, but before we move on, recognize what is in your control. You can choose to share responsibility and empower others inside your sphere of influence or span of control, regardless of your organization's norms or expectations. As a remarkable leader, you will be accountable for what is in your control rather than feeling powerless because you can't influence everything around you.

Empowerment is a big, complex, and important concept. This short section is meant to further your thinking about empowerment, but it won't complete your understanding of it. As a remarkable leader, you recognize the power and leverage that empowerment provides. I encourage you to continue your learning on this important concept.

Your Now Steps

There are few things you can do today (and any other time) to have a greater impact on your results and success than empowering others:

1. Look at the most recent situation when you feel you empowered others. Consider the factors outlined in this chapter (boundaries, resources, and latitude), and evaluate if and how well you provided these things. If you didn't do this as well as you could have, schedule a time with those people to rectify those gaps.

2. Consider your own beliefs relating to empowerment. Be honest with yourself. If you truly want to empower others as discussed in this chapter and your beliefs are in alignment with that goal, spend some time thinking about your next steps. If you feel your beliefs are in alignment, use the steps in this section to match your actions to those beliefs.

3. Talk to those you have empowered (or will) about the concepts of personal responsibility. Share some of your reflections with them.

 Remarkable leaders know that empowerment is a two-way street.

Creating Cultural Accountability

Many of the organizations I work with lament the fact that there isn't enough accountability across their whole organization. This manifests itself in a variety of ways, including projects that are always behind schedule, meetings held to make decisions that individuals could have made themselves, managers and leaders not truly holding people account-able (though they say they have), and action items identified in meetings never getting completed.

Because these concerns are most often expressed to me by people who don't sit in the executive suite or serve as a part of senior leadership, the conversation usually ends with descriptions of their helplessness in resolving the situation. They tell me that they'd love to change that part of their culture, but they aren't senior management, and those are the only people who could make that change really happen. This situation is quite a paradox: people are telling me they aren't able to be accountable to be accountable.

Although you might be able to have more impact more rapidly if you are a senior leader, it really doesn't matter what your job title is. You *can* have an impact on organizational accountability from any place in the organization hierarchy. How? Just like everything else in this chapter, it starts with you.

As you begin to take the actions described in this chapter, you will be role-modeling the behaviors that create greater accountability. As you model that yourself and create those opportunities for others in areas where you have influence, you will be creating pockets of accountability. As a remarkable leader, you know that these actions will lead to more committed, engaged, and productive people. Rest assured that your ef-forts will be noticed. At first, you may be looked at quizzically, as is often the case when people see something new or unexpected. Don't let that bother you; recognize that it is a natural result of change. People likely will wonder and be resistant at first.

Whether you are leading the accounts payable department, the loading dock, the marketing group, all of human resources, or your lunch group, the productivity and morale gains you will inevitably see from creating a more accountable and empowered environment will be seen by others. You will have created a ripple in the organizational landscape that will be noticed.

I've always enjoyed watching large displays of dominos placed in in-tricate patterns being set in motion by knocking over just one piece. Hundreds or thousands of dominos fall predictably because one piece is put in motion. In most of these displays, the one piece that is tipped over first is at the start or top of the display. Most people believe the same is true for organizational culture: that change must naturally start from the top. Culture change (or any other change) can of course start at the top. But just as the dominos could all fall by starting in different places throughout the maze, the same is true in organizations. You can begin where you are. You can hold people accountable around you. Your team can hold each other accountable. A company culture is a sum of all of the individual parts within it. You can create change by starting where you are. In fact, where you are, regardless of your title or position, is the only place you can start anyway.

If you want more accountability, start around you. Recognize what is in your control, and get started. Tip *your* domino.

Your Now Steps

You can get started in adjusting organizational culture only by getting started yourself. Here are some things you can do today:

1. Remind yourself that you can make a difference through your actions. Take a step toward greater personal responsibility now.

2. Take action on the other Now Steps in this chapter. Remember that cultural change can start with you.

3. Begin your next meeting on time.

4. At the next meeting you attend, ensure that every action item identified has an owner and an agreed-to time line. This action of making people responsible for the actions that come out of a meeting is an important step.

 To get ten specific tips and techniques for increasing accountability in meetings, download this Bonus Byte at www.RLBonus.com using the keywords "meeting accountability."

Remarkable Principle ▷ **Remarkable leaders know that they can have a positive impact on organizational culture, and they do.**

Some Final Thoughts

I hope that the key message of this chapter is clear. It all starts with you. You must be personally responsible. You must model these important behaviors for others. You won't be successful at these skills—skills critical if you want to build a highly productive, committed, and engaged team—unless you believe in the power and potential of others and then support its development through your actions.

There is far more to learn about these important topics than what I've been able to share in this short chapter. As a remarkable leader, you know that your growth and development are continual.

Go to remarkableleadershipbook.com/resources for more information, writing, tools, and other highly recommended resources to help you learn more about accountability and responsibility and how to engender it in others and throughout your organization.

15

REMARKABLE LEADERS MANAGE PROJECTS AND PROCESSES SUCCESSFULLY

MUCH HAS BEEN WRITTEN ABOUT project and process management in the past several years. Those who are invested in project management feel that more project work will increasingly be the norm. People will be assigned to project teams as needed, and work will be built around the structure of those projects. At the same time, several management theorists have espoused the view that all work is a process, and therefore work should be built around and analyzed from the perspective of the flow of work process steps. This view of "all work is a process" is a major underpinning of the quality movement that reshaped Japanese business and became popular in the United States in the 1980s and 1990s.

Before we go any further, let's define these two terms.

The Project Management Institute's Body of Knowledge defines a *project* as "a temporary endeavor undertaken to create a unique product, service, or result" (2004, p. 2). Four specific points should be drawn from this definition:

○ Projects have a defined and definite beginning and ending.

○ Projects are undertaken for specific purposes.

○ Projects have a customer (and likely other stakeholders).

○ There are best practices to help anyone manage project work more successfully.

It follows that project management is the application of these best practices to develop a project plan that will meet (or exceed) the requirements of the customers or other stakeholders.

At first, a *process* seems to be the opposite of a project. A work process is an ongoing series of steps that are repeatable. Processes usually contain a series of handoffs between internal suppliers and customers who together work together to reach the desired outcome. *Process management* is the management of these steps, improving them as appropriate, to ensure successful delivery of the end products.

Given those definitions, most people usually start wondering, "Is my work generally a project or a process?" I believe that is the wrong question. Is there work that is project oriented? Of course, and a case could be made that more work is designed this way than ever before. But if this is the case, it doesn't reduce the importance of process work. In fact, the management of projects themselves is a work process and can be improved using the tools of process improvement.

Remarkable leaders know there are skills in both of these areas that will have an important positive impact on the results they can produce. The rest of this chapter will help you think about these different but closely related skills.

Self-Assessment

Here is a quick assessment to help you think about your skills as a relationship builder. Use the following scale of 1 to 7 on each question:

1. Almost never

2. Rarely or seldom

3. Occasionally

4. Sometimes

5. Usually

6. Frequently

7. Almost always

I use the basic tools of project management.	_____
I provide project leadership.	_____
Projects I lead are seen as successful.	_____
I support and personally seek to improve processes.	_____
I think of processes and process improvements from the perspective of the customer.	_____
I seek process improvement ideas and help to implement them.	_____

Using Basic Project Management Skills

My goal with this chapter isn't to make you a remarkable project manager; rather, it is to help you think about your role as a leader as it relates to project management. Some leaders have project management as a big part of their role, and others less so, but remarkable leaders understand that project management is an important skill set and prioritize their learning in this area based on the relative frequency with which they use these skills.

Planning

Although some people are naturally open to and adept at planning, in my experience most people have a love-hate relationship with this activity. We know it is necessary but typically don't do it enough. When debriefing training exercises that have a planning component built in, participants almost always feel they should have spent more time planning—even if I had provided time specifically for planning and they chose not to use it.

In short, you can't manage projects successfully without planning. Every text I've read, every expert I've spoken with, and every experience I've had suggests the same thing: planning is the most important activity for a successful project manager. This planning needs to be detailed enough for both execution and communication, it must be systematic to ensure that everything is covered, and it must involve the team that will be completing the work.

The planning doesn't stop once the project is formulated and kicked off. We all know that events and projects often don't occur as we expect them to (or plan for them). So when the real world interferes with the plan, we must make adjustments, which means we must take replanning as seriously as preplanning.

The Three Dimensions of Success

Projects are successful when all project deliverables are completed on time, within budget, and at a level of quality that is acceptable to all stakeholders and sponsors. As a project manager you must focus on these three—schedule, budget, and quality—at all times. One of the biggest challenges (in fact, a major reason that a project manager is needed) is continually balancing those three dimensions.

There's an old adage that says you can easily get two of the three project management dimensions: you can get something cheap and fast at poor quality; you can get it cheap at high quality, but it will take forever; or you can get it fast and at high quality, but you'll pay for it.

When you build your project on a foundation of planning, you allow yourself a much better chance of successfully balancing those dimensions.

Use of a Model

Projects, even small ones, are complex. It is important to employ proven strategies rather than reinventing the wheel each time we begin to work on a new project. Most professional disciplines have models that help define the creation of a work product. When you compare your professional model to a model of project management, you will likely find great parallels. If you don't, take the models within your world and incorporate best practices from the science of project management, and you will be pleased with your results.

There are certifications and many training opportunities to help you become more proficient at the process of project management. The Project Management Institute (http://pmi.org) is a great place to start. That organization's best practices are compiled in the PMIBOK (Project Management Institute's Body of Knowledge, 2004), which outlines a five-step model that will correlate with any model you find. It arranges all of the work of project management into five groupings identified by the acronym IPECC: initiating, planning, executing, controlling, and closing:

> *Initiating.* An identified project is determined to be feasible, a project manager is selected, and a project charter is created.
>
> *Planning.* We've talked about this, so it shouldn't be a surprise.
>
> *Executing.* After adequate planning, the project work begins.
>
> *Controlling.* Here you keep the project moving or under control, dealing with any unexpected challenges or delays or other issues as they arise. This also is where project leadership becomes critical.
>
> *Closing.* This is the step for reviewing deliverables, determining lessons learned, and doing any other close-out work related to the project.

This overview of project management isn't designed to develop you into a world-class project manager, but rather to keep you focused on the most important factors related to creating successful projects. View these concepts as a starting point, and keep them in focus regardless of the amount of time you spend on project management, and you will be on the road to remarkable.

Your Now Steps

These steps will help you improve your project management skills immediately:

1. Make a list of all of the projects you are involved in, small or large, regardless of the role you play in each.

2. Consider one of those projects that is early in its life cycle, or one you know needs help, and apply some thoughtful planning time to it. You may not be able to drop what you are working on now and do all of the necessary planning, but you can take ten minutes right now to outline the next level of planning that is required.

3. Consider the three dimensions of project success for one of your projects, and work on balancing the dimensions. If you identify a challenge, work on it.

 Remarkable leaders use proven project management skills.

Providing Project Leadership

George had taken training in project management. He had learned all of the fundamentals, and his projects were more successful than in the past, but he knew something was missing: the talented people on his project team weren't as connected and committed to the project as he would like, and the results weren't what they could be. Over the course of several months, he began to understand that successful projects require more than management: they require leadership.

Beyond the scope and requirements, and time lines and milestones, and underneath the updates and Gantt charts lie the people working on the project. Project leadership focuses on the people, their challenges and opportunities, and how they create successful projects. I wrote about project management first because these skills and tools are the critical initial components of success, but it is project leadership that will take you from successful to remarkable.

Project leadership can be viewed as a microcosm of everything in this book: communication skills, team skills, and all of the other concepts. All apply to project leadership as well as any other leadership context, but here we explore some of these keys specifically in the project context.

Create a Clear Vision

A project manager creates a project charter or some other document to outline the deliverables, team members, stakeholders, and other important facts for any project. This is a critical document, but it doesn't create a vision. Remarkable leaders know they must do more than create the charter or contract; they must create a compelling vision of project success in the minds of the whole team. People need to know the context of the problem, the pain of the customer, and the benefits that a successful project will produce. The benefits could include monetary incentives for the team (for example, a bonus for project success or "we all get to keep our paychecks"). However, the vision needs to be more complete and customer focused than just what's in it for the team members themselves.

 For a list of tips to help you create clear team visions, download this Bonus Byte at www.RLBonus.com using the keywords "project vision."

Keep Focused on Customers

Much project management literature refers to *stakeholders* and *sponsors* rather than *customers*. In this case, I am using *customers* in a global way to include all of the people and groups who are interested in or will benefit from the project's results. In the daily grind of project work, it is easy to lose sight of why a project is being done and what the definitions of success are (beyond finishing).

Remarkable leaders keep the customer's needs and desires at the forefront of their team's mind, knowing that this will help keep them focused on the most important outcomes. When this focus is combined with a compelling vision, you have created an environment that allows people to truly excel in a project team. Remember that we are talking about customers in the global sense, so the customer for your project could be a client or other externally focused relationship, or internal customers, stakeholders, or management sponsors.

Remove Obstacles

As your project teams do their work, they will encounter obstacles from inside the project, other parts of the organization, and external forces. Obstacles can be resource constraints, changing expectations, or pressures of any kind. Your role as a project leader is to clear the obstacles from the path of your team members.

Removing obstacles can be as big a challenge as the obstacle itself. Not only do you have to be in tune with what is happening with your team (if you don't know what obstacles your team is facing, it will be hard to remove them), but you also must recognize obstacle removal as one of your most important roles. Staying in tune with your team can be very difficult if the team spans the country, continent, or world, and the larger your project team grows, the harder it becomes. Obstacles can come from anywhere, and they can be real obstacles (for example, not enough time, people, money, or other resources) or perceived ones (for example, we don't have universal approval for doing this project, my kids are sick and I can't be here today, it's too hot in this office for me to concentrate). Whatever the obstacles, when they are removed, people can focus on their project work.

Provide Encouragement, Energy, and Engagement

Many times, projects are long and grueling, and those working on them can get burned out as they work harder and harder to keep up with the deliverables in front of them. In the crush of the work, encouragement is often forgotten. As a leader, this is your job. You are often in the best position to see when people need encouragement.

Often people's energy gets sapped by the amount and nature of the work involved. All of the steps above—providing a vision, helping them see how their work matters, removing obstacles—can infuse energy into people and their project. Notice that if you do your work successfully as a leader by creating a clear vision, the rest of the steps will come more easily. It is easier to focus on customers when the big picture is clear. It is easier to identify obstacles when the focus is clear, and when people are already working successfully, there are clearly going to be more things to encourage people about.

In the end, though, all of these project leadership activities help create an internal sense of meaning and purpose for the team members. That is the essence of project leadership: by getting people to own the work, they will create their own energy through their personal engagement in and pride for the project and its outcomes.

Your Now Steps

Here are some things you can do right now to strengthen your skills as a project leader. These are actions you can take at any time to remind you of your project role beyond managing the tasks:

1. Make a list of all of the projects you are involved in, small or large, regardless of the role you play in each. (This is the same task from earlier in this chapter. If you have already made your list, you have taken this first step.)

2. If one of your projects is just starting, make sure you create a clear picture of the desired future with the project team. If you are past this step, be willing to step back and do that if you see major disconnects between people and the vision, or if you see people merely going through the motions. Building this clear vision is critical, and there is no time like the present to do this.

3. Find someone right now to encourage. Share some positive feedback or simply encourage the team member by saying how much you appreciate him or her and his or her contributions to the success of the project.

 Remarkable leaders do more than manage projects; they lead them.

Viewing Work as a Process

Work is rarely a discrete set of steps unconnected to something else. Rather, the output of one person's work is delivered to someone else, who uses it as an input to the next step. Most work also is repeatable. Since we seldom do anything just once, we have work processes (whether documented and managed or not) that exist and need to be understood. Once they are understood, they can be systematized and improved. Understanding work as a process and operating using this philosophy can open the door for phenomenal improvements in productivity and results.

Here's an example. All businesses make sales in some way. Regardless of your product or service, at some point a salesperson takes (or the customer places) an order. Once the order has been placed, a number of steps must be taken:

1. Order placed
2. Order reviewed
3. Inventory determined
4. Inventory reduced
5. Product shipped

6. Invoice created

7. Invoice mailed

8. Accounts receivable adjusted

9. Payment received

10. Order or invoice closed

Depending on the nature of your business, these steps might be automated or they might look a little different, but when you see them spelled out, it is hard to argue with the fact that the work is a process—even if you run your own business and do all of these steps yourself.

Don't dismiss this thought as either too regimented or passé. Creating a team or organization that truly understands the nature of work as a process and providing that team with tools for documenting, understanding, and improving their processes are the best ways to create ownership and engagement in work. When people understand how they fit into and contribute to the success of the organizational effort, they are much more likely to become remarkable contributors themselves.

Customer and Supplier

At the heart of a process is that every task requires input and creates outputs. When you receive an input, you are someone else's customer. When you add value to that input and hand it off to someone else as your output, you become the supplier, and that other person or team is *your* customer (Figure 15.1).

Figure 15.1 is a simple concept but an extremely powerful way to represent work. When people see their work as an input to someone else's work, they have additional reasons to take pride in it and do their best. Also, when they realize that they are a customer for the work of others, it empowers them to ask for what they need to improve the inputs they receive.

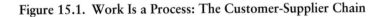

Figure 15.1. Work Is a Process: The Customer-Supplier Chain

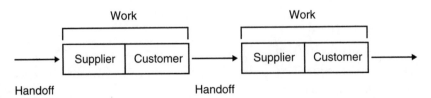

As a leader, you can ensure that those you lead see work in this way; then you can create conversations about internal customer and supplier relationships (discussed in Chapter Nine), as well as help people see more clearly how their work fits into the ultimate delivery of products or services to the external or paying customer.

The Context of Work

Providing this mental framework of work as a process gives people greater context or perspective for their own work and is the first step to helping to create individual alignment with organizational goals. Remarkable leaders want individuals to see the big picture of the organization regardless of the work that they do—from executive to janitor, marketer to administrator.

When people have this context of the bigger picture, they will make better independent decisions relating to their work and the adjustments of their own work processes. Providing this perspective is an underappreciated way of unleashing people's engagement by helping them see how they fit into the bigger picture.

Your Now Steps

Here are some things you can do right now to spread the concept of work as a process. These are actions you can take at any time to remind yourself and others of the value of thinking of work from a process perspective:

1. Using Figure 15.1 as a guide, identify a work process you are involved in, and create a high-level work flow of the steps. Don't include the details; just list the big chunks of work done by each person or department throughout the process. Either create this with the help of your group or team, or get their feedback after you have taken a first pass.
2. Identify your personal customers and suppliers on the diagram.
3. Have a conversation with one of your customers (internal or external) to discuss how you are performing compared to his or her needs and expectations.
4. Lead the process of steps 2 and 3 with others on your team.
5. Continue building process blocks to take the process all the way to its final completion.

Remarkable leaders see work as a process and lead based on that picture.

Enabling Process Improvement

Two things are required for process improvement: the realization that you have a process and the recognition that it could be simplified, streamlined, or otherwise improved. Your role is to create an awareness of both because everyone will be involved in process improvement efforts. As leaders, it is not our role to do process improvement for others; instead, we need to provide team members with the skills, experience, and opportunity to do it themselves.

A Basic Process Improvement Methodology

There are some fundamental pieces of any process improvement model:

1. Identify the process to improve.
2. Identify the customers of the output of the process.
3. Understand the needs of those customers (either internal or external).
4. Understand and document the current work process.
5. Determine the gaps or opportunity areas.
6. Identify areas for improvement.
7. Test those improvements to make sure they can be done and really are improvements.

There are many different models for process improvement, but they all can be boiled down to this fundamental set of tasks. You need to understand these steps, apply them yourself, and help others apply them as well.

 For a list of tips for facilitating these basic steps, download this Bonus Byte at www.RLBonus.com using the keywords "process improvement."

Allowing Your Methodology to Work

Knowing a model or being able to improve your own work processes isn't enough. You must create a whole cadre of people willing and able to do process improvement. There are some basic things required to make that happen:

○ *Training.* Whatever your model or methodology, people need training in order to use it. Effective training teaches the method, provides the tools, and creates the confidence to use the methods effectively in the workplace.

○ *Time.* Have you ever attended training, left excited to try it, and returned to work with no time to implement? It happens far too often. Remarkable leaders know that they are better off not providing the training at all if people won't have the opportunity to apply what they have learned.

○ *Resources.* Time may be the biggest resource people will need, but they may need other resources too, like backup (to cover for them while they are working on process improvement) or meeting space. Provide the resources, or your efforts to improve processes likely will fall short of your expectations.

○ *Belief and support.* Throughout this book, I've noted the importance of believing in the potential, value, and skills of those you lead. This is another time when that belief is critical. You must believe that your processes can be improved and that people will succeed in finding those improvements—both the small, incremental ones and the huge breakthroughs. Your expectations of people and the support and encouragement you provide them is at least as important as any training you provide.

○ *Flexibility and empowerment.* Although I have listed this last, it could come first. Ask yourself if you are willing to live with the changes people may identify in their work processes. Are you willing to let them do it a new way? Are you willing to fully empower them with the responsibility for improving their work? If not, do not start down this path. You will do far more damage to commitment, morale, and confidence by asking for help and then not allowing it to proceed than if you never asked at all.

Holding On to Improvements

The methodology described leaves out the final piece of the process improvement puzzle: locking in the improvements. Lots of people find ways to improve things. They look at their small piece of the process and make adjustments. Too often, unfortunately, those gains are lost, due to one of three factors:

1. *The changes weren't documented and standardized.* If people change or improve processes but don't document them or if they allow themselves to slide back into the old methods out of habit, the effort and improvement are lost.

2. *The ideas weren't shared and therefore replicated by others.* Especially in large organizations, improvements in one location or department often aren't shared as organizational improvements. Sharing those improvements across departmental or geographical boundaries will maximize the benefits of the improvements and improve the chances of those improvements sticking for the long term.

3. *The changes improved one person's work but not the entire process.* Sometimes a person or small group will work on improving their processes, but do so in isolation from the larger work process. When this happens, the work can be so internally focused that what appears to be an improvement may actually be to the detriment of the overall process.

As a leader, we can address each of these issues, and we must do so. It isn't enough for teams or individuals to make a process improvement. The work isn't done until they have locked in those gains every time the process is used.

Your Now Steps

Here are some things you can do right now to enable process improvement within your group:

1. Look for low-hanging fruit. Do you have an often-used or critical work process? Get the people together who do that work, and have them look for issues that could be easily resolved. Chances are that one or more things will be found that will improve the speed or quality of the task or reduce the effort expended to do it.

2. Identify some process improvement training to give to your team. Although this might not be a step you can complete quickly, you can begin the identification process rapidly. Try a Web search or visit our Web site (KevinEikenberry.com) for some suggestions.

3. Think about times when improvements have been made in the past, and notice if those are still in place. If they are not, start investigating why

they aren't. Once you have diagnosed a reason, work on eliminating that reason in the future.

 Remarkable leaders support and enable process improvement.

Some Final Thoughts

Projects and processes get to the core of our work and how we do it. As a remarkable leader, you must understand these concepts and support their application, regardless of your level within the organization. As a senior leader, you may feel this material is too elementary or not something you would personally be involved with. You would be wrong.

Can a singer sing without knowing the scales? Can a football team be successful if the players can't block and tackle? Can a salesperson be successful if he can't build rapport with customers? Managing projects and processes are fundamental skills. Without them, many of the other competencies in this book will be less effective.

 Go to remarkableleadershipbook.com/resources for more information, writing, tools, and other highly recommended resources to help you learn more about project and process management.

16

REMARKABLE LEADERS SET GOALS AND SUPPORT GOAL ACHIEVEMENT

ON MAY 25, 1961, in Houston, Texas, President John F. Kennedy gave one of his most famous speeches. Often called "the man on the moon" speech, the president made some remarkable statements:

> I believe that this nation should commit itself to achieving the goal, before this decade is out, of landing a man on the moon and returning him safely to the earth. No single space project in this period will be more impressive to mankind, or more important for the long-range exploration of space; and none will be so difficult or expensive to accomplish.

Imagine: putting a man on the moon in less than nine years.

But there is much more to this story than a bold proclamation of a goal (perhaps one of the boldest publicly stated goals ever). Being a skilled, goal-setting leader, President Kennedy had consulted with the best scientific experts of the time to determine if his bold goal was possible. In addition, his speech outlined the purposes for the goal, the benefits that would be received when we achieved it, and the resources required to accomplish it. (Incidentally, the budget for advanced man-in-space projects in 1961 was $6 million. In the speech, the president pledged an additional $500 million, and by 1963 this one part of NASA's budget was $863 million.)

Without this goal, would a person have walked on the moon? We'll never know for sure, but I'd be willing to bet the answer is no, even more than forty years later. After all, by all accounts, the Soviet Union was way ahead of the United States in the space race at that time–and no cosmonaut has yet stood on the moon's surface.

Without that bold goal, the marshaling of resources, and the tight time line, political and economic factors likely would have gotten in the way; leaders and priorities would have changed. Without that speech and that goal, if an American astronaut had walked on the moon by now, you can be sure it would not have been by July 1969.

You may never set a goal as monumental and world changing as Kennedy did on that day in 1961. But that doesn't change the importance of goals and goal setting to all leaders. Nor does it change the value of the lessons we can learn from President Kennedy and his speech.

Self-Assessment

Here is a quick assessment to help you think about your skills as a relationship builder. Use the following scale of 1 to 7 on each question:

1. Almost never
2. Rarely or seldom
3. Occasionally
4. Sometimes
5. Usually
6. Frequently
7. Almost always

> I set goals. _____
>
> I help my teams set goals. _____
>
> I support the goals of my teams and provide the resources they need to succeed. _____
>
> I help people see the big picture. _____
>
> I believe in and help others believe in their goals. _____
>
> I provide a process that teams can use to set and reach their goals. _____

The Importance of Goal Setting

Maybe President Kennedy read Maxwell Maltz's now famous book *Psycho-Cybernetics* (1960). Maltz gave us the most important key to goal setting when he wrote, "Man is by nature a goal-striving being. And because man is 'built that way' he is not happy unless he is functioning as he was made to function—as a goal striver. Thus true success and true happiness not only go together, but each enhances the other"(p. xvi). Goals work because, as Maltz said, we are "built that way."

The practical importance of goals goes beyond our psychological need for them. From a leadership perspective, goals are the ultimate productivity enhancer: they provide focus, direction, and (we hope) meaning to our work. Goals allow us to move from a state of activity to the point of accomplishment, where our work leads to valuable results. And if these are not reason enough, it is important as a leader to remember that goal achievement can create great satisfaction and confidence. These elements cannot be underestimated as factors to future improvement and success, as well as team morale and retention.

It takes more than recognizing the importance of goal setting to set goals successfully. Many people, teams, and organizations set goals, but their results are less than stellar due to mind-set problems. The five keys listed in the sidebar will make all the difference between goals set and goals achieved. As a leader, you lead the way in building this mind-set. Build it for yourself, and you will, through your communications and actions, begin to build it in those who work with you.

KEYS TO A SUCCESSFUL GOAL-SETTING MIND-SET

- *Size*. Goals must be large enough to be inspiring and yet believable enough to be achieved. (President Kennedy didn't state his goal without knowing there was some scientific possibility of success.)

- *Belief*. Everyone involved in the achievement of the goal must believe it's possible. That belief must start with you, the leader. (President Kennedy worked tirelessly to build that belief both before and after the speech.)

- *Investment*. People must be willing to invest the resources required to achieve the goal; that investment typically starts with you as the leader. (President Kennedy invested the money and committed the people who would be required to reach his large goal.)

- *Commitment*. Commitment is everything. Once the first three keys are in place, though, it is much easier to achieve across the team. (President Kennedy built a structure and organization that reinforced the commitment to the goal.)

> ○ *Action.* Setting a new goal and then continuing business as usual won't lead to goal achievement. Positive, directed, focused action is required.

Before we get to the nuts and bolts—the skills of this chapter—one more key to successful goal setting must be examined: purpose. President Kennedy gave the United States a purpose when he set his large goal. Dr. Martin Luther King Jr. stated his purpose with, "I have a dream ..." Andrew Carnegie drove many of his business pursuits based on the purpose of giving as much wealth back to the community as possible.

President Kennedy's purpose was stated more completely as a goal, while the others were more visionary and less goal specific. Purpose can be divided into specific goals. As the examples show, purpose itself should focus on the desired end result. Only with the desired outcome as a starting point can the specific means (step-by-step goals) be developed.

While I'll examine more about purpose when we discuss alignment later in this chapter, I share these thoughts here because this is where people often get stuck. Any leader can state a lofty purpose, but unless real goal setting and real work are placed behind that purpose, those words are empty and lost. One only has to think about Martin Luther King Jr.'s purpose and wonder how much more progress might have been made toward it had his life not ended so prematurely. Purpose matters, and it will be much more powerful when followed up with a goal-setting process that can focus energy toward that purpose.

> **PURPOSE IN ACTION**
> In 1989, Ken Derr became chairman of Chevron Corporation. Soon after, he stated a new purpose for the company and described his vision as the company becoming "Better Than the Best." As a Chevron employee at that time, I noticed much initial skepticism and confusion regarding this statement. People argued that it didn't mean anything, that it was just a slogan, and that it was hard to know what to do if you didn't know what the best was. During Derr's eleven-year tenure as chairman, I watched (partly as an employee and largely as an external consultant) the impact of his "Better Than the Best" purpose. It certainly was met with

some initial cynicism (as are many visionary ideas), but due to a belief, investment, and commitment to this idea, Derr's purpose had a significant impact on both organizational culture and financial results. Over time, through conversation and much communication, employees developed a vision of what "Better Than the Best" meant, and it played a role in the formation of strategies at more than just the corporate level, but for individual teams and groups. What started seemingly as a slogan became a point of reference, a source of pride, and the touchstone for actions that molded and improved the company for more than a decade.

If you want to improve your results, use a goal-setting process.

Personal Goal Setting

The importance and virtues of personal goal setting to our own growth should be obvious, especially to you as a reader of this type of book. So although this chapter is not a complete text on personal goal setting, it provides the foundation so you can be a highly successful goal setter. As a leader, you must think of yourself as a goal-setting role model. How can you help others develop goals and coach them on their goal-setting process if you aren't doing these things yourself?

If you want to be remarkable as a leader or in any other facet of your life, the fastest way to reach your vision is to become more skilled in setting goals. But more important than the exact method or model that you follow is that you *find a model and follow it*. No method will be successful if it remains in the book, in another resource, or on your to-do list.

Have you been stopped in the goal-setting process before? Have you known that you needed to set goals or wanted to set goals, but you either spent your time searching for ways to do the process or were stymied by the process you found?

If this is your current dilemma or past experience, download this Bonus Byte at www.RLBonus.com using the keywords "getting started."

Goal-Setting Basics

When you are ready to take action, follow these steps to set a goal and, more important, develop a process you can use to reach those goals you set. Once you have these components in place, creating the complete plan (or for a larger goal, one part of the new plan) will be easy.

Step One: Consider Your Dream, and Write It Down

The best question I know to start with is, "What is my fondest wish?" Let's say you need a new car. You should start with the fondest wish question. If your fondest wish is a jet black BMW 540i, then make that your goal. Too often people make the goal "buy a new car" or "buy a Buick." Why do they pick a Buick? (And before you write me a letter about your Buick, know that I don't think there is *anything* wrong with Buicks—unless your fondest wish is a BMW.) Is it because they think the Buick is possible, or practical, or (insert your own excuse, or the rationalization you've heard from someone else here)? The best goal-setting process starts with what we really want. The same applies in business. If you are setting a goal for service times, what is your fondest wish? What service time would make a real difference with customers, your team, or the bottom line? Regardless of the type of goal you are setting, get your dreams written down.

Step Two: Create a Specific, Tangible Goal Statement

Dreams are not goals. Rather, they are like a purpose and are motivating and inspiring. Goals are the specific statements that, when achieved, help you reach your dreams. This step is the translation of dreams into tangible, clear, actionable, and measurable statements. They should always be written as a present-tense description of a desired future state. Here are a few examples:

- On October 30, 2008, I will weigh 178 pounds.
- I smile as I turn the ignition key in my new jet black BMW 540i on September 10, 2008.
- I enjoy the feeling as I walk across the stage to be awarded my M.B.A. in spring 2009.

Notice that although each statement follows a slightly different format, all are desired, all are specific and tangible, and all are stated in the present tense. Why are these factors so important?

Your brain is designed to solve problems. When you state your goal in this way, you are setting up a gap between what you have and what you want. The more clearly defined this gap is, the easier it is for your brain to close the gap. So you have to build a picture— a description of what it is that you want, what it looks like, what it feels like, what it tastes like, and what it's like to really achieve this goal.

You've probably heard or read about processes that say that if you have a goal to acquire something, have a clear picture of it: put a picture of that car on your refrigerator, or post the blueprints for your remodeled kitchen on the kitchen wall. Those great suggestions are related to this idea of clearly and specifically visualizing a picture of what you really want.

The more specific you can make it, the more your brain's conscious and subconscious efforts will be put in motion to close that gap. Make it detailed, make it specific, and make it about what you want, not about what you don't want.

STATING YOUR GOALS POSITIVELY

When my children were younger, I didn't want them to play in the street (I don't really want that now that they are older either!). One day I found myself saying, "Don't go in the street, don't go in the street, don't go in the street." Unfortunately, this was not the best possible approach.

Our brains are not designed to think about the negative of an idea. So when I said, "Don't go in the street," what my children's brains were hearing was, in effect, "in the street, in the street, in the street." When I recognized what I was doing, I started saying some variation of, "Stay on this side of the sidewalk." If they stay on this side of the sidewalk, will they achieve the ultimate goal? Absolutely. I've put it in a positive frame of what I want as opposed to what I don't want.

If your goal is to lose weight, don't say, "My goal is to lose twelve pounds," because then the focus is on twelve pounds. Instead, set the goal to describe what you want to weigh. What is your desired future weight? Or what is your desired future revenue for the business? What is your desired future profitability for that product line? What is your desired future in terms of team productivity?

State your goal in terms of what you want, not what you don't want.

Step Three: List the Benefits You'll Acquire

Technically after step 2, you have set your goal. The rest of these steps are actually about goal *getting*—planning for and achieving the goal that you've set. A lot of people never set goals or don't set them successfully. Setting them is important, but it is only one step in the process. Next, you need to build a plan for getting them. The first step in that process is to think about how you will benefit from achieving it. What will the benefits be when you reach your weight loss goal? How will you feel, look, and be different as a result? When setting a personal goal, most of these benefits will likely be personal. When setting a professional or business goal, make sure to consider benefits to the business, the team, the customer, and anyone else who is relevant. This builds your motivation to achieve the goal; thinking about this ahead of time sets you up to succeed. Write down a list of these benefits.

Step Four: Identify the Barriers

Now it's time to roll up your sleeves and get started. If all your goals were easy to achieve, you would already have the results. If they were easy to achieve, there would be few obstacles and challenges. But when you identify those challenges up front and see what the mountain ahead looks like, you put yourself in a much better place to get past it. At this stage, you may hear yourself saying things like, "You can't reach this goal because of this, this, this, this, and this." Once you hear those voices, write down all of the this, this, this, this, and thises. Then you will recognize which are real and which are perceived. Either way, once they're written down, they are exposed and identified, and you can purposefully build a plan to eliminate or overcome them.

Step Five: Identify the Resources Required

Just like President Kennedy when he set the goal of a man on the moon, you must identify the resources required to succeed. What will you need? How much money will be required? The nature of the resources will vary greatly based on your goal. But asking this question is an important part of your goal-planning process.

Step Six: Identify What You Need to Learn

I'm guessing that the most important resources you will need are new knowledge and skills. Identify what those skills are, and recognize what knowledge will be required. Determine what learning you will need. Remember that a goal change is required, and underneath all successful change is learning. Identify what you need to learn, what you need to know, what you need to change, and how it relates to achieving the goal. Then determine how you will achieve this learning. It may require a training course, a new certification, knowledge in a specific book, the help of a mentor, or any of many other approaches. As you move toward your goal, you may identify other things you need to learn, and you can add those at that point. Your challenge now is to create an initial plan, and plans can always be updated and modified.

Step Seven: Set a Date

Because we are so busy with so many competing priorities, we raise our chances of success in goal achievement when we place a deadline on it. Always set a date.

Step Eight: Get Committed

You need to commit to your goal. When you are 100 percent committed, your chances for goal achievement skyrocket.

 To get a template of these steps for goal setting and getting, download this Bonus Byte at www.RLBonus.com using the keywords "goal template."

I started this section by saying that personal goal-setting skills are critical for you as a leader. If you want others to set individual or team goals, you must first role-model that behavior. These steps will work for you within any organizational goal-setting process.

Your Now Steps

Here are some things you can do right now to begin improving your personal goal-setting process. This is a great opportunity to be selfish and work on something you really care about. Remember that learning to use this process for yourself will make you far more successful in using it as a leader:

1. Use the steps outlined in this section for setting a personal goal. It can be in a professional context, but make sure it is your goal.

2. Ask the fondest wish question now (or as soon as you possibly can). Allow yourself to dream, and write down your fondest wishes in the life area you have chosen.

3. Take advantage of the momentum you have gained in steps 1 and 2 by completing the rest of the planning steps within forty-eight hours.

 Remarkable leaders set (and reach) goals.

The Goal-Setting Leader

Once you have mastered the goal-setting steps for yourself, it is easy to translate those steps into your work as a leader. Remember that as a leader, your job is to help other people reach their goals. To reach this objective, you have three basic roles to play: creating a vision, setting collaborative goals, and providing ongoing support.

Creating the Vision

A typical organizational approach is for leaders to decide on the goals and then communicate those goals to the people who will be responsible for achieving them. Based on what you have learned in this chapter, you should already know that isn't going to be the most successful approach. To be the most motivating, team goals must be co-created by the team. However, to be the most successful, those goals must be placed in context. As the leader, you provide that context. How much time have you spent thinking about:

o Your fondest wishes for your team?

o The future of your industry?

o Technological changes that might impact you?

o New opportunities?

You get the idea: you are your team's Dr. Martin Luther King Jr. If you are a vice president, director, or C-level executive, this certainly is meant for you. But make no mistake: this is also meant for you if you are a first-line supervisor or don't even hold a typical leadership position within your organization yet. No one is in a better position to create that vision for your team or department than you are.

Collaborative Goal Setting

I have already noted that your job as a leader is to help people reach *their* goals. The key word in that sentence is italicized. Again, to be the most motivating and successful, the goals must belong to the people responsible for creating the results.

FOUR REASONS TO SET GOALS COLLABORATIVELY

1. *To gain agreement.* When everyone has the same goal, you can take advantage of clarity and focus. Strive for agreements on the goals themselves, and ensure that everyone agrees they are the right goals for the team. (See Chapter Twelve for more information.)

2. *To set collective consciousness.* Once the goal is clear, people will begin to look for opportunities related to the goal, see the goal being achieved, and create new connections that spark goal achievement.

3. *To create engagement.* When people are engaged in a common task or goal, their commitment, ownership, and buy-in will grow.

4. *To manifest synergy.* By getting a group to collectively work on a goal, you are hoping for the sum to equal far more than the total of the parts.

Use the framework we've already discussed (and you've already begun to put into action) to create group goals. Start with your vision, and allow others to add to, expand on, and talk about that vision and its impact on the group. Recognize that your vision may not be perfect or complete, and be open to the ideas that come from the group conversation.

Create a dialogue with the group as you walk through each of the steps in the goal-setting and planning process. Recognize that as the leader, your most important job might be to shut up because if you are talking, the group isn't creating the goal. Make sure to lead or facilitate the process, adding your commentary only when necessary. Solicit *their* input, gather *their* ideas, value *their* contributions.

Here are some special points to note about doing goal setting and planning in a collaborative way:

○ *Help them create a desire.* The most effective goal inspires you when you read it. You want this process to be one that inspires each person, so time must be spent during the benefits stage helping people understand how the organization benefits, how the team benefits, and how they personally will benefit from this process.

○ *Help create belief.* Your success will be limited by the degree that people don't believe the goal is achievable or lose sight of the goal. Always strive for complete goal agreement. When you have true goal agreement belief can follow.

○ *Gain commitment.* Consider having everyone on the team sign the goal statement and implementation plan as a form of commitment, to themselves and each other, to invest their hearts and souls in the achievement of the goal.

Ongoing Support

As a leader, you have a significant supporting role to play in the goal achievement of your team. Some of the tangible ways you can support both individuals and the team include:

○ Being a role model by being a goal setter yourself
○ Listening to their concerns and helping to remove obstacles
○ Providing resources when possible
○ Valuing and using their expertise
○ Keeping their focus on the big picture
○ Helping them see progress
○ Celebrating successes (large and small)

Your Now Steps

Once you feel comfortable with the goal-setting process for yourself, it's time to help your team set some goals and plan for goal achievement. Here are some steps to get you started.

1. Spend some time thinking about the vision for your team. Brainstorm and capture your thoughts regarding what is possible and desirable for your team. Think about this from your perspective, your customer's

perspective, the organization's perspective, and your team's perspective. Make some notes in your journal, and continue with step 2 in a couple of days.

2. Review your work. Look back at your personal visioning exercise, and make any adjustments and clarifications that you see. Make sure you haven't been overly prescriptive because your team's success will be much more difficult if you set the goals before involving the team.

3. Once you have completed these visioning steps, meet with the team, and begin the collaborative goal-setting process.

It doesn't matter when this exercise takes place. Don't worry about your formal organizational goal-setting calendar. Recognize where you are now, and focus on how you can move forward from today. Of course this exercise will be valuable leading into a new calendar or fiscal year, but you can start at any time. No matter the time of year, it will be more valuable to do it now than to wait for the what you think is the right time.

 Remarkable leaders help their teams set and achieve goals.

The Power of Alignment

When doing personal goal setting, the only alignment that matters is the alignment of your goals with your personal values and ethics. If you are leading a team, your concern will be the alignment of the group goals to the values and mission of the organization. The larger the organization is, the more important and challenging alignment becomes.

Earlier in this chapter I talked about Chevron chairman Ken Derr's vision of "Better Than the Best." That vision became valuable and highly effective in the organization once operating companies, departments, teams, and individuals saw how to connect their work to this idea. One of the great callings of leaders is to understand the organization's larger goals and connect those organizational goals with the everyday work activity of the people they lead.

Alignment is building the linkage among the organizational, team, and individual goals and work activities. Once those linkages are clear and understood, great leverage will be attained. Now people will be working on the right things from the organization's perspective.

It is far more than just a mechanical exercise, however. Do you think the people at NASA had a stronger sense of purpose, greater enthusiasm and energy, and a higher likelihood of success and job satisfaction before or after President Kennedy set a goal to put a human on the moon before the decade's end? The answer is clear: alignment creates energy, alignment creates synergy, and alignment can create magic.

One of our clients is embarking on some significant organizational change that is being led by the CEO. At a recent meeting of the cross-functional steering committee, there was much discussion of creating better methods for setting goals within the organization. It became very clear that many employees found it hard to see how their work contributed to the organization's goals and objectives. On a practical level, this makes the organization's well-designed bonus structure hollow: if employees don't know how their work contributes to the goals, how can they do more of the right things? The team improved its process based on this practical matter.

Beyond the practicality, strong alignment creates power through meaning. As a leader, you can give people more meaning in their work when you help them align their work with the purpose and vision of the organization.

What You Can Do

There are several ways you can create or ensure alignment:

1. *Understand the alignment yourself.* Spend the time required understanding alignment between your group's work and the organizational goals. The larger the organization is, the harder this may be, but it can be done. Think about it, ask questions, and do what is needed to better understand the organizational goals so that you can clearly understand and articulate your team's place in the big picture.

2. *Ask people.* Ask people how they see their individual goals connected with the team and organizational goals. Get their ideas on the table for conversation.

3. *Create conversation.* Use more questions to generate joint understanding and agreement across all members of the team about their contribution to the success of both team and organizational goals.

4. *Identify examples.* Have examples ready to discuss if needed. Remember to let the group discover the connections themselves as much as

possible. When possible, use your examples as a means of corroborating and confirming their thoughts.

5. *Make a list.* Have people make a list of all of their job tasks and roles. Then encourage them to make two lists: the tasks they see in alignment with team goals and those in alignment with organizational goals. Identify any items from the first list that aren't on the second list.

6. *Question everything else.* What about those items that didn't make the second list? Question their relevance to the team's progress. As the leader, allow people to question whether these tasks should be continued. After all, discontinuing any tasks currently being done that are not required frees up additional time to work on higher-value, goal-driven activities. As the leader, make it okay for people to do this questioning.

7. *Be willing to eliminate.* Once the questioning has been done, if no clear reason can be found for the remaining tasks, reassure people that these tasks can be eliminated.

Your Now Steps

Creating greater alignment within your team is an important task, to be sure. Following the steps in this section will take some time. Since Your Now Steps are designed to be things you can get started on now, your team's success starts with you, no matter what your position or job title.

1. Look at the alignment between your work and the team's and organization's goals and objectives. In your journal, list how your tasks relate to these goals. If you find items that aren't in alignment, investigate how you might be able to eliminate these tasks.

2. Use your personal exercise as the impetus to start this process with the whole team. Use your experiences as a model for others to do the same.

3. Make time in your team calendar to look at alignment from the group perspective.

Remarkable leaders create alignment because they know that goal alignment can create magical results.

Creating a Process

This competency is about more than setting goals; it's really about goal achievement. Remarkable leaders make goal setting and goal achievement an integral part of the work, not something done once a year and then forgotten in the crush of the "real work." Leaders must support goal setting and make it relevant to each person's everyday work.

When people and teams have clear alignment between their work and the team and organizational goals, it is much easier to see goal work as the real work. After all, the process just discussed provides a way to reduce work that isn't goal connected.

There are at least five things you can do on a regular basis to create and maintain a process for goal setting and achievement.

- Keep the picture clear.
- Communicate continually.
- Invest time personally.
- Be enthusiastic.
- Track progress.

Keep the Picture Clear

Continually provide a clear picture of the goals. We started the goal-setting process with a fondest wish, and your process made the goal clear while it identified the benefits to its achievement. The importance of those steps extends beyond the setting of the goal; they are useful throughout the life of the goal too. This process creates motivation for everyone involved. By keeping the picture of the desired future state clear in people's minds, motivation can remain high.

Challenge the team to come up with several ways to describe the end state clearly. Use those visions to maintain clarity throughout the life of the goal.

 For some creative ways to make the goal compelling and visible, download this Bonus Byte at www.RLBonus.com using the keywords "compelling vision."

Communicate Continually

It's nearly impossible to communicate too much (see Chapter Six). This is as true for keeping people mindful of goals as for anything else. Remind people of the goals and the benefits that will come from achieving the goal. Continually connect them back to the overall purpose and vision as well. We all need those reminders, and as the leader it is your job to do the reminding.

Invest Time Personally

You must invest time to assist others (supporting them in the ways described earlier), and you also must invest time in working on your own goals. As you continue to move toward your personal goals, you will be reenthused and reinvigorated in the process and therefore even more eager to help team members with theirs. Of course, your positive example may be the best reason of all to invest your personal time.

Be Enthusiastic

This advice doesn't mean you have to be a cheerleader, though you can be in your own way. Enthusiasm is a contagious, positive energy that you can spread through your actions. The previous three steps (keeping the picture clear, communicating, and investing your time) can all be done with enthusiasm. Choosing to do so will send a powerfully supported message to your team. Be yourself, but be positive and upbeat about the goals themselves, the team's progress toward them, and your belief in their ultimate achievement.

Track Progress

Many organizations set goals as an exercise and wonder why nothing happens. You now have all the tools you need to make sure that you not only set goals but have a plan to achieve them. Because you set tangible, specific goals to start with, they can be measured. As a leader you can help the team track progress along the way to goal achievement. Use your plan to identify the measurements, and then help people measure and communicate progress.

Your Now Steps

You now have a process to create tremendous results. Any of these five suggestions can help tremendously, but your first Now Step is meant for you to truly start now:

1. Take five minutes right now to review your team's goals. Identify the most important of those goals.
2. Get up from your desk, and have a conversation with someone on the team about that goal, its importance, and its current status.
3. If you aren't at work while reading this, resolve to do step 2 as soon as you return to work.

 Remarkable leaders know that goal setting is an ongoing process and must be supported continually.

Some Final Thoughts

This is the thirteenth competency in this book, but it is by no means the least important. You could make a case that after learning, it is the most important. Your ability to set goals and support goal setting among your team can pay huge dividends for you and your organization. But more important than ability is willingness. This book provides you with the tools, techniques, and ideas, but you must put them to work.

 Go to remarkableleadershipbook.com/resources for more information, writing, tools, and other highly recommended resources to help you to set and achieve goals for yourself and your team.

EPILOGUE

CONGRATULATIONS!

You have completed one step in your journey to becoming a remarkable leader. While every journey begins with a step, it is just one step. It should be exceedingly clear to you now that you have read this book, reading alone is barely a step at all. The real first step is taking action. This book has provided many steps that you can take on your journey and subtly suggested many more.

Get started on taking those steps.

I believe that you can become a remarkable leader once you take those steps. Once you begin your journey, 1 believe you will change the world. I look forward to meeting you, shaking your hand, perhaps signing your marked-up and dog-eared copy of this book, and learning from your lessons as a remarkable leader.

Yours in learning,

KEVIN EIKENBERRY

REFERENCES

Albrecht, K. *The Only Thing That Matters: Bringing the Power of the Customer to the Center of Your Business*. New York: HarperCollins, 1992.

Amabile, T. *The Social Psychology of Creativity*. New York: Springer-Verlag, 1983.

Baker, D. *What Happy People Know: How the New Science of Happiness Can Change Your Life for the Better*. Emmaus, Pa.: Rodale Press, 2003.

Bell, C. *Managers as Mentors: Building Partnerships for Learning*. San Francisco: Berrett-Koehler, 1996.

Bryan, J. "The Mintz Dynasty." *Fast Company*, Apr. 2006, p. 56.

Buckingham, M., and Clifton, D. *Now, Discover Your Strengths*. New York: Free Press, 2001.

Carnegie, D. *How to Win Friends and Influence People*. New York: Pocket Books, 1998.

Cotton, K. *Expectations and Student Outcomes*. Portland, Ore.: Northwest Regional Educational Laboratory, 1989. Retrieved from http://www.nwrel. org/scpd/sirs/4/cu7.html.

Dirks, K. T., and Ferrin, D. L. "Trust in Leadership: Meta-Analytic Findings and Implications for Research and Practice." *Journal of Applied Psychology*, 2002, *87*, 611–628.

Drucker, P. "The Way Ahead: Get Ready for What Is Next." *Executive Excellence*, 2004, *21*, 3.

Gitomer, J. *Customer Satisfaction Is Worthless, But Customer Loyalty Is Priceless*. Austin, Tex.: Bard Press, 1998.

Greenleaf, R. *Servant as Leader*. Westfield, Ind.: Robert K. Greenleaf Center, 1970.

Hogan, K. *The Science of Influence: How to Get Anyone to Say "Yes" in Eight Minutes or Less!* Hoboken, N.J.: Wiley, 2004.

Jenkins, J. N.d. Retrieved from http://www.parapublishing.com/sites/para/ resources/statistics.cfm.

Leeds, D. *Smart Questions*. New York: Berkley, 1988.

Lewis, R. T. *The Psychology of Losing and How to Profit from It*. Gretna, La.: Wellness Institute, 2000.

Magrath, A. J., and Hardy, K. G. "Building Customer Partnerships." *Business Horizons*, 1994, *31* (1), 24–28.

Maltz, M. *Psycho-Cybernetics*. Upper Saddle River, N.J.: Prentice Hall, 1960.

Maurer, R. *Beyond the Wall of Resistance*. Austin, Tex.: Bard Press, 1996.

Maurer, R. *Resistance to Change—and What to Do About It*. White paper, 2006.

Nolan, V. *The Innovator's Handbook: The Skills of Innovative Management: Problem Solving, Communication and Teamwork*. New York: Penguin, 1989.

O'Toole, J. *Leading Change*. New York: Ballantine Books, 1996.

Peters, J. D. *Speaking into the Air: A History of the Idea of Communication*. Chicago: University of Chicago Press, 2000.

Project Management Institute. *A Guide to the Project Management Body of Knowledge*. Newtown Square, Pa.: Project Management Institute, 2004.

Rath, T., and Clifton, D. O. *How Full Is Your Bucket? Positive Strategies for Work and Life*. Princeton, N.J.: Gallup Press, 2004.

Rogers, E. *Diffusion of Innovations*. New York: Free Press, 1962.

Sanders, T. *The Likeability Factor*. New York: Crown, 2005.

Say, R. *Managing with Aloha: Bringing Hawaii's Universal Values to the Art of Business*. Waikoloa, Hi.: Ho'ohana Publishing, 2004.

Schank, R. *Tell Me a Story: A New Look at Real and Artificial Memory*. New York: Atheneum, 1991.

Screenvision.com. "Fact Sheet." 2007. http://www.screenvision.com/m/audience/fact/2007.

Seligman, M. *Learned Optimism*. New York: Knopf, 1991.

Stein, S. J., and Book, H. E. *The EQ Edge: Emotional Intelligence and Your Success*. Hoboken, N.J.: Wiley, 2006.

Stevens, M. *Extreme Management: What They Teach at Harvard Business School's Advanced Management Program*. New York: Warner Business, 2002.

Suzuki, S. *Zen Mind, Beginner's Mind*. Boston: Shambhala, 2006.

Terez, T. *Twenty-Two Keys to Creating a Meaningful Workplace*. Avon, Mass.: Adams Media, 2002.

Tracy, B. *The 100 Absolutely Unbreakable Laws of Business Success*. San Francisco: Berrett-Koehler, 2002.

Tracy, B. Brian Tracy's Blog: "Thinking Outside the Box." Mar. 1, 2007. Retrieved from http://blogs.briantracy.com/public/item/160313.

Tuckman, B. W. "Developmental Sequence in Small Groups." *Psychological Bulletin*, 1965, *63*, 384–399.

Vitale, J. *The Attraction Factor: Five Easy Steps for Creating Wealth (or Anything Else) from the Inside Out*. Hoboken, N.J.: Wiley, 2006.

Wallas, G. *The Art of Thought*. (Abridged ed.) New York: Watts, 1949.

Walton, S. N.d. Retrieved from http://en.wikiquote.org/wiki/Sam_Walton.

Welter, B., and Egmon, J. *The Prepared Mind of a Leader*. San Francisco: Jossey-Bass, 2005.

Zemke, R., and Bell, C. *Knock Your Socks Off Service Recovery*. New York: Amacom, 2000.

Ziglar, Z. *See You at the Top*. (2nd rev. ed.) Gretna, La.: Pelican Publishing Company, 2000.

ACKNOWLEDGMENTS

I ALWAYS READ THE ACKNOWLEDGMENTS IN BOOKS for the insight they give into the author. My main observation in reading so many acknowledgments in so many books is that everyone says that they couldn't have written their books alone.

They are all correct.

I have many people and groups to thank, and while I will share some names here, they certainly aren't the only people in these groups who have had an impact on my evolution as a consultant, leader, learner, author, and person. These people have helped me become who I am today, and therefore by extension they play a significant part in the creation of this book.

From a leadership perspective, there are those who led me as a manager, supervisor, coach, or mentor. First on this list of coaches and mentors are my parents. No one has had a greater impact on my life than these two people. I grew up on a farm, and many of my earliest lessons on leadership came from Dad, who was both my dad and my boss. This list also includes Bob Strawn, Steve Furbacher, and Paul Rushing, all of whom showed business acumen and a deep underlying focus on people and leading from the heart.

I've learned much from the leaders I have coached and consulted with over the past seventeen years. These people have provided opportunities for me to observe and test many of the ideas set out in this book. Outside the conference rooms and offices of clients, I have honed my ideas in hundreds of training workshops—in the conversations, exercises, and questions from participants in all sorts of training sessions. I acknowledge all of those learners for their role in the creation of this book.

A book comes not just from those experiences and thoughts collected in these ways, but also from a broader network of people. There are far too many important colleagues to mention here without risking leaving someone important out. If I have done my job as a remarkable leader (and human being), they know who they are. My thanks go to each of them.

I acknowledge and thank the entire team at Jossey-Bass for believing in this project, helping it come to life, and making it a better book.

More directly and more recently, there are people who have helped and will help with the success of this book. There are bloggers, editors, journalists, and reporters who will perhaps be responsible for your reading these words. There will be people who will write kind words for the cover of this book, and there will be countless others whose efforts will help this book have an impact in the world. I thank all of these people, both those I can name and the many I'll never meet.

My team has helped create this book in many ways. The Web site materials you can access and the entire online presence of this book is the responsibility of Brett Atkin, my long-time friend and colleague. Jenny Pratt provided a valuable sounding board for ideas and word choice, as well as being the first editor to touch everything you read here. I'll never fully be able to show my appreciation to her for her impact on this book, though I hope these words help.

Three people need the most acknowledgment. Parker and Kelsey put up with their dad doing work that requires him to be away from home at times. They tolerated with understanding the time I spent in the final weeks of this project while at home but not fully present with them. These two wonderful children have also helped create this book, because it is often in the lessons of parenting that we can find the deepest principles of leadership at play.

And the person who should come both first and last is Lori, my wife, best friend, and partner. Her belief, support, understanding, patience, and love are truly remarkable. Thank you, honey.

Finally, I thank God as the ultimate source of the blessings I have been given. I thank him for the potential he placed in me, for the people placed around me (and mentioned here), and for the opportunities to use my talents to improve the lives and results of others.

KEVIN EIKENBERRY

Indianapolis, Indiana
January 2007

THE AUTHOR

KEVIN EIKENBERRY IS THE CHIEF POTENTIAL OFFICER of the Kevin Eikenberry Group, a learning consulting company that provides a wide range of
services, including training delivery and design, facilitation, performance
coaching, organizational consulting, and speaking services.

Since 1993, he and his team have been helping organizations and
individuals worldwide reach their potential—becoming remarkable by
succeeding at their highest level. Emphasizing the power of learning,
Eikenberry's specialties include leadership, teams and teamwork, organizational culture, facilitation, and training trainers.

He has worked with Fortune 500 companies, smaller firms, univer-
sities, and government agencies, among others. His client list includes
the American Red Cross, Chevron, Chevron Phillips Chemical Company,
IHOP, John Deere, OPTI Canada, Purdue University, Sears Canada, Shell,
Southwest Airlines, Telus, the U.S. Marine Corps, and the U.S. Mint.

Eikenberry gives keynote talks to organizations on leadership, lifelong
learning, developing human potential, teams and teamwork, creativity,
and other topics. He has presented to the National Institutes of Health,
the American Farm Bureau Federation, the National Speaker's Association, the International Society for Performance Improvement, the National Association for Experiential Learning, the American Society for
Training and Development, the International Society for Performance
Improvement, and many others.

He is the author of the best-selling book *Vantagepoints on Learning and
Life* (2006) and a contributing author to the *Handbook of Experiential
Learning* (2007), *101 Great Ways to Improve Your Life* (2006), and
Walking with the Wise (2003). He has been a contributor to thirteen
training and development sourcebooks since 1997.

Eikenberry offers four e-mail-based publications: *Unleash Your Potential*, a weekly publication to assist organizations and individuals in
turning their potential into desired results; *Powerquotes,* a weekly publication featuring a quotation along with questions to reflect on; Powerquotes Plus, a fee-based daily publication that adds personal coaching

to the *Powerquotes* offering; and *Vantagepoints*, an essay on learning from everyday events and activities.

He developed the Remarkable Leadership Learning System, a virtually delivered leadership development process that expands the work of this book. Eikenberry is also the developer of the Million Dollar Skills Learning System, a learning system on valuable life skills delivered in bite-sized pieces that create powerful and productive habits. He hosted an Internet radio program for two and a half years, *Magical Movies with Kevin Eikenberry*, on the leading Internet radio site, VoiceAmerica.com.

ABOUT THE KEVIN EIKENBERRY GROUP

THE KEVIN EIKENBERRY GROUP

If you have just finished reading any portion of this book, you will be clear about my belief in learning. I run my business based on the philosophy that we are at our best and achieve our best results when we are learning. All of our products and services support this philosophy: to help you as a continuous learner achieve success at the highest level. Read on to learn more.

Wow Your Audience with Kevin as Your Speaker

Kevin Eikenberry has delivered keynote speeches and training across the United States and Canada. His presentations give inspired solutions, relevant approaches, and interactive fun. Visit www.KevinEikenberry.com/speaking.asp to learn more.

> His dynamic presence and presentation both energized and informed the group. People left not only more knowledgeable, but more importantly, believing in themselves. They were clearly going to try out what they had learned.
> —Chris Saeger, manager of program development, American Red Cross

Learning That Lasts: Effective Customized Training

You will receive a customized training plan to meet your specific needs and provide learning that lasts. This training leads to powerful skills, increased productivity, loyal employees, and delighted customers. Visit www.KevinEikenberry.com/training.asp to learn more.

> You won't regret using The Kevin Eikenberry Group for your next training. And you will realize that you wasted your money on the last trainer when you use Kevin.
> — Kendall Barrow, shift supervisor, Chevron Phillips Chemical Company

Helping Your Organization Succeed with Consulting Services

Our consulting services lead to real change, empowered organizations, productive teams, and greater business success through coaching, customer service, facilitation, instructional design, organizational change, strategic planning, or team building. Visit www.KevinEikenberry.com/consulting.asp to learn more.

> Kevin Eikenberry is clearly a catalyst to higher levels of achievement. When we launched a fresh company-wide cultural initiative, Kevin provided the spark to initiate momentum. He was able to deliver the message in a way that was energetic, interactive, and most importantly, real-world applicable. I would recommend Kevin to any organization that is looking to accomplish great things.
> — Dave Fechter, executive vice president, Shamrock Companies

Leadership Development

The Kevin Eikenberry Group offers a wide variety of delivery methods for its leadership products, including teleseminars, learning systems, downloadable MP3 recordings, and audio CDs to cater to different learning styles. Visit www.KevinEikenberry.com/products/leadership.asp to learn more.

Unleash Learning

These products expand on some of the competencies in this book, including creativity, learning, and teamwork. Visit http://KevinEikenberry.com/products/index.asp to learn more.

Remarkable Leadership

LEARNING SYSTEM

The Remarkable Leadership Learning System

The Remarkable Leadership Learning System is an ongoing process to help you dive deeper into the concepts and ideas in this book and put those ideas into action . . . It is a virtually delivered leadership development program for individuals and organizations and is designed around the realities of work and learning:

- **Focus.** When we can focus on one thing at a time, we will be more successful. A traditional multi-day leadership training program provides too many new things to work on at once, leaving people too often working on none of them.

- **Limited time.** Leaders are busy people with an overflowing plate of work. They don't have the time to go to a three-day workshop on leadership skills. And if they do manage to carve out the time for the class, they can barely find time to respond to all the e-mails they have received since leaving the office, and so they quickly forget about being able to apply what they've learned.

- **Incremental improvement.** Leaders don't become remarkable overnight. They work every day to get a little bit better. By giving them a limited number of competencies to work on at a time and helping them integrate those new ideas and techniques into their ongoing work, they will be more successful in making improvements.

- **How we learn.** We learn by taking new ideas, trying them, repeating what worked, and changing what didn't. This learning system provides new ideas, avenues to try them, and a process for reflecting on their effectiveness.

Each month, the Remarkable Leadership Learning System focuses on a different leadership competency or skill from this book. Along with this focus, participants continue to build a thirteenth competency: learning continually, which is important for anyone who aspires to be a remarkable leader.

Leaders can join the program at any time. They receive an initial learning portfolio that will acclimate them and help them get the most out of the Remarkable Leadership Learning System, and they begin participating in the live program from the month they register.

For more information about this leadership learning process, go to http://remarkable-leadership.com.

Online Resources for Your Success

Unleash Your Potential with Kevin Eikenberry A weekly newsletter delivered by e-mail with recommended resources and an article from Eikenberry for developing professional and leadership skills. Learn more about this at www.kevineikenberry.com/uypw/.

Powerquotes Delivered weekly by e-mail and featuring a quotation and questions to ponder. Not every Powerquote is directly about leadership-related issues, but all contribute to growth. Learn more about receiving this for free at www.powerquotes.net.

Powerquotes Plus This is the premium Powerquotes Service. Each daily quote and questions comes with actions to consider. Learn more about this at www.powerquotesplus.net.

Remarkable Resources At the close of each chapter in this book is information about online resources. These resources will continue to be available to help you in your journey toward remarkable leadership. Learn more about this at www.remarkableleadership-book.com/resources.

Bonus Bytes All of the Bonus Bytes in this book are available by keyword at www.RLBonus.com.